SALTS AND SUITS

How a bunch of surf bums created a multi-billion dollar industry
... and almost lost it

PHIL JARRATT

hardie grant books
MELBOURNE · LONDON

Published in Australia in 2010 by
Hardie Grant Books
85 High Street
Prahran, Victoria 3181, Australia
www.hardiegrant.com.au

National Library of Australia Cataloguing-in-Publication data:
  Jarratt, Phil.
  Salts and suits / Phil Jarratt.
  ISBN 9781740667401 (pbk.)
  Surfing—History. Surfing—Economic aspects. Surfers.
  Leisure industry. Sporting goods industry.
797.32

Design by Phil Campbell
Typesetting by Megan Ellis
Cover image by Getty Images
Printed and bound in Australia by McPherson's Printing Group

10 9 8 7 6 5 4 3 2 1

CONTENTS

PREFACE

Big is the enemy of cool ... or is it?

Always an early riser, former pro surfer Danny Kwock, forty-three, president of Quiksilver Entertainment, was out of bed with the first light of Thursday, 30 June 2005, hoping to catch a few uncrowded waves near his new Montecito, California home before getting down to the business of the day.

A great believer in 'know before you go', he tapped his Mac and clicked onto the Surfline.com surf report while downing a bowl of muesli and fruit and a cup of herbal tea. The wave cams were okay, not too thrilling. Kwock clicked onto the New York stock markets, just a few minutes into the trading day, and keyed in VLCM on the NASDAQ. This was more exciting. Making its debut in the market, Volcom, surfing's 'youth against the establishment' brand, had opened at $26.01, well above its $19 initial public offering price, and was headed for the sky.

Kwock, a founding shareholder in Volcom back in 1991, had already made millions before breakfast. By the end of the trading day he would be more than $50 million richer. He allowed himself the smallest of smiles, slipped his board into the back of the SUV, threw his wetsuit on the seat beside him and headed for the beach, careful not to wake his sleeping family as he backed the car out of the drive.

That Danny Kwock, the 'rainman' of the $10 billion surf industry market leader and one of its most influential marketing executives for more than two decades, should be a beneficiary of the successful public offering of a rival surf brand is unusual in business, to say the

1

least, but no more so than the story behind Kwock's emergence as a force in the industry over a quarter of a century earlier. In the world of surf, however, stuff like this is standard operating procedure.

One afternoon in the spring of 1978, Bob McKnight, Jeff Hakman and Peter Wilson, the then-partners in a company that held the American licence for Quiksilver, an Australian brand of surf trunks, (or 'board shorts' as the Aussies called them) sat in their makeshift office at the front of a Quonset hut in the industrial backblocks of Costa Mesa, CA, feeling pretty pleased with themselves. The three young men, one a business major, one an architecture graduate who had already made money in property development, and one a big-time pro surfer just retired, could see that their fledgling company had survived the first hurdles. Summer orders were good, the brand was gathering momentum.

Suddenly car doors slammed at the rear entrance and tyres screeched as a car took off at speed. The three men ran to the far end of the hut and found a sliding door open and their entire stock of size 36 board shorts gone. One hundred pairs, a tenth of their inventory. 'Unbelievable,' said McKnight.

'Kids,' said Wilson.

'Maybe,' chuckled Hakman, 'but they'd have to be really chubby little buggers.' No one else found this amusing.

A few days later a scrawny kid turned up at the factory. 'I know who ripped you off,' he told McKnight. 'It was Danny Kwock and Preston Murray.'

The Kwock monster. McKnight and Hakman knew who he was, a pint-size surf terrorist who operated between 52nd Street and 56th Street in Newport Beach, blatantly stealing every wave he could paddle into without fear of reprisal, because no one would hit such a shrimp. Perhaps his luck had just run out, thought McKnight. He made a couple of investigative calls, then dialled the number he had been given.

Of Hawaiian, Chinese, Dutch and Japanese ancestry, Daniel Christopher Kwock II was born in Honolulu in 1961 and spent his early years living in rooms behind his aunt's store, Helena's Hawaiian

Foods. His father, who ran Hawaiian entertainment at fairs and travel shows around the world, had accumulated eleven children from two marriages. As Danny would later recall: 'He was too old to play catch, and then he wasn't around anymore, so I was raised by my four sisters while Mom went to work.'

Danny learned to surf on the South Shore beaches of Oahu, but just as he was starting to make progress his mother moved the family to California, to the hot, smoggy, land-locked San Fernando Valley, where Danny was enrolled at a Catholic prep school. 'Nuns hitting you with rulers, man,' he recalled. 'It was heavy!'

One day, Mrs Kwock, deciding she could stand the smog and the heat no longer, put Danny in the care of an aunt while she and the girls lit out for the cooling breezes of the coast. When they ran out of road at the tip of Newport's Balboa Peninsula, they rented what Danny remembers as a 'thrasher pad' opposite the infamous Newport Wedge surf break. On his sixteenth birthday Danny quit school and went south to join them.

The Wedge, where ocean swells refracted around the Newport Harbor entrance and broke with ferocity in a doubled-up shore-break, was frequented by hard-arsed Vietnam vets, tattooed marines on leave, and other surfing freaks. It was a staple of the early surf magazines and movies because of the visual spectacle of body-surfers hitting its back-wash and elevator-dropping headfirst into the sand. Danny Kwock started surfing the place standing up on a borrowed body-board, then, as he grew in confidence, on a proper surfboard. His reputation growing along the strip between Balboa and the River Jetties, Danny soon graduated to the beach between 52nd and 56th streets, home to the hottest young surfers in Orange County, and within a matter of months he was king of the kids, leading the way in mutating the latest fashions depicted in the surf magazines and movies.

Kwock and Preston Murray, his school pal at Newport Harbor High, pestered a local surf shop proprietor to 'flow' (or give from a promotional stock) them pairs of Quiksilver trunks, the hottest new thing to hit the California coast. When the retailer refused, Preston told Danny: 'I know where their factory is, man.' The plan wasn't really thought out. They just 'borrowed' Preston's mum's car and drove up the hill to Costa Mesa. They parked a few blocks from the Quiksilver factory and Preston explained to Danny that he would be the getaway driver. Barely able to drive or to see over the dashboard, Kwock edged up on the factory, Murray disappeared inside and emerged running, his arms filled with trunks. The passenger door slammed and Danny put the pedal to the metal.

Danny was lucky that it was he, not his mother, who picked up McKnight's call. 'Listen to me, you little asshole. We know it was you and your buddy and unless you get your scrawny butts up here right now, you're goin' down!' An hour later the Quiksilver partners faced off against the two trembling kids. Murray toughed it out but Kwock was quickly in tears as McKnight read the riot act. They would pay for all the trunks they couldn't return. They would become company slaves, spending all their time outside of school hours at the factory, cleaning the washrooms, washing cars, running errands. And whenever the partners appeared in the surf at Newport, the two thieves would quietly paddle to the beach until their elders and betters had finished their session.

Murray made a couple of appearances at the Quonset, borrowed money from his parents to repay the debt and was never seen there again. Kwock reported for duty every afternoon, sold his surfboards to pay off part of his debt and reached an agreement to work off the rest. After a while the partners conceded that it was kind of cool having him around. Danny was their conduit to the kids on the beach. He was the guy with his finger on the pulse of the new generation. By the end of the year he was a team rider, being flowed not only Quiksilver board shorts but also Rip Curl wetsuits and McCoy surfboards. Within two years he was Quiksilver's marketing manager, and when the company went public in 1986, he was one of the highly valued inner sanctum of employees whom McKnight rewarded with company stock.

By the beginning of the 1990s California's surf industry had ridden a wave of unprecedented growth for more than five years. Not yet the market leader, Quiksilver USA was nonetheless closing on $100 million in sales revenue and was negotiating to acquire the

European Quiksilver licensee, thus giving it a stranglehold on the brand's lucrative northern hemisphere markets. But not all Quiksilver's employees felt that bigger was necessarily better. In Danny Kwock's marketing department, for example, a young assistant named Richard Woolcott made no secret of his view that 'big is the enemy of cool', a catch-phrase that was bandied around the marketing department like a mantra of youth. Woolcott implored Kwock and – whenever he got his ear – CEO McKnight to resist the pressure to 'go corporate'.

Finally Woolcott and another Quiksilver employee, Tucker Hall, decided to strike out on their own with a new brand that reflected their interest in surf, skate and music. McKnight and Kwock wished them well, and when one of Wooly's personal loans fell through, Kwock even invested $15,000 of his own savings to help out his young buddy. Kwock's investment was an open secret at Quiksilver. Not sure what the business practices manual would say, but it was pin money, for God's sake, and the start-up was unlikely to go anywhere. So went the talk at the Quiksilver water-cooler, and in a few weeks the matter had been all but forgotten.

A month or two after his $50 million Volcom windfall, Danny Kwock's freezing out of Quiksilver was well under way. Nothing personal, of course, but he could hardly expect to continue on his merry way as both a key executive of one company and a major shareholder of its rival, not now that everyone knew. He would remain a marketing 'guru', 'guiding light', 'elder statesman', whatever, but the truth was that within the Quiksilver management hierarchy he would carry about as much weight as a Roxy bikini. Kwock was privately telling friends: 'I love Quiksilver, always have. I'll go, stay, whatever is best for the brand.'

In fact Danny Kwock and his ilk, perhaps the last of the free-bootin', salt-stained, sun-drenched entrepreneurs of the surf industry – the ones who back in the day had smoked reefers for breakfast and showed up for work only when the surf was flat – had been placed on an exit path (whether they were aware of it or not) quite some time before this. The battle of the 'salts and the suits', seen by many of the most influential people in the industry as an inevitable consequence of growth, had been well and truly won by the suits. Even Quiksilver's McKnight, hailed as the 'most powerful person in surfing' by *Surfer* magazine in 2002 and a lifelong surfer, fiercely proud of the salt running through his veins, conceded to *Transworld Surf Business* magazine in 2004 that his company's focus, since attaining $100 million in sales in the mid-nineties, had been on bringing in 'professional managers who aren't dripping salt'.

In the same interview McKnight said:

> The tools that come from being [a public company] are wonderful ... Everybody wants to grow in their career ... You can't just sit there and be cool and groovy ... That's why I can't wait to watch [what happens to] Volcom. Richard [Woolcott] and I talk about it all the time ... [I tell him] you're going to get to that point ... of going places that are a little more uncomfortable, and bringing in non-salt people to help you grow, and what's your posse going to say then?

McKnight's premise – that companies reach a point in their growth where certain fundamental characteristics just have to change – is in a sense confirmed by events at Nike, the one time bad boy of sports marketing whose rebellious disposition had been an inspiration to several surf brands. (Quiksilver even adopted the Nike affectation and started referring to its corporate headquarters in Europe and the US as 'campuses' in the nineties.) In a cover story in September 2004, *Business Week* magazine noted:

> With revenues exceeding $12 billion in fiscal 2004, the company that Philip H. Knight started three decades ago by selling sneakers out of the back of a car at track meets has finally grown up ...

In the past few years, the company has devoted as much energy to the mundane details of running a business – such as developing top-flight information systems, logistics and (yawn) supply-chain management – as it does to marketing coups and cutting edge sneaker design. More and more, Nike is searching for the right balance between its creative and its business sides, relying on a newfound financial and managerial discipline to drive growth ... To many of the Nike faithful, these sorts of changes smacked of heresy. Lebron James is cool. Matrix organization and corporate acquisitions aren't. But cool or not, the new approach is working.

As the company that Australian Alan Green founded in Torquay, Victoria, in 1970, and Robert B McKnight took to California in 1976 – selling surf trunks out the back of a VW van – also finally grew up, there were plenty ready to call that heresy too.

The argument over the corporatisation of the surf industry – inevitable or not? – is not confined to Quiksilver. It's just that the long-time industry leader, which hit a billion dollars in global sales in 2003, was the first of the surf brands to reach a size where big versus cool became a real issue. (Billabong joined the billion dollar club in 2006, Rip Curl was nudging it as the global financial crisis kicked in and sent it backward.) And with its 2005 acquisition of the venerable but ailing French ski brand Rossignol, taking the Quiksilver group to $2.2 billion and requiring a corporate repositioning into the bigger world of the 'outdoors' market segment, the brand that once tagged itself 'the board shorts company' had crossed a conceptual river and would have to push hard against the current to ever go home again. By 2008, with the stock price down seventy per cent, a lot of investors and more than a few people within the company were wishing that Quiksilver could simply paddle back. 'This [buying Rossignol] is the bell that can't be unrung,' one sceptical and highly placed Quiksilver executive told me then, throwing another metaphor into the mix.

The point was that Quiksilver had gone where no surf company had gone before – right out of its comfort zone. But the question of how corporate is too far is not the only one of consequence for the surf industry. Every season surfwear manufacturers from California to Cornwall, Biarritz to Bali, Sydney to Sao Paulo, ask themselves the same question: how much longer will kids continue to wear the clothes their fathers wear and how can we convince them they're not? And out in the water at the slow-moving point breaks that will still tolerate their slow-moving presence, the dads are asking their own question: 'How did my old beach buddies get so frickin' rich and why am I helping them get richer by continuing to wear their stupid uniform?'

More than fifty years since it gurgled into existence under seaside piers and in backyards and garages along the coast, the $10 billion surf industry knows few commercial or cultural boundaries. Surfing has its own language, its own media, its own icons and its own mythology, most of it largely unfathomable to those outside the cognoscenti. Indeed, the expert financial advice sought by the industry in its formative years in the 1970s and 1980s gave surf a short shelf life in a geographically limited niche market defined by the sport's daredevil participants. Not only were there very few of these anyway, the experts said, but they would be done with the beach by the age of thirty, when familial responsibilities like gardening, junior soccer and little league would kick in. Have fun with this surf thing, guys, but don't expect to get rich. That was the clear message.

But in fact the market for surfwear has turned out to be merely window-dressed by surfing's actual participants, who represent just a tiny percentage of the global market. The real market, analysts and cool hunters alike now agree, is that vast and growing tribe of urban dreamers who aspire to an action lifestyle, whether they actually ever lead one or not. And furthermore, the core market of surfers is not giving up at thirty. Even sixty doesn't see too many off these days, as this author, now sneaking up on the twilight years, can joyfully attest. Californian industry researchers Board-Trac recently released a survey that showed fifty-three per cent of American surfers are now over the age of twenty-five, and thirty-one per cent are over thirty-four. Industry sources in Australia concur that the demographic is ageing rapidly. So there is now no shortage of role models at any age.

Having seen where all this is heading, corporate America has been chasing its piece of the surf pie for several years now, sometimes through acquisition of genuine surf companies (such as Nike's 2002 purchase of Hurley, Warnaco Group's purchase of Ocean Pacific and VF Corp's 2005 Reef buy) and sometimes through blatant plagiarism, as in retail giant Abercrombie and Fitch's creation of the bogus surf brand Hollister in 2000. But so far, in most parts of the world, the authentic companies have kept control of the industry, albeit at the cost of pushing volume sales a little more than might be healthy for their core credibility.

In 2009, despite the significant thrashing handed out by the global financial crisis, three brands, all founded in small Australian beach communities about forty years ago, controlled sixty per cent of the global surf market and commanded huge influence over every aspect of the industry. Rip Curl (10%) started as a surfboard factory in Torquay, Australia, in 1968, and the following year went into wetsuit production. In 1970 it spawned Quiksilver (30%) when the brand's wetsuit designer decided to try his hand at manufacturing surf trunks. Spurred on by Quiksilver's early success, a surfboard shaper at Burleigh Heads, some 2000 kilometres north of Torquay, launched Billabong (20%) into the trunks business in 1973.

In each case the decision to go into business was based on life-style rather than the profit motive. Brand founders 'Claw' (Doug Warbrick), 'Sing Ding' (Brian Singer), 'Greeny' (Alan Green) and 'Greasy' (Gordon Merchant) were all committed surfers who had seen how the workaday world worked, and didn't like it. They wanted to spin the wheels of industry on their own terms, and basically that meant downing tools when the surf was up. Against all odds, their companies succeeded and eventually transformed the entire industry.

Reluctantly at first, the Australian-founded 'big three' pioneered the new structure of the modern surf company, crossing category and demographic boundaries to brand an ever-increasing array of garments and products, offloading production to the Third World and ploughing their profits back into the creation of vast dream factories to entice the increasingly homogenised global youth market.

This book tells the amazing true story of this band of young beach bums and hippies, and how they turned their passion for riding waves into the world's fastest-growing leisure industry, surviving wipeouts, drug busts, rip-offs, recessions and the constant pressure to dress and act like grownups. Despite tough times in the GFC, they are (mostly) still the darlings of Wall Street and stock exchanges around the world. Surfing's biggest brands have crossed the billion dollar threshold by thinking big and staying cool … and that's a hell of a balancing act.

As I write (in late 2009), all the major surf companies and their leading retailers are facing huge challenges. Chances are, they will survive the shakeout, even Quiksilver (which had the furthest to fall), although probably not with its current empire intact. But the landscape for the surf companies has definitely changed since the GFC. The surf industry's big three will now have to prove they are as innovative as they have been telling us they are for years.

With this realignment of market forces, it seemed timely to focus on the hugely colourful history of the surf industry in Australia and around the world. For the most part, it's a story that begins with the baby boomers following their dream to build a life around surfing, and ends with them departing the boardrooms of major corporations, mostly kicking and screaming as they go. But it also takes us back in time to the infancy of the culture of leisure, and follows a century or more of the evolution of Hawaii's ancient sport of kings, and its eventual impact around the world.

Above all else, like the simple yet empowering act of riding a wave, the story of the surfing industry is nothing less than a grand adventure. Enjoy the ride!

Phil Jarratt
Noosa Heads, December 2009

1 PAGAN RITES

The decline and discontinuance of the use of the surfboard, as civilization advances, may be accounted for by the increase in modesty, industry and religion.
Hiram Bingham, Calvinist missionary, 1820s

The first surfers carved their boards from trees – either koa or wiliwili – and fashioned them according to their caste. The *a'ali*, or Hawaiian royalty, rode *olo* boards of perhaps seventeen feet in length, while the commoners rode the *alaia*, less than half that length. For more than a thousand years the Hawaiians rode their surfboards naked, standing cross-armed and majestic as the surf carried them across the coral-cased bays of their beautiful island chain, preferably against a backdrop of the setting sun. And when day was done, invigorated by their surfing, they would casually couple in the shallows or in the shade of the palms with the beautiful naked women who had surfed with them or awaited their return.

Given the way that a similar sex-on-the-beach hedonism was to evolve in white Anglo-Saxon communities in southern California and on the east coast of Australia in the post World War II years, it is supreme irony that it was the white man who came along and spoiled the party for the Hawaiians. Captain James Cook's discovery of the islands (which he named Sandwich) in 1778 signalled the beginning of the end for Hawaiian surf culture in its original form. Lieutenant James King, Cook's first mate, wrote in his journal after watching surfers in action at Kealakekua Bay on the Big Island of Hawaii: 'The boldness and address with which I saw them perform these difficult and dangerous manoeuvers was altogether astonishing and is scarcely to be believed ... They seem to feel a great pleasure in the motion which this exercise gives.' Well, we couldn't have that, could we! Reading of this blatant paganism, the muscular Christians of the Mother Country were galvanised into action. Over the next century, Calvinist missionaries attempted to stamp out surfing and other allegedly pagan rituals in Hawaii, while introducing not only their new god, but also misery, disease, poverty, alcoholism and, inadvertently, that mortal enemy of cultural authenticity – tourism.

Cook's historian, the Reverend William Ellis, also wrote accounts of the surfing that day at Kealakekua Bay (and of Cook's bloody demise the following year) that he published in different forms more than thirty years later. It is interesting to note that Ellis, a man of the cloth, seemed not the least offended by the exhibitions of paganism he witnessed. In fact he seemed enthralled by the sport, and his eye for detail provides us with the first descriptions of the surfboards the Hawaiians rode and the unbridled enjoyment wave-riding gave them:

> Native men, and women alike, enjoyed it ... the waves broke out about one hundred and fifty yards. Twenty or thirty natives, each with a narrow board with rounded ends, would start out together from the shore and battle the breaking waves to a point out beyond. The surfers would then lay themselves full length upon the boards and prepare for the swift return to shore. They would throw themselves in the crest of the largest wave, and be driven towards shore with amazing rapidity. The riders must

ride through jagged openings in the rocks, and, in the case of failure, be dashed against them.

The higher the sea and the larger the waves, in their opinion the better the sport. They use a board, which they call *papa he naru* (wave-sliding board), generally five or six feet long, and rather more than a foot wide, sometimes flat, but more frequently slightly convex on both sides. It is usually made from the wood of the erythina, stained quite black, and preserved with great care. After using, it is placed in the sun until perfectly dry, when it is rubbed over with coconut oil, frequently wrapped with cloth and suspended in some part of their dwelling house.

Ellis's prescient account was not only the first to use the words 'surfer' and 'surfboard', but he was also the first to document the lifestyle his peers would work so tirelessly to destroy. Ellis was, in fact, the first writer to describe the 'stoke'. Any modern surfer reading the above extract would identify exactly with the Hawaiian pioneer, surfing all day, then returning home to carefully tend to his board before hanging it on the rack until tomorrow.

There were several more published accounts of surfing, even as it entered its 'dark age' of prohibition, including one spirited defence of it. In 1838 WRS Ruschenberger, in a book called *Narrative of a Voyage around the World*, questioned the right of the missionaries to interfere. 'A change has taken place in certain customs … I allude to the variety of athletic exercises, such as swimming, with or without the surfboard … all of which games, being in opposition to the strict tenets of Calvinism, have been suppressed … Can the missionaries be fairly charged with suppressing these games?' But it took someone of the stature of Samuel Clemens (writing under his literary *nom de plume* Mark Twain), the first modern travel writer, to focus broader attention on surfing (and thus assist its renaissance), in an article first published in the *Sacramento Union* in 1866 after a visit to the Kona Coast on the island of Hawaii:

In one place we came upon a large company of naked natives of both sexes and all ages, amusing themselves with the national pastime of surf-bathing. Each heathen would paddle three or four hundred yards out to sea (taking a short board with him), then face the shore and wait for a particularly prodigious billow to come along; at the right moment he would fling his board upon its foamy crest and himself upon the board, and here he would come whizzing by like a bombshell!

Twain actually tried the sport with predictably painful results, concluding: 'None but the natives ever master the art of surf-bathing thoroughly.' But the fact that he tried it gave the banned sport a much-needed boost, just as Hawaii's new king, David Kalakaua, tried to reassert Hawaiian culture over the pious groans of the Calvinists.

In the last years of his life, David Kalakaua put together a fascinating collection of myths and stories he had discovered in his travels through the islands as monarch. *The Legends and Myths of Hawaii*, published by Webster & Co in New York in 1888, was seen by the various missionary agencies as advocating a return to the paganism they had all but stamped out, but in fact Kalakaua was a cultural visionary who saw that, denied their heritage, his people would disintegrate. His book put the old stories into a context that encouraged an acceptance of traditional Hawaiian ways, including surfing.

In 'Kelea, The Surf-rider of Maui', the king tells the story of the sister of the king of Maui in the fifteenth century, whose beauty was equalled only by her athleticism on a surfboard. Using exhibitions of her surfing skills to open doors, as it were, she not only scored a husband of suitable royal lineage, but managed also to unite warring factions on Maui, Molokai and Kauai. In his interpretation of this and other island myths, the king's message was clear: surfing was a cultural tool that could be used as a force for good.

By the time of the arrival of Jack London, a next-generation travel writer of similar stature to Twain, the rebirth of surfing in Hawaii had begun in earnest, and now the 'surf-bathers' wore clothes. Adventurer London's account of attempting to master the sport at Waikiki in 1907 was first published in the *Women's Home Companion* and later in his 1911 compilation, *Cruise of the Snark*: 'When a breaker curled over my head, for a swift instant I could see the light of day through its emerald body; then down would go my head, and I would clutch the board with all my strength. Then would come the blow, and to the onlooker on shore I would be blotted out … I should not recommend those smashing blows to an invalid or delicate person.'

When he wrote these words, London was already a famous adventure novelist, and a boxer, swimmer, fencer and cyclist as well, but, like Twain before him, he could not stand on a surfboard and seemed almost in awe of those who could. His description of this heroic endeavour, published at a time when the western world was only beginning to see the leisure potential of the ocean, was widely read and extremely influential, giving surfing a romance that few, apart from Cook's Reverend Ellis, had noticed previously. And just as Ellis had marvelled at every minute detail of the surfing lifestyle, London seemed almost obsessive about the 'physics of surf-riding':

> When a wave crests, it gets steeper. Imagine yourself, on your board, on the face of that steep slope. If it stood still, you would slide down just as a boy slides down a hill on a coaster. 'But,' you object, 'the wave doesn't stand still.' Very true, but the water composing the wave stands still, and there you have the secret. If you ever start sliding down the face of that wave, you'll keep on sliding down it for a quarter of a mile, or half a mile, and not reach the bottom … And it is because of this that riding a surfboard is something more than mere placid sliding down a hill. In truth, one is caught up and hurled shoreward as by some Titan's hand.

When film-maker and adventurer Robert Bonine's two-minute 1906 'actuality' *Surf Board Riders, Waikiki, Honolulu, Hawaiian Islands*, began showing on the Edison Company's lecture circuit across America the same summer that London's article was published, the modern age of surfing had truly begun. While this first 'surf movie' was not seen by the mainstream public, it was viewed by many of the opinion-makers of the intelligentsia, including the Californian tycoon Henry Huntington, who hired an Irish/Hawaiian surfer named George Freeth to give surfing exhibitions at Santa Monica in October 1907, to promote Huntington's Red Car Trolley transport service from downtown Los Angeles to the beach.

While it is not known whether Huntington paid for a passage to the mainland for the fair-haired Freeth, it is known that the surfer received a fee for his performances, thus becoming the first professional surfer. And Huntington had picked his mark astutely. Freeth, a natural on a surfboard despite being only one-quarter Hawaiian, had been Jack London's tutor the previous summer, along with Honolulu-based writer Alexander Hume Ford, and, despite his notable failure to get London upright and flying on the face, he was a natural promoter. Huntington was so impressed he invited Freeth back to LA the next two summers for a series of exhibitions, the most significant of which was his 1909 surf in front of Huntington's Redondo Plunge swimming baths, which drew more than a thousand spectators. Freeth was also picked up as a media-sexy booster by other millionaires on a mission, including the tobacco tycoon Abbot Kinney to promote his futuristic 'Venice' canal development on Santa Monica Bay.

So successful were these promotions that for many years it was believed that George Freeth was the first to ride a surfboard in California, but in fact three young Hawaiians of noble blood achieved this distinction more than twenty years before Freeth sold his soul to Huntington the 'railroad king'. In 1885 three nephews of the enlightened King David Kalakaua and Queen Kapiolani were attending St Matthews Military School in San Mateo, south of San Francisco. Homesick, they made boards from local redwood and rode them at Santa Cruz. When they left town, their boards stayed and a few hardy locals braved the cold water in forlorn attempts to emulate the feats of the young princes, but surfing didn't catch on. However, it is interesting to note that while the missionaries continued to suppress surfing in Hawaii, Kalakaua had managed to slip one under the net and introduce the pagan rite to the mainland.

Alexander Hume Ford was a worldly, outgoing and rather preposterous scion of a wealthy South Carolina plantation family when he arrived in Hawaii early in 1907. Despite no previous evidence of athleticism, he fell in love with surfing, shaped his own board and, with a little help from the small band of Waikiki surfers and four hours' water time a day, taught himself to surf proficiently within three months. It was he who recognised Jack London sunning himself in front of the gleaming new Moana Hotel and convinced him to try surfing, subsequently enlisting young Freeth to give the more advanced lessons. The following year, buoyed by London's championing of surfing's rebirth, Ford established the world's first surfing club, the Hawaiian Outrigger Canoe Club, with the stated aim of 'preserving surfing on boards and in Hawaiian outrigger canoes'. The club operated from a property leased from the Queen Emma estate, just along the beachfront from the Moana Hotel.

Ford's intentions were good but there was no escaping the fact that the Outrigger was a gentlemen's club, created by and for the resident *haole*, or white expat community, at a time when the Hawaiian surfing resurgence was enticing more and more locals to take up (or take back) their sport. Following the publication in *Collier's* magazine in New York in 1909 of an article called 'Riding the Surf in Hawaii', Ford shared the spotlight with George Freeth as surfing's frontline PR men, and, as the rich and powerful started flirting with the new concept of South Seas tourism, they sought out Ford and his club on the beach, which soon had a stock of surfboards to rent or sell to tourists, arguably making it the world's first surf shop.

The small Hawaiian surfing community began to feel they were losing their culture yet again, and, in a move that was to be echoed down through the new century and beyond, they responded by starting their own club, the Hui Nalu (the club of waves), which was formalised in 1911. The Hui had no flash clubhouse like the *haoles'*, just a space under a hau tree in front of the Moana and a downstairs bathroom in the hotel they could use as a change room. The founding members of the Hui formed the nucleus of the Waikiki beach boys who were to introduce surfing to the tourists all day every day for the next hundred years, and can still be seen today, chilling between sessions in the shade in front of the Moana.

Co-founder and number two [after Ford] member of the Hui Nalu was Duke Paou Kahanamoku, the best and the brightest of the Waikiki beach boys and the fastest swimmer in the Islands. Born in Honolulu in 1890, Duke took his name from his father, who in turn had been named in 1869 for the Duke of Edinburgh, who happened to be visiting Hawaii at the time of the birth. The royal title was to cause confusion all of Duke's life, not least because he had the bearing of royalty, and he came to personify the romantic vision of the little tribal monarchy beneath the swaying coconut palms, long after the real monarchy had passed on.

The eldest of nine full-blood Hawaiian children, Duke's maternal lineage went back to the 'Vikings of the sunrise', the Polynesians who settled Hawaii, so it was his destiny to be a waterman. Mentored as a teenager by George Freeth, the powerfully built Duke first made headlines not in the surf but in the harbour, when he clipped almost five seconds off the world record for the hundred yards. Sceptical of such a swim in tidal conditions by a complete unknown with a radical and untried new style, the Olympic selection committee disallowed the time, but Duke was on his way regardless, eventually taking the one hundred metres gold ahead of Australia's Cecil Healy at the 1912 Stockholm Olympics. (Having proven himself to be possessed of 'the right stuff', in 1917 Duke was admitted to the Outrigger Canoe Club, whose membership now topped a thousand of Hawaii's leading citizens and regular visitors. But he also retained his Hui Nalu membership.)

The first 'surf trunks' worn by the Hawaiian watermen were little more than loin cloths, fashioned to escape the wrath of the missionaries in the last years of their campaign to take the heathen out of Hawaii, but by the time a 'Hawaiiana' craze swept the United States between 1912 and 1915 – bringing with it grass skirts, the hula, ukulele bands, elaborate stage productions such as *Bird of Paradise*, and silent pictures such as Universal's *Hawaiian Love*, romanticising the free love and surfing high times of the pre-missionary era – surfers had adopted the woollen 'tank suit'. Posters of Duke Kahanamoku around the time of his Olympic gold feature an artist's impression of a well-endowed young man wearing nothing but woollens that stretch provocatively from high on the thigh to just under the navel. But in many parts of the world, Duke's attire would have gotten him locked up, as he found on a tour of Australia in 1914–15, when he had to cover his chest and hide the shape of his genitals behind an attached skirt while introducing surfing to the stunned locals. (Ironically, it would be Duke's younger brother Sam who introduced the prototype modern and topless surf trunk at the Outrigger Canoe Club a decade or so later.)

As much as the flappers of New York, Los Angeles and San Francisco had embraced the Hawaiian craze, wearing leis and grass skirts to the new hula dancing clubs and posing for photographs with Waikiki beach boys during their Matson Line summer vacations (now bringing a stunning five hundred plus tourists to Honolulu each month), the actual sport of surfing needed much longer to take root. Having introduced many Californians to surfing over a decade of lifeguarding and wandering the coast from Santa Cruz to San Diego, George Freeth died a lonely death in a San Diego hotel room in 1919, succumbing to the influenza epidemic that was sweeping the world. By this time Duke Kahanamoku was unquestionably surfing's frontman, having introduced the sport to Australia and the US East Coast, but while people marvelled at his skill, few persisted with the sport, finding the heavy redwood boards too difficult to manoeuvre.

The surfer who most credit with laying the foundations of the modern sport was Tom Blake, born in Wisconsin in 1902. In 1910 the young Blake saw one of Robert Bonine's surfing 'actualities' at a cinema in Milwaukee and decided he too would become a surfer. In

1920, the dream very much alive, Blake chanced to meet the great Duke Kahanamoku, who, having just won two more gold medals at the Antwerp Olympics, was on a promotional junket through the Midwest. The following year Blake moved to Los Angeles and rode his first waves in Santa Monica Bay. Strangely, he seems to have taken a few early wipeouts to heart, and did not surf again until 1924. This time, however, the thrill of the slide caught him by the throat, and he soon made his first trip to Hawaii, where he fell in with the Kahanamoku brothers and became a *haole* beach boy, eventually becoming the only white member of the Hui Nalu.

Blake was fascinated by the ancient *olo* boards he saw in Honolulu's Bishop Museum, and decided that the long rakish template of the royal surfcraft was the way to go for future surfboard design. In 1926 he designed and built a fifteen-foot replica of the *olo*, halving the weight of the board by drilling hundreds of holes through it and sealing them with thin wood veneer. As keen on distance paddling as he was on surfing, Blake took the next step and built a fully chambered hollow board of similar dimensions, which he took back to California for the inaugural Pacific Coast Surf Riding Championships at Corona Del Mar in 1928. This event, in part devised by Blake himself, judged competitors on speed paddling as well as time spent riding a wave and, perhaps not surprisingly, he won.

The Pacific Coast titles were not the first surfing championships of modern times. As Blake himself noted in his 1935 book, *Hawaiian Surfboard*, the first book specifically about surfing: 'On one occasion, about 1918, a riding contest was held, the winner being judged on form, etc. Everybody disagreed and that led them to believe surfing contests were impracticable.' More than ninety years later, people were still arguing about how to judge aesthetics in surfing, but at the time he published his landmark book, Tom Blake was confident that there would be a revival of surfing contests 'under the ancient rules'. The ancient rules were pretty loose, but they did take into account both form and function, judging riders on style and distance travelled. The results were taken very seriously too, since the Hawaiians usually wagered high stakes on the outcome, with losers forfeiting a domestic animal, a house, a wife, and even their lives. This wasn't quite what the frequently didactic Blake had in mind, and, in fact, his concept was more or less what was adapted when surfing contests finally came of age in the 1950s.

Buoyed by his success at Corona Del Mar, Blake continued to develop the hollow *olo*, and in 1929 he changed his construction technique from chambering to casing a wooden frame. When he introduced the board at Waikiki as a combination of 'the ancient Hawaiian type of board and the English racing shell', a reporter derisively described it as a 'cigar', and the name stuck. But the sleek, hollow cigar performed beautifully, and in 1931 Blake filed for a US patent, calling his invention the 'Water Sled'. The patent was granted in 1932 and Blake thus became surfing's first industrialist.

But, much like a surf industry start-up in 2008 or 2009, Blake's timing was not as great as his vision. The Great Depression was in full cry, and the Water Sled manufacturing licence moved from company to company as its owner tried to broaden the application of his invention. In this he met with some success, and the Honolulu *Star-Bulletin* of 28 September 1934 noted:

> Tom Blake, surfboard expert of Waikiki beach, has just returned from a year's tour of the mainland introducing his development, the new Hollow Surfboard, to the public on the mainland United States for lifeguard work, surfriding, paddling and aquaplaning purposes. Blake holds the US patent on the Hollow Surfboard and has been fortunate in interesting eastern capital and a large Cincinnati, Ohio, manufacturing concern in the making and distribution of his board ... A very enthusiastic reception of the Hollow Hawaiian Surfboard in the States is reported.

By Tom Blake, no doubt. While Blake's 1935 book is still regarded as the beginning of a dedicated surf media, a cynic might also regard it as the beginning of surf spin. Blake talks up his invention a treat, explaining its many and varied applications, particularly its lifesaving potential. (In his own brochures from the period, Blake even hypes its application to water polo!) But the lifesaving gambit worked, with the Red Cross endorsing Blake's design for use around the world, so that even when his designs fell from favour, the inventor had enough loose change to continue his humble existence, moving with the seasons from Waikiki to southern California, trading one grass shack for another.

An extraordinarily innovative and resourceful businessman, Tom Blake never ever traded the salt in his veins for a suit, nor a ride on a board for a seat on a board, and for that alone he should rightly be regarded as the soul father of the surf industry. But not everyone bought the hollow board theory, and through the mid-1930s surfboard design innovation flourished in California, despite the pitifully small market.

The Depression had hit the West Coast housing market hard, and no company more so than Los Angeles–based Pacific System Ready Cut Homes. Founded in 1908, Pacific Systems had capitalised on the postwar boom in California when, seemingly overnight, orange groves were transformed into tract housing estates. When the market stalled, the company had stocks of wood and machinery lying idle. A young man named Meyers Butte, son of one of the founders, was called home from college to assist in a time of crisis. Butte the younger had been to Hawaii and experienced the thrill of riding a wave with the Waikiki beach boys, and when he saw his father's massive lumberyard and machine shop, he thought of one thing: surfboards.

There being no West Coast–based manufacturer of Hawaiian style solid boards, Pacific Systems leapt into the breach. It's not known which marketing wizard was responsible, but Pacific decided to adopt as its brand name and logo an ancient symbol familiar to many eastern cultures and denoting good fortune. In the late summer of 1931, as an Austrian former house painter named Adolf considered ways and means of creating a new world order, in Los Angeles, Pacific Systems launched the 'Swastika Surfboard Company', with the soon to be familiar reverse cross on every printed item. The company's business card proudly announced, 'Look for the Swastika emblem on every board'.

This was not your perfect start-up, but Swastikas turned out to be well-crafted boards, first made of redwood and later of redwood and balsa. They sold well in California and even started shipping to Hawaii, and, wonder of wonders, the brand became a status symbol even as Hitler's army started storming through Europe, holding the logo aloft. (Here again, astute observers of the surf industry might have detected an early indicator. In 2010 if you named a surf brand after a mass-murdering dictator, you'd probably do very well.)

As the world approached the brink of war, in 1938 Pacific Systems changed their surf brand to 'Waikiki Surf Boards', but it was too little too late. When their lumberyard was commandeered by the military, company management breathed a sigh of relief, but the ultimate failure of their surfboard division was not about an unfortunate choice of name. It was about the lack of a workable market.

By the time the United States entered World War II in December 1941, there were still only two or three hundred active surfers in California, most of whom rode boards of their own construction, and lived a surfing life of their own design. Californian historian Kevin Starr wrote of the surf cult of the era in his book *The Dream Endures*:

> At San Onofre, Hermosa, Palos Verdes, or Malibu, perhaps a hundred surfers and their wives and girlfriends ... would converge on a weekend in their wood-paneled station wagons ... and proceed to erect tents or lean-tos of driftwood and palm fronds ... They would plant their tall surfboards, twice the length of ordinary human height, upright in the sand in rows and circles, thereby creating a surfers' Stonehenge ... By night

there were campfires and beach parties into the late hours, with singing and ukelele music.

Old timers remember it less innocently, with alcohol-fuelled sex playing a major part in the festivities. Certainly this small cell of social rebels shared a bohemian outlook – their abiding philosophy derived from the pre-missionary Polynesians – but the free spirit did not seem to influence their clothing. The snapshots taken by pioneer surf photographer, the late Dr Don James, between 1936 and 1942 reveal a motley crew of handsome, tanned misfits, dressed in ill-fitting garb from high camp sailor gear to army greatcoats ... nothing to label them a tribe. Only after the war, with decades of prosperity ahead, would the style of the surfer start to emerge, for better or for worse.

2 THE DUKE AND HIS DUCHESS

He paddled onto this green wave and, when I looked down it, I was scared out of my wits. It was like looking over a cliff. After I'd screamed, 'Oh no, no!' a couple of times, he said: 'Oh yes, yes!' He took me by the scruff of the neck and yanked me on to my feet. Off we went, down the wave.
Isobel Letham, 1993

While Hawaii was witnessing the first stages of the renaissance of surfing, across the Pacific in Australia, beach culture was struggling to find its feet in a new nation that was becoming increasingly eager to promote its differences from the 'Mother Country', Great Britain, while at the same time clinging to the comfortable similarities. This was a paradox nowhere more obvious than at the beach, where on any given Sunday afternoon, rugged bronzed Aussies promenaded above the tide line in their finery while the surf went unridden.

Along many parts of its vast coastline, the Australian beach offered leisure opportunities that were obvious only if someone with salt in the veins pointed them out to you. It was somewhat ironic, therefore, that a nation built on convict labour should come to realise one of its own natural treasures through people more recently deprived of their home, their freedom and their birthright.

New Hebridean Tommy Tanna was one of many victims of the late nineteenth century 'blackbirding' of native labour from the Pacific islands, a practice for which there were many apologists among the descendants of Australia's first wave of slave labour. Working as a gardener for a wealthy family in Sydney's northern beach suburb of Manly in the late 1880s, Tommy took to body-surfing the rolling waves as he had done since early childhood on his home island of Tanna, and the children of his employer (one of whom was a young lad named Freddie Williams), and their friends, and their friends' friends, watched in awe as the athletic young Islander rode wave after wave for more than fifty metres. Soon, the more adventurous of them were joining in, despite the fact that ocean bathing was technically illegal, courtesy of a series of colonial laws put in place in 1833. Although these archaic laws were not always enforced, surf swimming was generally discouraged as dangerous and déclassé. The real deal at the beach was to dress to the nines and swagger along the boardwalk with a bustled and bonneted babe.

But in the final years of the century, again thanks to the imported Polynesian and Melanesian Islander population, a swimming culture began to gain strength in Australia. Even as Tommy Tanna faded into oblivion, other young Islanders rose up to take his place, notably Alick Wickham, a Solomon Islander whose unique swimming style inspired former British champion turned swimming instructor Fred Cavill and his three champion swimmer sons to develop the Australian crawl, which was used to great effect by Australia's best turn-of-the-century swimmers, and exported to America, where it became the 'American crawl', and came back to bite us. Moreover, young Australian swimmers like Fred Williams were inspired to take their skills to the surf and to start riding waves.

After Federation, as historian Manning Clark noted, 'Australians were hypnotized with pleasure', but beach culture, not yet part of the pleasure principle, still had its battles to fight. While policing of the daylight bathing bans seemed increasingly to be a lot of hard work for no common good, it took a media campaign to actually instigate the change of laws. In 1902 William Gocher was the editor of a parish pump called *Manly & North Sydney News*. While he was not a surf bather, he was an English newspaperman with Fleet Street sensibilities, and he sensed the public mood. At the start of summer 1902–03, Gocher promoted a public protest against the daylight ban over several weeks, and on the first Sunday of the season, he led the way into the surf at Manly at high noon. The police watched and did nothing as Gocher and friends emerged from the waves, even after the journalist pleaded to be made an example of, his photographer waiting with box brownie to capture the moment of arrest. In a matter of weeks the bathing laws had been repealed.

But while the new freedom to swim in the sea, albeit in neck-to-knee woollens, brought prosperity to beachside towns (Manly's population jumped by fifty per cent and property values by 300 per cent in less than two years) there was also an immediate downside. Seventeen people drowned while swimming in the surf at Manly in 1902–03 alone, prompting a local fishing family, the Slys, to launch their dory each weekend and unofficially patrol the line of breakers. All the popular Sydney beaches had the same problem, but Bondi, soon to become Australia's beach culture capital, was the first to respond, establishing the Bondi Surf Bathers' Lifesaving Club to protect its own. The concept of volunteers patrolling the surf beaches would soon spread around Australia and the world, and for the next half-century most young Australians who aspired to ride the waves would learn to do so through a strictly regimented process that put work before play.

But for some the call of the surf was more elemental. Freddie Williams was the first Australian surfer to adopt the beach as a way of life, amusing some and appalling others. Having learnt the basics from Tommy Tanna, Williams went on to develop his own unique style of body-surfing, and became leader of the beach push at Manly, and later at a 'bush camp' he created over the hill at Curl Curl to escape the crowds. Curl Curl was an outpost of civilisation on the northern beaches back then, and Williams treated it as such, living rough and loving it. As he got older he became ever more reclusive, eventually retreating to a humpy at Dobroyd Point, inside the Heads, where he was to die alone just before World War II. Great surfer, style-setter, recluse, tragic – this was to become an all-too-familiar characterisation in surfing down the years.

As the beach lifestyle became more popular, there was the vexing question of what to wear in the surf, modesty and decency being higher priorities than comfort and function. In 1907 three Sydney councils introduced laws requiring men and women to wear skirts over their swimmers. As Waverley's Mayor Watkins told the *Daily Telegraph*: 'Some of these surf bathers are nothing but exhibitionists, putting on V trunks and exposing themselves ... they are in worse manner than if they were nude. Their garments after contact with the water show up the figure too prominently.'

The new requirement was 'a Guernsey with trouser legs, reaching from the elbow to the bend of the knee, together with a skirt, not unsightly, attached to the garment, covering the figure from hips to knees'. Secretary of the newly formed Manly Surf Club, AW Relph, summed up the reaction of the surf bathing community: 'Our beaches will become a laughing stock.'

Not only was bathing attire laughable, but it was considered suitable only for the specific act of surf bathing, not lounging around on the beach, which was destined to become a far more popular activity than surfing. When Hawaii booster and journalist Alexander Hume Ford visited Sydney in 1907, he fell foul of the law at Manly: 'I was arrested at Manly Beach before I had even stepped into the breakers. I had committed the unpardonable offense of sitting in the warm sand in my bathing suit.'

Nothing was surer than that authorities' fixation with 'public lewdness' would encourage some to exploit the notoriety, and first out of the blocks was film-maker and entrepreneur TJ West, a Scottish immigrant who in 1911 produced the world's first bathing beauty film, *Sirens of the Surf!*, which predated Mack Sennett's American efforts by several years. It featured 'Mermaids from Manly, Beauties from Bondi, Charmers from Coogee' disporting themselves in daring one-pieces. The film opened to packed houses at Sydney's Alhambra Theatre at Christmas 1911, but the enthusiastic crowds may have come for the live action, a nightly beauty contest (first prize twelve pounds) featuring girls in swimsuits.

Although he was by now a keen surfboard rider, there is no evidence that Hume Ford brought a board with him to Australia, or that he used one while he was here, but some of the pioneer surf shooters, who had perhaps seen photos of surfing in Hawaii, had been aware of the potential of using a board to launch onto a wave – if not to ride it – as early as the 1890s when Islander Alick Wickham used a piece of driftwood. According to surf lifesaving historian C Bede Maxwell, the Bell brothers of Manly tried to ride a toilet door in the surf at Freshwater at the turn of the century. But no one had fashioned a board good enough for the idea to catch on. Charles D Paterson, president of the Surf Life Saving Association of Australia (SLSAA) since 1910, returned from a world trip in 1912 with a heavy redwood *olo* he had acquired in Hawaii. Paterson couldn't ride it, as much as he tried, and nor could his beach mates at North and South Steyne. The board was consigned to decorate the rafters of the clubhouse, and there it might have stayed had not another of the Manly surf bathers been about to collide with a man who could not only ride such boards but was regarded as the best surfboard rider in the world.

Cecil Healy, born in Sydney in 1881 and tragically to die on the battlefield of the Somme in 1918, equalled the world record for the 100 metres freestyle in 1905 and was Australian champion at that distance for the next seven years. Lack of finance kept him out of the 1908 Olympics, but he was Australia's great white hope at Stockholm in 1912, where he was expected to fight out the gold with the new Hawaiian swimming sensation, Duke Paoa Kahanamoku. In the lead-up to the Games in Stockholm, Healy became friendly with the big, smiling Hawaiian, for they had in common an extraordinary love of surfing, and Healy was fascinated by Duke's photos of himself and others riding the breakers at home in Waikiki.

In the pool, Healy saw that Duke was everything the media had claimed, charging through the water with a radical version of the Australian crawl, supplemented by a frantic two-time kick that would become known as the Kahanamoku kick. Cec Healy knew that only one thing stood between him and the gold, and there it was, smiling up at him from the pool.

There are several versions of what happened next to cement the friendship between Healy and Duke, but the one that has found its way into swimming folklore is that the finalists were on the blocks when it was noticed that Duke was nowhere to be seen. The officials were set to mark him as a forfeit when Healy stepped off his block and refused to race until his rival showed up. Soon enough a sheepish Hawaiian ran into the pool with the excuse that he had slept in, then proceeded to beat Healy for the gold by half a head. More likely, but less colourful, is the version that has the entire American team missing the semifinals through an inaccurate timetable being posted in their quarters, and Healy and the Australian officials urging that they be given a chance with an additional time trial, which Duke won.

However it went down, Healy's sportsmanship was never forgotten by Kahanamoku, and when Cec persuaded the New South Wales Swimming Association to invite him to compete during the 1914–15 summer season, Duke was delighted to come. Unfortunately, shortly after Healy issued his invitation, the Great War that was to claim his life broke out in Europe and there was speculation about calling the tour off. But Duke was keen and, with his friend and fellow swimmer George Cunha and manager Francis Evans, he set sail from Honolulu on the SS *Ventura* on 30 November 1914.

Cec Healy, now writing for the leading sports newspaper *The Referee*, did his best to whip the Sydney sporting public into a lather of expectation, not just to see the Olympic champion in the pool, but to see him surf:

Kahanamoku is a wonderfully dexterous performer on the surfboard, an instrument of pleasure that Australians have so far been unsuccessful in handling to any degree. Reports have been brought back from overseas of his acrobatic feats executed while dashing shorewards at great speeds, but one doubts the possibility of Duke, or anyone else, duplicating such feats in Australian surf. Still, if he should give one of his rare exhibitions for our edification, be sure it will create a keen desire on the part of our ambitious shooters to emulate his deeds, and it goes without saying that his movements will be watched intently. Personally, I am convinced that the natural amphibious attitude of the Australians will enable one or another to unravel the knack. But it must not be forgotten either, that massive boards could cleft a person in twain, so that if the sport should become popular, certain portions of the beaches will need to be set aside, and a new set of regulations will have to be framed.

Cec Healy must have been bitterly disappointed when the ship docked on 14 December and he found his friend hadn't brought a surfboard. Healy reported in *The Referee* that Duke's response was 'I was told that surfboards were not permitted in Australia'. Having been arrested for sunbathing just a few years earlier, perhaps this was Alexander Hume Ford's take on it. But Duke was not concerned. 'Get me some wood and I'll make one,' he told Healy.

Despite a hectic three-state schedule of more than fifty swimming meets in which Duke and Cunha were to participate, surfing was given such priority in the program that the swimming officials might have begun to wonder about Cec Healy's motives, but it helped that several of the committee members were equally surf-stoked. The Hawaiians were installed at 'Boomerang', a beach camp at Freshwater, just over the hill from Manly, where a couple of surfer/swimmers named Roy Doyle and Don McIntyre 'dispensed memorable hospitality', as C Bede Maxwell put it. While Duke cased the beach for surf, a slab of sugar pine, nine feet by two feet and three inches thick was fetched from North Sydney timber mill George Hudson's and, working late into the evening, Duke carved an eight foot eight inch *alaia* from it.

No doubt Duke would have preferred to carry his new board over to the beach and slide a few by himself, but Cec Healy had other ideas, and a public exhibition of 'breaker-shooting and board-shooting' was promoted for the following Wednesday, 23 December. With school out for summer and many Sydneysiders already on their Christmas vacation, a big crowd lined Freshwater at the appointed hour of eleven. The surf was small and choppy but Duke was not deterred. He laughed when organisers told him the Manly surfboat had been rowed around the headland to tow his board out to the break, and ran to the water's edge and effortlessly paddled the pine slab into the break.

Duke enjoyed several long rides that day, but none impressed the crowd more than when he paddled Manly teenager Isobel Letham out on the front of his board, turned and caught a wave and held the tiny girl aloft in his big arms. Duke was so impressed with Isobel's courage and balance that he took her with him on his tour, hoisting her above his head in waves from Cronulla to Torquay, but it was that initial thrill of riding from one end of Freshwater to the other in the arms of the Hawaiian hero that was to define Isobel's life, and she never stopped talking about it, even into her nineties.

As the tour went on, the press found it increasingly difficult to find superlatives to shower on the Hawaiian great. In fact surfing probably scored more mainstream column inches in its first month than it has at any time since. The *Sydney Morning Herald*, whose reporter saw the Cronulla exhibition, gushed: 'The Hawaiian proved himself a master of the art. On one occasion the board carried him a distance of four hundred yards, and he balanced on his head while shooting towards the shore. On another occasion, and whilst sitting on the board, he finished the shoot broadside on. He also carried a lady passenger a distance of a hundred yards.'

Another youngster who was profoundly changed by what he experienced that first day at Freshwater was Claude West, who managed to get Duke to give him a private lesson later. When Duke finally left

Australia in February 1915, he gave his board to young West (with the proviso that Isobel be allowed to share it), who subsequently won the Australian title on it and was unbeaten until 1925. Competition can't have been too tough in 1915, with only a few pine Duke imitations in existence, but by the mid-1920s, the surf lifesaving movement had fully embraced the solid surfboard, not only as a sporting surfcraft but also as a lifesaving tool, thanks to Claude West's pioneering use of Duke's board to rescue swimmers during his working hours as Manly's permanent lifesaver.

Louis Whyte, a doctor from Geelong, Victoria, was another who witnessed Duke's exhibition at Freshwater, and subsequently visited Hawaii to learn more about surfing. After an extended stay in Waikiki, during which he was taught the basics by the beach boys, Whyte sailed home with four redwoods he had bought from the Kahanamoku brothers. The boards were put to good use throughout the 1920s at the Whytes' beach house at Lorne, but by the 1940s, one of them had been converted to a mantelpiece above the fireplace. At least two of the others, however, found their way into good and loving hands. (One is an exhibit at the Surfworld Museum in Torquay.)

Meanwhile, outside working hours on the beach at Manly, Claude West had another project. Having apprenticed as a carpenter (making coffins) before he became a lifeguard, West took to shaping boards with ease, but all of his early models shared the same problem – they were too heavy. As early as 1918 he experimented with a hollowed-out redwood, screwing a thin deck into it, but in the days before plywood, the sheets cracked and let in water. Nevertheless, Claude West became Australia's first surfboard manufacturer, turning out solid boards in a range of shapes for the young Sydney surfers of the 1920s. One of them, CJ 'Snow' McAllister, became one of Australia's finest surfers, snatching the national title from West in 1925 and memorably winning it again at Newcastle in 1928 with a headstand all the way to the beach. (Surfboard contests were point-to-point races in those days, but the 'stunting' boardriders liked to add a flourish whenever they could.)

Adrian Curlewis, later to become president of the Surf Life Saving Association and a High Court judge, was another of West's protégés who, like Snow, preferred 'stunting' to surfboard racing, and in later years often lamented the passing of the trick riders as Australian surfboard riding became annexed by the lifesaving movement. Curlewis rode West's boards at first, but later switched to the second starter in the nascent surfboard industry, Les V Hind, whose redwood shapes, fashioned in his father's toolshed in Manly, became quite popular in the twenties, with even West riding one for a time.

News of Tom Blake's patented hollow board was slow to get to Australia, but by 1934 Frank Adler of Maroubra was winning surfboard races by healthy margins on a long, hollow racer that appeared to be based on Blake's designs. Adler, a mountain of a man, had found the solid boards bogged down as he paddled into waves, whereas the hollow racer allowed him to streak into green ocean swells long before they broke. Adler's board was ridiculed at first, but its competitive advantage soon became obvious, and the Blake hollow board – both the short 'cigar' and the long 'toothpick' versions – became standard, in Australia and around the world.

Keightly 'Blue' Russell was another Sydney surfer who went into backyard production, making hollow boards at Palm Beach, on the furthest tip of Sydney's northern beaches peninsula, where a small but significant surfing community had taken root. Blue Russell, an enigmatic fellow, notched up a string of firsts in the 1930s, pioneering the kneeling position for paddling (and developing a set of 'board bump' calluses under his knees for his troubles), becoming the first Australian to win a surfing event in Hawaii in 1939, and the first Australian surfer to hit the big time as a US expat, establishing a recording company in Los Angeles and thereafter dividing his time between business on the coast and surfing in Hawaii.

If Blue had moved on from making hollow surfboards in his backyard, there were plenty of others learning the skills to take his place. And while production of toothpicks flourished, Australia also led the way in other forms of surfcraft. In 1933 Dr GA 'Saxon'

Crackenthorp of Manly developed a wider, shorter, thicker version of the hollow board which kept the rider above the water where he could propel it using a paddle. Crackenthorp called it a 'surf ski', and after its adoption by the Surf Life Saving Association as a lifesaving tool in 1937, the surf ski took off, almost outselling the surfboard in Australia and South Africa.

While Crackenthorp was gluing and laminating in Manly, across Sydney Harbour at Bronte another doctor was fooling around with rubber moulds. In 1934 Dr Ernest Smithers introduced an inflated rubber raft he called a 'surf-o-plane'. Simple to use and basically indestructible, the 'surfos' were an instant hit and remained a part of Australian beach culture for more than forty years, with many beaches featuring surfoplane hire outlets. The somewhat eccentric Smithers, who was also to give the world the stainless steel steak tenderiser and a contraceptive gel, years earlier took a summer job at a Palm Beach boatshed where the flotation devices used on yachts caught his attention. That same summer he tried unsuccessfully to ride a heavy redwood surfboard. Bingo! Why not a small rubber 'surfboard' that anyone could use? After the war, Smithers sold his design to North Australian Rubber Mills, which added handles and marketed the NARM surfo successfully around the world.

World War II brought surfboard production to a virtual halt in Australia, but as life returned to normal in the late 1940s, surfers got back on their 1939 model toothpicks. While in postwar California and Hawaii change was in the wind, with surfers using wartime technological advances to improve their surfboards, in Australia nothing had changed, nor did it seem likely to, because surfboard riding was firmly in the grip of the fundamentally conservative surf lifesaving movement. In 1945 a group of Sydney surfboard riders had formed the Surf Board Association of Australia, to run their own surfboard riding contests, but when they applied for affiliation with the SLSAA, the establishment came down on them heavily, refusing affiliation and refusing to allow its own membership to compete in the new association's events.

At the same time, Australian surfers, like their American counterparts, were starting to identify as surfers and develop styles of dress, speech and behaviour that set them apart, even from the surf clubs they belonged to. A final, somewhat belated attempt to make men cover their chests while bathing had failed in 1935 when no one took any notice of Eric Spooner, the New South Wales Minister for Local Government's ridiculous proclamation that trunks had to be 'skirted and no portion of the stomach to be seen'. After the war, beachgoers felt they had licence to shed their workaday garb and enjoy life. At Sydney's North Bondi a group of young surfers led by top boardrider Jack 'Bluey' Mayes was known as the 'Cornel Wilde Boys', for the hairstyles and cool strut they had borrowed from the Hollywood actor. In Torquay, Victoria 'China' Gilbert led the 'Boot Hill Gang', the members of which belonged to the surf club but preferred surfing to lifesaving and their own rowdy company to club meetings.

Surfing and surf lifesaving seemed to be on a collision course, but at the start of the 1950s they were held together by two things – surfboard design and fuel rationing. Boards were still huge and heavy, and with few young people being able to afford cars or fuel, the most sensible thing a surfer could do was keep his board at the surf club, and to do that, he had to be a member. But all of this was about to change.

In 1950 the Hollywood actor Peter Lawford arrived in Australia to start shooting the movie *Kangaroo* in the Flinders Ranges in South Australia. He brought with him a Dave Rochlen balsawood and fibreglass, finless surfboard – a prototype of what was soon to be known as the 'Malibu chip'. Spending a few days in Sydney before filming began, Lawford rode the board at Bondi and left it in the care of beach inspectors and surfers Bluey Mayes, Ray Young and Aub Laidlaw, who later became the scourge of the brief bikini at Bondi, ordering scantily clad young women off his hallowed sand. Just as Charlie Paterson's redwood board attracted little attention in 1912, Lawford's Rochlen seems to have done little for the Cornel Wilde Boys, even though they saw themselves as cutting-edge surfers.

Much the same thing happened when Phillip 'Flippy' Hoffman, a pioneer big wave rider and later surfwear fabric king, visited Sydney in 1954 or 1955, probably doing business for the family firm, Hoffman California Fabrics. While in Sydney, Flippy became ill with yellow jaundice and was hospitalised, leaving his balsa semi-gun surfboard in the care of young Sydney surfer Scott Dillon, who rode it a few times but was not overly impressed.

The status quo was safe, for the moment at least.

3 THE ALOHA FACTOR

*Honolulu's noted shirt maker and kimono shop. 'Aloha' shirts, well
tailored, beautiful designs and radiant colors. Ready-made or made to order,
95 cents up.*
Ad in the *Honolulu Advertiser*, 1935

In beachwear, the shirt came before the shorts, and it all happened
in Hawaii where, from the 1930s on, tourists began to feel relaxed
enough to wear clothes they would never have dreamt of wearing at
home. Upon this slender thread an industry was born.

The first Hawaiian, or 'aloha', shirts as they soon became known,
were a by-product of the Great Depression. The Chinese and Japanese
tailors of old Honolulu found there was a diminishing market for their
traditional bread and butter lines of business attire and plantation
worker garments, but noticed that there was a growing tendency
among the young to wear brightly patterned, imported Japanese silk
and cotton shirts to social functions. The trend was picked up on by
fashion-conscious tourists, but the shirts were difficult to come by.

Just which tailor first plunged into the manufacture of Hawaiian
print shirts is still in dispute some eighty years later, but we can say

with reasonable certainty that by 1932 Ellery Chun, just graduated from Yale, had converted his family dry goods store at the corner of King and Smith streets in downtown Honolulu into King-Smith, manufacturers of 'Aloha' and 'Waikiki' sportswear, and that Ti How Ho had established Surfriders Sportswear Manufacturing just down the road. Both companies made print shirts featuring the familiar motifs of the islands – palm trees, grass shacks, tropical flowers and, increasingly, surfboard riders.

But aloha shirts were no overnight success story, as can be judged by newspaper photos of US President Roosevelt's 1934 visit to Honolulu. A huge luau was thrown for the distinguished visitors, at which almost everyone wore floral leis teamed with 'regular street or afternoon wear as would have been worn on the mainland', as Emma Fundaburk noted in her 1965 history of the Hawaiian garment industry. The following year, however, Pan American World Airways began its China Clipper service from the West Coast, and as tourist numbers increased tenfold, so did the market for aloha shirts and the number of suppliers. When stars of the day like Bing Crosby and John Barrymore began wearing them, the age of beachwear had begun.

At some point in the 1920s men's swimming trunks began to evolve from shapeless woollens to stylised high-waisted and belted affairs worn from Biarritz to Bondi, but the Waikiki beach boys preferred a more casual style of drawstring shorts of solid colour with stripes down each side, supplied locally by Linn's Clothing. In a famous photo of Duke Kahanamoku and Tom Blake at Waikiki in 1929, Blake is shown in standard belted trunks while Duke sports a cool pair of Linn's, which became the prototype for all early surf trunks. But if Linn's had the inside running on surf trunks, they didn't necessarily have Duke, who in 1937 signed a five-year contract with Hawaiian company Branfleet to endorse its 'Duke' line of trunks and aloha shirts, for a royalty of about three cents per piece sold. Branfleet, named for founders Georges Brangier and Nat Norfleet Sr, sounded more like a breakfast cereal than a clothing company, and wisely changed its name to Kahala as it started to become one of the major players in the beachwear industry. When US *Vogue* ran a surfing shot on the cover of its 1938 travel edition, the Duke lookalike, shown tandem surfing with a pretty girl, was wearing a pair of Polynesian print 'Duke Swim Trunks by Kahala'.

Surfboard design also took a leap forward in Hawaii in the mid-1930s. First, Tom Blake experimented with a 'rudder' or 'keel' on the back of his hollow boards to facilitate sharper turning. The keel, which eventually became known simply as a fin or skeg, was a brilliant idea but it didn't work on Blake's 'cigar box' boards. At the same time surfers John Kelly and Fran Heath were surfing ever larger waves on their solid redwoods. They didn't buy into the Blake hollow theory for big waves, but they did find that their redwoods tended to 'slide ass' when the waves got too steep. After one day of frustration at a break called Brown's Surf, they retired to a shack on the beach and took an axe to the tail of the plank, trimming its width to less than five inches and changing the rail contours in the process. Even without the benefit of a fin, the board worked like a charm. It was the first 'Hot Curl', a performance design that lasted for more than twenty years.

The attack on Pearl Harbor in December 1941 brought barbed wire barricades to the beachfront at Waikiki and a halt to the beachwear and tourism industries. In California barbed wire barricades also began to appear at popular breaks like Malibu, but few surfers noticed. Most of them were in boot camp or on transport ships to the battlefields. There were some who managed to avoid service and surfed on through the war, but surfboard manufacturing completely stopped, with companies like Pacific Systems being seconded to the war effort.

By war's end many Californian surfers felt they had been robbed of some of the best years of their lives, and proceeded to live the vagabond surfing lifestyle with a gusto they would not have considered before Pearl Harbor. Soldiers who surfed came home to California and found that South Sea Island culture had taken root in their backyard. In Los Angeles, clubs like the Hula Hut, Club Zamboanga and Coconut Grove attracted surfers with nightly live music by Hawaiian ukulele, slack key and steel guitar players, who travelled back and forth as entertainers on the Matson Line cruise ships. As limited as their numbers were, the postwar Californian surfers felt an emerging tribalism. One of the pioneers, Dr John ('Doc') Ball had his dental surgery above Club Zamboanga and his dramatic surfing photos (he had taken over the mantle of surfing's leading documentarian from Tom Blake) adorned an entire wall of the bar. It became the unofficial headquarters of the Palos Verdes Surfing Club.

One of the postwar surfers who began to make a mark was Bob Simmons, a goofy-foot from Pasadena who surfed despite severe disabilities to an arm and a leg. Simmons dropped out of school early but somehow later gained admission to the California Institute of Technology and studied engineering, gaining straight As. During the war he worked as a machinist, then as a mathematician at Douglas Aircraft. He learnt the rudiments of surfboard shaping from Gard Chapin, the leading and least popular Californian surfer of the period, then applied his mathematics knowledge to the design of planing hulls for surfboards.

To look at an early Simmons board today (a styrofoam/balsa 'sandwich' sold at auction for US$40,000 in 2009), it is difficult to appreciate how revolutionary his design concepts were, but he was the first surfboard designer in the world to apply hydrodynamic principles to what was, after all, a hydroplane. Simmons was also the first to coat his balsa boards with protective fibreglass, and the first to use two fins. Simmons's radical ideas were widely copied and he inspired many of the leading Californian board designers of the 1950s, but he failed to make commercial capital from his undoubted genius, and became embittered and reclusive. Surfing alone at Windansea, San Diego, in 1954, he was struck on the head by his own board and drowned at thirty-five.

In the immediate postwar years, the South Bay of Los Angeles, a surf rich area that stretched from the airport in the north to the Palos Verdes peninsula in the south, became one big party town, the dance halls and bars stretched along the front and on Manhattan and Redondo piers attracting not only surfers but bikers, hot-rodders, party animals and ex-servicemen – cashed up from the veterans' '52/50' compensation package ($50 a week for a year) – who felt they were overdue a lost youth.

Dale Velzy was all of the above. Discharged from the Merchant Marine in 1946, nineteen-year-old Velzy was rough, tough, handsome and capable of great charm. A keen and talented surfer since before the war, he had steamed around the Pacific and Far East with a redwood surfboard strapped on the deck and had surfed alone at remote reef breaks in Sumatra and the Philippines that would not be 'discovered' for another forty years. Velzy was a legend in the making. When his surfing buddies started painting popular cartoon characters on the noses of their boards, he responded by fibreglassing onto his board a pair of lace panties souvenired from his latest conquest.

According to Velzy's biographer, Paul Holmes, Velzy had seen fibreglass used on a surfboard for the first time when he found himself surfing alongside Bob Simmons one day at Palos Verdes Cove. Velzy, who died in 2005, told Holmes: 'When I saw that stuff, I just went, I gotta have it.' Simmons, not usually one to divulge trade secrets, gave him the address of a supplier. Velzy went to work shaping and glassing boards on a couple of sawhorses under the Hermosa Beach Pier, while the county paid him as a lifeguard.

Velzy wasn't the first postwar Californian surfboard manufacturer – in Orange County to the south, George 'Peanuts' Larson and Lorrin 'Whitey' Harrison had been building traditional redwoods since well before the war, Simmons was producing cutting edge prototypes out at Pasadena, and in Santa Monica, Preston 'Pete' Peterson was building surfboards and paddleboards, while Malibu surfers Dave Rochlen, Matt Kivlin and Joe Quigg were among the backyard shapers – but he was the first to make a song and dance about it, and the first to hang a shingle outside a place on Pacific Coast Highway.

In 1950 Velzy's employers finally had had enough of the piles of wood shavings and the smell of resin under the pier and gave him his marching orders. Velzy first moved his operation to the adjacent Manhattan Beach Pier, where the local surfers allowed him use of their small clubhouse, but his business was growing and eventually he borrowed some money and took a lease on a former shoe shop a stone's throw from the pier, hanging up a sign that said, 'Surfboards Designed by Dale Velzy'. It wasn't much, with surfboards shaped, glassed and sold in one room with a naked light globe hanging from the ceiling, but it was California's first surf shop.

In 1952 San Francisco surfer Jack O'Neill opened 'The Surf Shop' in a beachside garage on the Great Highway. Initially, it too sold only surfboards, but O'Neill had enough faith in his big idea to trademark the name. In January 1954, Hobie Alter, who had been building boards at Laguna Beach, opened Hobie Balsa Fiberglass Surfboards at Dana Point, the first purpose-built surf shop, with more floor space than its two predecessors combined. More shops followed, but all faced the same problem. There were not enough surfers to go round. To survive, the retailers had to attract a broader market.

Despite these issues, the surfboard market continued to grow as balsa replaced redwood as the material of choice and fibreglass coating replaced varnish. Less than half the weight of the redwood planks, waterproof and resilient, the balsa boards were easier to ride, inspiring more novices to take up the sport. The development of the 'Malibu chip' board by Bob Simmons and Malibu surfers Joe Quigg and Matt Kivlin accelerated the process, and Dale Velzy's wide-backed 'pig' (so named for their unattractive dorsal aspect) shapes also proved popular. The surfboard industry was still rude, crude and undesirable to outsiders (particularly those who might happen upon an inebriated Velzy sitting on a resin drum outside his shop, finishing off a six-pack and shouting obscenities at passing girls) but the manufacturers were servicing their small market, and the market was responding by buying branded surfboards rather than making their own. By the early 1950s there was a living to be had in the surfboard industry in California, but only just. Velzy, the leader in the field, made ten boards a week and sold them for $55 apiece almost as fast as he made them.

One thing that was holding the surf industry back was the Californian climate. Frequently depicted as a subtropical beach paradise, the California dream becomes a nightmare when you put a foot in the water. Even at the height of summer, the ocean temperature remains chilly in southern California and downright cold north of Santa Cruz. When they chose their big, buoyant boards, prewar California surfers had always factored in the need to sit high above the waterline in winter or risk hypothermia if they stayed in for more than a short time.

In the 1930s the DuPont Corporation had developed a synthetic plastic 'rubber' they named neoprene, which, because of its heat-resistant qualities, was soon being used in many insulating applications. In 1951 a physicist at the University of California (Berkeley), Dr Hugh Bradner, began testing neoprene suits for heat retention so that US Navy divers might be able to work in comfort in all climates. Bev Morgan, a student at Scripps Institute of Oceanography near San Diego (and a former surfboard glasser for Dale Velzy), read about Bradner's successful trials of the neoprene suits in a scientific newsletter in early 1952, managed to get hold of some neoprene and by the end of the year was making copies of the prototype for his friends. Because the suits were designed to admit water and heat it to body temperature, they were known as 'wetsuits', as opposed to the diving 'drysuit' of latex rubber developed during the war years.

In 1953 Morgan went into partnership with surfboard builder Hap Jacobs and opened a shop called Dive 'n' Surf in Redondo Beach, Jacobs building balsa boards on one side of the room while Morgan glued neoprene on the other. 'It wasn't such a good idea,' Morgan told writer Paul Holmes more than half a century later. 'The sawdust and fibreglass got all over the suits. It was a mess.' Morgan shared dreams of cornering the emerging Californian diving and surfing market with two other surfer/divers, Bill and Bob Meistrell, so ultimately a deal was brokered with Jacobs heading up the road to build surfboards with Velzy, and the Meistrell twins paying US$1800 for one-third of Dive 'n' Surf.

As it turned out, both new partnerships thrived. Velzy Jacobs became the biggest name in surfboards in the US until the partners amicably split in 1960. The Meistrells bought out Bev Morgan in 1957 and plodded on with their wetsuits, which they had named 'Thermocline'. Business did not boom until eventually they hired a young man who was making a name for himself as a marketing consultant to the new surf companies. Duke Boyd asked them what the key innovation was in their wetsuits. 'Well,' said Bob Meistrell, 'they fit like a glove.' Bingo! Body Glove Wetsuits took off. Duke Boyd picked up a cheque for two hundred bucks on his way out the door.

Meanwhile, in San Francisco, Jack O'Neill had become aware of neoprene when he enquired about the foam carpeting used along the aisles of DC3 aircraft. He managed to buy some of it from the Rubatex plastics corporation and started making vests for the Bay Area's hardy surfers. Because year-round surfing was virtually impossible without them, wetsuits became accepted in San Francisco much sooner than in southern California, and while the Meistrells continued to focus on the dive market, Jack O'Neill's product soon became known as the wetsuit for surfers.

By the late 1940s, California surfers had begun to reinforce their identity as a tribe of outsiders by wearing outlandish gear, usually purchased for next to nothing from disposal stores and thrift shops. Pea jackets and navy caps were part of the look, but the main deal was to buy a pair of navy whites and cut them off under the knee. Worn for all occasions, including surfing, these were the original 'baggies'. Dale Velzy was again the leader of the pack, and one summer he initiated a contest to see who could last longest without removing his baggies. According to Greg Noll, later a famed big wave rider and surfboard designer but then just a South Bay 'gremmie' (or novice), the rules were that the baggies could come down to the knees for ablutions and sex, but otherwise had to remain worn at all times. Velzy was declared the winner after a month.

Despite these unsavoury beginnings (or perhaps because of them), baggies were to have many commercial lives in the years ahead, the first of them coming when Hawaii's Kahala brand introduced an under-knee trunk it called the 'Sailormoku', referencing the naval origins of the style and, somewhat cheekily, Duke Kahanamoku, who had just defected to Cisco Casuals of New York. These were short-lived, with surfers in Hawaii preferring the beach boy short trunks they could buy from Linn's and Taki in Waikiki. In the 1950s, however, as more visiting surfers began to explore the possibilities for surf beyond Honolulu, two small country tailors became the first cool 'surf' brands, distinct from the broader beachwear by virtue of the fact that they were sourced, designed and worn exclusively by surfers.

The first of these was 'M Nii Tailor', a label as simple and humble as the roadside store in dusty Waianae where they were custom made to the specifications of surfers on their way to the big waves of Makaha on Oahu's Westside. After the Waikiki Surf Club and the Waianae Lions Club initiated the Makaha International surfing contest in 1953, word got out about the trunks that could be ordered from the one-legged Japanese tailor up the road. Pioneer big wave surfer Walter Hoffman, whose family company would become surfing's biggest fabric supplier, recalled the M Nii experience in a 2005 interview with the author:

> You'd walk into this tiny little room where there's just two sewing machines, and this little Japanese guy with one leg is behind one and his wife is behind the other. Mrs Nii would take your measurements while Mr Nii shouted instructions. Then you'd wait forever for your order, but it was always worth it. They were good quality trunks and, at the time, they were what you had to have.

The M Nii trunks, basically gym shorts with a stripe down the side and a pocket for a block of board wax, became a prized object on the US mainland, and many visiting surfers helped fund their fares by coming home with a suitcase full of them. Their value skyrocketed when footage appeared in the very first surf movies of Greg Noll wearing his striped 'jailhouse' Niis. Noll was still wearing the trademark stripes when he rode his farewell 'biggest wave in history' at Makaha in 1969, but by then the little one-legged tailor had gone back to making 'Sunday bests' for the locals, and become a mere footnote in surfing history.

By the late 1950s more surfers were making the longer trek through the pineapple fields to Oahu's North Shore, where huge and challenging waves broke every winter. Along the way they had to pass through the historic old village of Haleiwa, driving right past the shopfront of H Miura, who had opened the doors of his country store in 1918. Husakichi Miura first worked in the Kahuku sugar plantation while his wife, a seamstress, ran the store, but when he realised the demand for plaid (or 'palaka') shirts for plantation workers, he learnt to sew too. By the 1950s, H Miura had also become known for its aloha shirts, and when surfers dropped in to check out the shirts they also discovered that Miura trunks were available. Just as M Nii's brand became a status symbol for surfers who had been there, H Miura became synonymous with braving the North Shore. And when their day in the sun was over, the Miuras simply went back to what they had always done. Husakichi's daughters, Jane and Katherine, finally closed the doors of the family store in 2005.

While the majority of surfers who defined 'cool' in the 1950s by wearing custom Hawaiian trunks were from the mainland, California was strangely slow to pick up on surfer style. Again the impetus came first from cottage industry, when a twelve-year-old surfer named Charles 'Corky' Carroll approached his neighbours in Surfside, near Long Beach, to make him some surf shorts out of tough canvas. As it happened, the neighbours, Walter and Nancy Katin, had canvas to spare. Their small business specialised in canvas boat covers. Childless, the Katins had a special relationship with young Corky, later to become an American champion, and Nancy delighted in making him a pair of sturdy red trunks with a drawstring fly. The trunks became the Corky trademark and, as he established himself as a junior surf star, Kanvas by Katin grew into a full-time business, California's first legitimate surfwear brand. It was soon copied by Birdwell Beach Britches, which were made of lightweight sailcloth, but otherwise identical.

The fledgling surf industry of the fifties existed almost entirely through word of mouth. Although the imagery of surfing had been adopted wholeheartedly by the tourism industry and other glamour factories of the era, there was virtually no means of communication of ideas between surfers themselves. Unless you were a part of the very small cognoscenti who commuted between Hawaii and the mainland on a regular basis, and pounded the coast highway from San Diego to Santa Cruz, you had no idea what was happening beyond your home beach. The surf movie changed all of that, but it had a very slow gestation.

Bud 'Barracuda' Browne was a forty-year-old schoolteacher studying film part-time at the University of Southern California (USC) when, in 1953, he decided to give himself a practical lesson in film editing by splicing together the best of the 16-mm footage he'd shot while on vacation in Hawaii each year since the end of the war. Browne was also a good surfer, a former captain of the USC swim team (1934) and regarded as one of the best body-surfers in California, so his surfing footage was taken with an expert's eye.

Encouraged by friends to show the film publicly, Browne rented the auditorium of John Adams Junior High in Santa Monica, charged sixty-five cents admission and showed the 45-minute film he imaginatively titled *Hawaiian Surfing Movies* to a packed house. Browne sat in the projection booth and provided a live narration over the school's PA system, occasionally adding a music track or two from his state-of-the-art reel-to-reel tape recorder. It was basic, to say the least, but the crowd loved it, and the commercial surf film had been born.

The following summer, Browne released *Hawaiian Holiday*, which featured a lot of the same footage but with new big wave surfing at Makaha added. Again he sold out John Adams, and then took his show on the road, finishing his run in San Francisco, where Jack O'Neill promoted the showing vigorously at his Surf Shop. Browne quit teaching and embraced his new role as the godfather of surf film, and the annual offering improved commensurately with his camera skills. Soon he was alternating between beach positions and shooting from the water, either on outrigger canoes or swimming with his camera waterproofed inside a primitive housing.

Browne also pioneered the surf film format that would become standard – big waves, big wipeouts, a few bikini-clad babes and the mandatory slapstick comedy sequence in which a bunch of surfers would lose control of their woody coming down a steep hill, or their boards would fly off the roof on the freeway. He also pioneered the star system, featuring big wave heroes like George Downing, Buzzy Trent and Buffalo Keaulana. Another of the stars of the early Browne flicks, Greg Noll, watched the reaction of audiences at Browne's showings with great interest, and when the opportunity arose for him to travel to Australia in 1956, he took along an 8-mm camera he had bought from ski film-maker Warren Miller.

On the way back from Australia, Noll wintered in Hawaii, capturing some good big wave footage at Makaha and on the new big wave frontier, the North Shore. In California, he hastily edited the footage, leaning heavily on the formulaic presentation used by Bud Browne and by his friend Miller in his ski movies. Big, loud, exuberant Greg Noll was a man of many talents but he was not a creative film-maker. His 1957 debut release, *Search for Surf*, was a pale imitation of Bud Browne's work in every respect except one, and it was an important one. Whereas Browne had visited the same locations every year, Noll had created a surf travelogue, introducing exotic new locations in Australia and on Oahu's wave-rich North Shore, and he had even thrown in an excursion to the island of Molokai where he filmed animals in the wild in an off-limits ranch. Noll upped the ante on Browne, charging a dollar admission, and played to packed houses everywhere.

The following year, for his 1958 flick, also called *Search for Surf* (as all of his five films would be known), he found more exotic locations around Mazatlan, Mexico, where surfing was unknown. Needing surfers to ride the perfect small waves for his camera, he telegrammed friends in California to join him. One of these, Bruce Brown, was to do to Noll what Noll had done to Bud Browne – watch, listen, learn, copy. But Brown had a cinematic sense that far surpassed the others, and he was to make the surf travelogue genre his own.

Art major John Severson was yet another young surfer who saw the possibilities of film, making his first feature, *Surf*, while doing compulsory military service in Hawaii in 1958. Unlike the others, Severson couldn't roadshow his product along the coast and do live narration because he couldn't get a release from the army. But Severson had other strengths, which came to the fore when he got out of the army. A painter with a distinctive style that married surf with modern jazz record covers, he created wonderfully attractive posters and handbills for his first films. Seeing how printed material worked to promote his films, Severson decided to take it one step further, producing a 36-page black and white magazine full of grainy surf shots and stylised pen and ink drawings to promote his 1960 release, *Surf Fever*. He named the magazine *The Surfer*, spent every cent he had to print five thousand, and sold them up and down the coast at his showings.

Discussing this bold start-up with Severson at his Maui studio in July 2009, I was struck by the similarities with another kitchen table magazine creation a few years earlier – Hugh Hefner's *Playboy*. 'Yes,' said Severson, 'but there were a lot more people interested in sex than interested in surfing!' True, but surfing's audience was growing, and the magazine, intended as a one-shot with the possibility of doing it annually in conjunction with his movies, sold out before the summer roadshow was over. Surfing's first dedicated magazine was a hit, and Severson found a distributor and prepared to publish *Surfer* (having dropped 'The' from its title) quarterly.

By the end of the 1950s surfing was beginning to find its voice along the Californian coast and in small pockets elsewhere in the world, but its industry and nascent media were still very much cottage affairs. Surfing's devotees loved the sport, lifestyle and culture to death, but there were too few of them for the real business world to take any notice, and there were vast centres of population – notably the heartland of the US and most of Europe – where no one had even heard of surfing, or if they had, could certainly not grasp the power it exerted over its adherents, nor understand the dream factory its imagery could inspire.

For the most part, surfers were more than happy with this situation, preferring to regard themselves as rebels and outsiders. But there was also an increasing number who aspired to make a living out of the thing they loved to do, and in order for this to happen, surfing needed a circuit-breaker – a social and cultural breakthrough that would make the world at large sit up and take notice. Who could have guessed that it would take the form of a tiny, precocious sixteen-year-old girl from Brentwood who decided to devote the summer of '56 to learning to surf at Malibu?

4 THUNDER DOWN UNDER

After the paddling events were over we grabbed our boards and paddled out to the break. There had been thousands of people watching from the shore, and they had started leaving. Word got around in the parking lot, 'The Yanks are surfing, you ought to see the Yanks.'
Greg Noll, 1989

In the southern spring of 1956 the tiny Victorian fishing village and seaside resort of Torquay, one hundred kilometres south-west of Melbourne at the start of the Great Ocean Road, hosted the biggest event in its history, an 'International and Australian Surf Championship Carnival' held in conjunction with the Melbourne Olympics.

This was the first time that sports-crazy Australia had hosted an Olympic Games, and with the introduction of television occurring almost simultaneously, public and media alike were in a frenzy of anticipation. But the Australian surf lifesaving movement, now almost fifty years old, was smarting over the fact that the International Olympic Committee had rejected a proposal to make their sport an official 'demonstration sport' within the Olympics (they lost out to Australian Rules football), and the governing bodies in New South

Wales and Victoria were at loggerheads over which of them should host the consolation prize carnival. The answer was fairly obvious, given that the Olympic Games were in Melbourne and Torquay was the nearest surfing beach, but a compromise was found, with Sydney also being granted two international carnivals, at Maroubra and Collaroy.

Teams from Great Britain, South Africa, New Zealand, Ceylon (now Sri Lanka), the United States and the Territory of Hawaii were invited, the latter two at the instigation of Judge Adrian Curlewis, president of the Australian Surf Life Saving Association, who had taken a deep personal interest in lifeguarding and surfing in the US and its Pacific territory, not just because of his position in the SLSAA, but because he had been one of Palm Beach's leading hotdoggers of the 1920s, and he had followed Tom Blake's surfboard design developments ever since. Under the guidance of Curlewis, there had been greater communication between Australian and American lifeguards, with a large squad attending the Pacific Games in Hawaii in 1939, and an Australian national team touring California and Hawaii in 1953. Three years later, the reciprocal tour attracted a huge contingent to Australia, with the US team including elite swimmer Tad Devine (the son of actor Andy Devine) and surfer/lifeguards Mike Bright, Bobby Moore and a nineteen-year-old Greg Noll, the Hawaii team's star being the renowned surfer and paddling champion Tommy Zahn.

The American and Hawaiian teams flew into Sydney together on 13 November and were billeted at the Balmoral navy barracks, not far from Manly Beach, prior to their first public appearances the next weekend. In his 1989 memoir, *Da Bull, Life over the Edge*, Greg Noll recalled that the team members were bundled onto a bus for the journey across Sydney Harbour, while their paddleboards and surfboards were loaded onto a flatbed truck. He also noted that he, Bright, Zahn and Moore had paid the extra freight for their balsa chip surfboards, which 'we intended to take with us to the paddle meets and, during our time off, try out in the Australian surf'. Several other members of the US team also brought balsa boards with them.

On Saturday 17 November, the two teams travelled south of Sydney for a training session at Cronulla Beach, where they were watched by about four thousand people, including the media, who picked up on the alarming story that the lightweight American boards might prove an advantage over the Australians'. The following day, the lifeguards joined New Zealanders and the cream of Sydney's surf clubs at Avalon Beach on Sydney's northern peninsula for a surf carnival watched by more than 20,000 spectators. The Americans demonstrated exciting new paddle-racing techniques on their short, lightweight boards, but for some on the beach, the real excitement began when the carnival was over and Greg Noll and Mike Bright took their balsa chips out to surf a lefthander just up the beach.

Among the Australians watching that day at Avalon were surfboard builder Gordon Woods and surfers Bob Evans and Bob Pike. All three were amazed at the stunts performed by the Americans, particularly Noll, who flamboyantly flicked his board around in a style never seen before in Australia. By the end of the day, all three had gained assurances from the Americans that they would sell their boards at the end of the tour. Realising the pressures they would be under to sell their boards in Victoria, Gordon Woods paid a deposit on the Velzy-Jacobs pig board that had caught his eye and booked a flight to Melbourne to protect his investment with his fists if necessary. (Evans and Pike made similar arrangements to buy Hawaiian boards at the end of the tour.)

The American and Hawaiian lifeguard teams took a train to Melbourne, where they were housed in a tent village at the Melbourne Showground. Despite media reports that the accommodation was cramped and the food 'worse than horsemeat', Greg Noll had pleasant memories: 'I almost got sent home for screwing around,' he wrote in *Life over the Edge*. 'One night ... no less than five different ladies decided to bestow their warm, Australian hospitality on this poor ol' Yank.' Noll also claimed to have gone AWOL for three days on a beer-drinking binge with his new Australian mates. But by the time they got to Torquay, the lifeguards were on their best behaviour for the return of the patron saint of surfboard riding in Australia, Duke Kahanamoku, now sixty-six, who was accompanied by his wife, Nadine. (On his way home from Victoria, Duke was reunited at Freshwater Beach with the two Australian surfers he had mentored back in 1915. Duke attended a reception in his honour at the Freshwater Surf Club, posed for photos with Claude West and Isobel Letham, then joined West for a surf on his original sugar pine board.)

In different reports in the Australian media, the crowd at Torquay for that memorable surf carnival on Saturday 24 November 1956 was estimated at somewhere between 40,000 and 70,000, an extraordinary crowd for a one pub town, and although the international lifeguards, bussed in and out for the day, may not have had time to form a real impression of Torquay, Torquay never forgot them. While the lightweight boards of the Americans had already made their impact in Sydney, that day in Torquay exposed them to surfers from around Australia and around the world. Queensland lifesaver (and later boardbuilder) Hayden Kenny was there and managed to borrow a board for a few waves. 'I was hooked,' he recalled many years later. Reg Blunt of South Africa was another who saw the boards in action, took notes and sketched plans.

Some of the Americans, still encamped in Melbourne, returned to Torquay the following weekend, when the SLSAA championships were held, and on this occasion a local teenager named Peter Troy, whose father owned the general store, was co-opted to demonstrate the art of riding a surfboard for the visitors. Troy dexterously guided his long 'toothpick' hollow board to the beach on several waves before triumphantly hauling it up the sand. Then Tommy Zahn lent him his Malibu chip to ride a few waves with Greg Noll. The experience changed his life. 'We couldn't believe the way the Americans walked casually up and down the board and turned and trimmed with ease,' he told this writer in an interview for the *Australian Surfers Journal* in 1998. 'We had to have boards like theirs, and if we couldn't have theirs, we'd have to copy them.'

In early December the American and Hawaiian teams returned to Sydney for the two final surf carnivals of the tour, and were shadowed by a growing posse of Australian surfers determined that their boards could not leave the country. In the end, all the boards remained, with Woods, Evans and Pike among the lucky buyers. But Gordon Woods had no intention of keeping the design innovations to himself. He saw the potential of the new shorter, lighter boards to take surfing to the masses and wanted to be the instrument of that change, but his immediate problem was that there was no adequate supply of balsawood in Australia, and no immediate means of importing it.

So, as he followed his Velzy-Jacobs pig from state to state, rarely letting it out of his sight, Woods took measurements, drew plans and, when he returned to Sydney, and even before the Americans had left the country, and before he had actually taken delivery of the Velzy, he made a prototype hollow wood version of the Malibu chip that would soon become known as the 'okinui'. The board followed the plan shape of the Velzy, but its rail shape had to be carved from solid wood panels, which added considerably to its weight. But it had rocker, a fin, and it worked. Woods got his first order immediately, from fellow surfer and boardbuilder Scott Dillon.

The other Sydney boardbuilders of the 'toothpick' era – Barry Bennett, Bill Wallace and Norm Casey among them – all soon followed suit with okinui production, as an Ampol-funded documentary of the Olympic surf carnival (with Noll and the others featured riding the new boards) did the cinema circuit and helped fuel the market. But their inability to source balsa remained a frustration, particularly when a surfer named Roger 'Duck' Keiran, who apparently had little or no boardbuilding experience, started riding a balsa Malibu he had built in his garage. The board was rough but effective. Keiran had got hold of a limited supply of balsa from Melbourne timber wholesaler Arthur Milner, and when the Sydney boardbuilders drew blanks in trying to buy balsa at its source – notably from Ecuador – Milner was summoned and subsequently became the balsa middleman for the

Australian surfboard industry, operating out of offices in Double Bay in Sydney as well as Melbourne.

The first major shipments of balsa arrived in time for the Australian summer of 1957–58, but its quality varied wildly and the local surfboard craftsmen were also still grappling with how to shape the softwood, and how to use the new coating materials of resin and fibreglass cloth. A few, notably Greg McDonagh and Scott Dillon, began experimenting with polystyrene foam (used for insulation products and later for 'Coolite' mini-boards) coated with epoxy resin. This was radical stuff, with many a trial-and-error experiment ending with spontaneous explosions and fires. But McDonagh, in particular, persisted and eventually pioneered the modern foam surfboard in Australia.

While the surfboard manufacturers tried to sort out how to make a buck without blowing themselves up, their market was steadily growing, due in large part to the arrival in Australia of the surf movie. Pre-television, rival newsreel companies Cinesound and Movietone had featured surf and beach culture segments every summer, but there had been no dedicated coverage of the emerging sport of surfboard riding. In 1956, while he waited to lay claim to his new surfboard, Sydney surfer Bob Evans found himself deep in conversation with Tommy Zahn about the movies shot and shown by the great body-surfer Bud Browne. Zahn waxed so lyrical about the power of Browne's home movies that Evans, a sometime lingerie salesman with a keen commercial instinct, contacted Browne and invited him to screen his films in Australia the following summer.

Browne travelled to Australia by ocean liner, spending the two-week voyage in his cabin doing a re-edit on the best of his previous offerings. The resulting features, *Surfing in Hawaii* and *The Big Surf*, premiered at Queenscliff Surf Club in Sydney to an exuberant packed house of more than six hundred, and subsequently played to full houses right along the coast, including one show in a tent at Whale Beach, where a teenage surfer named Paul Witzig watched, fascinated, much like Greg Noll had a year or two earlier.

Browne shot enough surfing footage while in Australia to make it the focal point of his 1958 offering, *Surfing Down Under*, and after his summer roadshow tour, which followed in the wake of Greg Noll's Down Under footage of the previous year, the genie was out of the bottle. California's surf film-makers – all three or four of them – made plans to head for the promised land, a camera and last year's movie under one arm, a surfboard under the other. John Severson won the race, beating Bruce Brown by at least a month. Severson planned to use his time in Australia to shoot material for his next movie and still photos for his new magazine, *The Surfer*, with showings of his current movie, *Big Wednesday*, to fund the trip. But he had no idea what sort of reaction his relatively humble 16-mm flick would engender.

'Sevo' premiered his movie, supported by a compilation reel of his previous efforts, *Surf Safari* and *Surf Fever*, at Anzac House, a small inner-Sydney venue owned by the Returned Soldiers and Sailors League (RSL) on 20 November 1961. The foyer was packed well before the advertised starting time, and Sevo and his assistants, surfboard builder Barry Bennett and photographer Ron Perrott, began to worry about events getting out of hand. As surf film historian Albie Thoms observed in his 2000 filmography *Surfmovies*:

> The story of what followed has become another of surfing's legends, with accounts varying according to the teller, so it's uncertain whether it was because of the enthusiasm of the audience in response to the movies, or their frustration at not being able to get in to see them, but somehow the Anzac mural in the foyer … was dislodged from its supports …

An editorial in *The Australian Surfer* a couple of months later claimed that more than twelve hundred people had stormed the auditorium when the doors opened, a riot had broken out and police were called. The magazine noted that 'the glass mural in the foyer had been smashed, seats had been ruined and someone had written "Tourists

Go Home" on the foyer floor in indelible ink. Damage to the hall was estimated at three hundred pounds.'

In a conversation with this writer in 2009, Severson was still gobsmacked a half century later, not only by the violent scenes at Anzac House, but by the reaction of the media and the RSL, which promptly banned surf movies from its auditoriums. The Anzac House showing not only demonstrated that surfing had touched a chord with the general public, it also marked surfing's drift into the zone of unacceptable behaviour, which of course heightened its popularity as the generation gap began to define itself in Australia.

Bob Evans was impressed by the pulling power of the surf movie. Who could have failed to be? The modern era of surfing in Australia had just begun, yet youthful audiences could barely contain their excitement as the new heroes of world surfing free-fell down the face of huge waves as big as houses, and laughed in the face of danger. The surf movie gave the sport a wider audience because it represented a much bigger social shift than wave-riding itself. Like motorcycle riding, it was the action side of teenage rebellion against the social mores of their parents.

But Evans did not rush out and buy a movie camera immediately. His financial partner in the Sydney showings of Bud Browne's movies in 1957 had been Joe Larkin, a larrikin surfer and pioneer boardbuilder. Larkin had purchased an 8-mm camera a couple of years earlier from Vic Joyce's Dee Why Camera Store, had a hurried lesson from the proprietor (himself an early surf snapper) and had shot surfing around Sydney. When Duke Kahanamoku made his historic return to Freshwater in 1956, according to historian Albie Thoms, Larkin was shooting but had forgotten to take the lens cap off. This was pretty much the way of Joe Larkin's movie-making career, and eventually he sold his camera to Evans and returned to the shaping bay, where he enjoyed a long and distinguished career.

Meanwhile Bob Evans became Australian surfing's biggest booster. He organised Australia's first surf contest of the modern era with the Winter Surf Board Rally of 1958 at Long Reef, Sydney, and subsequently, not much past thirty years of age, he had the key to some of Sydney's wealthiest boardrooms and was able to secure corporate sponsorships for surfing's first big events. Evans was Australia's first real surfing entrepreneur, and it would have seemed logical for him to follow in Severson's footsteps and capitalise on surfing's growing popularity by packaging movie and publishing interests together and taking a stranglehold on the emerging market. But, on the publishing front at least, another Sydney surfer beat him to the punch.

Lee Cross, from Bronte, near Bondi, was one of about half a dozen surfers who started documenting their sport in still and movie photography towards the end of the 1950s. This group, which included Evans and Larkin, and the southside's Dennis Elton, Dennis Milne and Jack Eden, sometimes got together to view their images over a beer, but there seems to have been little or no discussion about the commercial possibilities of surf media. Perhaps they were all just holding their cards close to their chests, because three of the group would soon become publishers.

Clearly inspired by Severson's June 1960 publication of *The Surfer*, in 1961 Lee Cross and a graphic designer friend from Avalon, Dave Letts, began planning their own version, *The Australian Surfer*. Australia's first surf magazine (if you exclude the short-lived *The Surf*, a newsprint 'journal of sport and pastime' that appeared in 1917) copied Severson's in format, style and content, without licence to do so, and came on sale, coincidentally, a few weeks before Severson arrived in Australia. But surfing was not yet a 'business', and who could afford a lawyer?

Cross's publication was doomed from the start, selling for an outrageous seven shillings (a week's salary for a school leaver in 1961) and having no distribution network beyond the small number of businesses that had advertised in it, and therefore felt compelled to offer it for sale from the unattractive sales offices of their factories. Like Severson's first publication, it tried to present a picture of the domestic surf scene through photos, comic illustrations and very few words, but unlike the first *Surfer*, it had no beatnik era design flair and, worse, it had no conduit to its small and far-flung potential readership. In fact the most interesting thing about Lee Cross's debut publication was its advertising content.

The inside front cover was claimed by Bill Wallace Surfboards, still operating from Waverley in the eastern suburbs, while most other pioneer manufacturers had already clustered in Brookvale, an industrial enclave bordering Manly. Wallace, a fine paddler throughout the forties and fifties and a toothpick builder, had moved on to the new game, with 'boards personally hand-shaped from expanded hard foam'. Wallace also offered 'sun proof' clear foam boards (as distinct from the early foam boards that yellowed quickly with exposure to the sun) with 'spruce, cedar or maple stringers'. A footnote to the ad was the availability of balsa boards.

From being unattainable in 1957 to passé in 1961, balsa's fifteen minutes of fame in the surf industry seemed to have passed very quickly, but there were many, like Joe Larkin, who thought in the early days that wood would triumph over plastic, and that foam pioneer Greg McDonagh was barking up the wrong, ah, tree. The argument is played out in the pages of that first Australian surf magazine. While Wallace is lauding his foam boards on the inside front cover, Barry Bennett is singing the same song on the back, offering 'high density, non-yellowing foam', and inside Scott Dillon offers 'unlimited designs and colours' in '3.5 density foam'. In a half-page ad bereft of logos or graphics of any kind, McDonagh simply claims the territory as 'Australian pioneer in foam plastic fibreglass board construction'. But on page 20, Arthur Milner & Co, the importers of balsa, state over a full-page advertisement that 'balsa is the wonder wood of the world'. 'Dead Air' is the attention-grabbing headline of the ad, referring to some technical waffle about balsa cells, clearly trying to make wood sound as sexy as plastic.

Elsewhere in the publication, other ads provide a thumbnail portrait of the state of the industry. Bob Evans had apparently moved on from lingerie, and is promoted as a rep for Legal & General Insurance. In King George Square in the heart of Brisbane, Ken Wiles had opened Australia's first retail surf shop, which, in the spirit of Jack O'Neill a decade earlier, he had named 'The Surf Shop'. The Surf Shop advertised 'surfboards, togs, tracksuits, board racks, wetsuits etc'. Apart from the fact that a city surf shop was probably an idea whose time had yet to come, the ad is interesting for its reference to 'wetsuits', some time before they had really been marketed as such in Australia. On other pages, the Ferris Surfboards company, on Sydney's southside, stakes a claim as the first branded surf empire in Australia, offering Ferris boards in both foam and balsa, Ferris bermuda shorts and Ferris wetsuits. As the ad says:

> Look like a rider ... in Ferris Bermuda shorts
> Feel like a rider ... in a Ferris Rubber Suit
> Be a rider ... on a new 1962 Ferris Surfboard

While Graeme Ferris never became the mogul his advertising hinted at, he may have given others some ideas.

The second (and final) issue of *The Australian Surfer*, published in January 1962, was a far better magazine than the first, with lively news and humour pieces, better photos and new cartoons. Although the print run was down – from three thousand to two thousand, even though magazine distributor Gordon & Gotch had agreed to take on a small number – the advertising count was up, with new ads from Keyo and Gordon Woods in Sydney and Vic Tantau in Melbourne, and many of them improved by the unmistakeable touch of surf artist Gary Birdsall. But a keen eye can see that the jig was up. The printer credit on the back page had changed, usually a sign that the publisher can't pay the bill for the previous issue. While Australian surfing hovered on the verge of the big breakthrough, clearly Lee Cross wasn't going to cash in on it.

5 THE LITTLE GIRL WITH THE BIG IDEAS

A huge fire was going and suspended over it hung a black kettle. The great Kahoona stood over the kettle with a ladle and tasted the chowder he had brewed from sand crabs, sea mussels and rock oysters ... They had already annihilated kegs of beer and started to get fractured on Gallo wine. I saw a lot of guys I had never set eyes on before and they were decked out in what was unquestionably the screwiest collection of rags ever assembled anywhere.
Frederick Kohner, *Gidget*, 1957

In the northern hemisphere summer vacation of 1956, Fred Kohner noticed some alarming changes in his fifteen-year-old daughter, Kathy. One, she was never around. Two, when she was, she may as well have spoken in tongues for all he could understand of her gushing about 'gassing' and 'humps' and the like. Three, he knew she was hanging about on Surfrider Beach at Malibu where all manner of undesirables gathered. Kohner, a well-heeled Czechoslovakian Jew who had made good in America after fleeing the Holocaust, did what any dad would do. He sat his daughter down and they talked it out.

But Kohner was also a screenwriter of note, so, having heard all about Kathy's summer adventures, he did what any writer would do. He sat down and wrote a book about them. *Gidget*, published by Putnam in September 1957, was the surprise hit of the fall season, selling almost half a million copies worldwide within two years. The book's subtitle, *The Little Girl with the Big Ideas*, seemed to have struck a chord with teens all over the country, and Kohner was hired by Columbia Pictures to write the screen version. The book, considered racy at the time, is slight in every respect – plot, characterisation and credibility. But it was fictionalised only very lightly, and the coming-of-age summer adventure, played out against a beach full of wine-swilling, wave-ripping, sex-crazed surf bums, accurately reflected what was happening at Malibu, San Onofre and around other beach campfires up and down the Californian coast. *Life* magazine hurriedly sent a team to report on the story behind Gidget (so named because she was referred to by the beach crowd as a girl midget). The resulting article, featuring photos of Kathy Kohner surfing, was memorable for a quote the reporters got from a Malibu surf bum: 'If I had a couple of bucks to buy the [Gidget] book, I wouldn't. I'd buy some beer.' This seemed to capture the mood of 1950s Malibu far better than the book did.

Gidget, the book, kindled the beach bonfire, but *Gidget*, the movie, threw petrol on the flames. As surfboard manufacturer Greg Noll said in 2008: 'The surfboard business was just ticking along nicely, then the Gidget movie came out and fucked everything! We couldn't keep up demand so people were buying anything and calling it a surfboard.' But Noll learned to live with the boom. As his biographer Andrea Gabbard noted in 2001: 'To the chagrin of surfers suddenly having to share waves with the hordes, and to the delight of those who would create business out of surfing, *Gidget* lured inland America to the beach.' Well, at least LA's Inland Empire, if not the great heartland beyond.

Gidget starred Sandra Dee and James Darren, who couldn't surf, and co-starred Cliff Robertson, who could. Malibu surfers Miki Dora and Mickey Munoz were paid as stunt doubles for the lead actors, with the diminutive Munoz never living down his star turn in an orange bikini. It was a summer hit, and when the Four Preps released the title song as a single, that was a hit too.

Hollywood's first surf movie, trite and predictable as it was – the Great Kahuna (sorry, 'Kahoona') burns down the evil shack and joins President Eisenhower's workforce at the end – unquestionably took surfing and its underpinning (and tiny) industry into a new dimension. The Gidget franchise spread across the entire media spectrum and continued for years. The movies were dubbed into a dozen languages, opening up markets in dormant surf cultures like France. Even after the TV version's Sally Field swapped her surfboard for a nun's habit and a pair of wings, the production line continued. And when Gidget's first generation of fans became middle-aged, the retro-nostalgia stuff kicked in.

In the beginning it had very little to do with surfing and, by the end, nothing at all. But that was not the point. The Gidget phenomenon opened the doors for the entire beach movie genre, which even Elvis Presley was drawn into, albeit mightily uncomfortably, sucking his gut into a tight pair of Linn's boardies for 1961's *Blue Hawaii*. Something was going on at the beach, and it was cool for girls as well as guys. And you didn't have to go to the beach to be a part of it. You could just buy it!

Published just a few months after the first Gidget movie premiered, John Severson's debut magazine, *The Surfer*, steered well clear of the emerging Hollywood phenomenon, despite heavily featuring Munoz and Dora, who had worked on the film. Then, as now, surfers were quick to judge what was crass and what was cool, despite the fact that crass was more likely to put a buck in their pockets. America's first surf magazine carried just seven and a half pages of advertising, and that included a back cover 'house' ad for Sevo's new movie, *Surf Fever*. Of the rest, all but a page and a quarter were ads for surfboards. (The most interesting of these was a full page ad for Robertson/Sweet Surfboards, a short-lived partnership between actor Cliff Robertson and shaper Roger Sweet, designed to capture the Hollywood wannabe market.) The page and a quarter not for surfboards was given over to wetsuits, but there was not a single ad for clothing.

Jack O'Neill's San Francisco Surf Shop took out a half-page that mentioned their foam surfboards but concentrated on 'custom-tailored thermal barrier diving and surfing suits'. The Meistrell brothers' Dive 'n' Surf Shop advertised 'Thermocline Wet Suits', while La Jolla Divers Supply (open Sunday) took out a quarter page to plug their 'custom tailored surfing suits in aqua, yellow, red and black'. These were core ads for core surfers, a cool crew of a few thousand tops. It was business as usual, despite the fact that the barbarians were at the gates, brandishing bankrolls. The whole deal smacked of a commercial stand-off, with corporate America wanting to capitalise on Gidget but not trusting surfing's own fledgling media to communicate the message, and core surfers wanting to make a buck out of surfing but not trusting the corporate world.

Meanwhile, another aspect of the teenage cultural revolution – pop music – was discovering surfing. At the Rendezvous Ballroom in Newport Beach, California, resident band Dick Dale and the Del-Tones had built up a huge following of surfers throughout 1960 with their highly charged, guitar-led instrumental sets, which Dale said were inspired by his surfing experiences. Dale had a minor regional hit in 1961 with 'Let's Go Trippin'', but other instrumental bands had already made a bigger impact on the charts with similar music, notably The Ventures, from Seattle, with 'Walk Don't Run' and English pop idol Cliff Richard's backing band, The Shadows, with 'Apache'. Dale's trump card was that, unlike the others, his music was actually inspired by surfing, and with his second single, 'Misirlou', in 1962, he went to the top of the charts and took on the mantle of 'King of the Surf Guitar'. The 'Surfer's Stomp', which became a dance craze to rival the Peppermint Twist, also originated with Dale at the Rendezvous.

Other instrumental bands picked up on the surf theme with considerable success, notably The Surfaris with 'Wipeout' in 1962, and The Chantays with 'Pipeline' in 1963, but the greatest airplay, and therefore biggest record sales, was reserved for two-minute pop songs with inoffensive lyrics, so the biggest hits of the surf music genre came from the manufactured sounds of boy bands who carried on the tradition of 1950s bands like the Four Preps. The first and the most successful of these was the Beach Boys, whose amazing harmonies emerged from a garage in the South Bay of Los Angeles in late 1961.

The Beach Boys' first single, 'Surfin'', covered both bases for the surf market by having an instrumental B-side, but as soon as the public heard those magical harmonies, the writing was on the wall. Surfers loved the instrumentals, but everybody loved the Beach Boys when they sang about fun in the sun. And the only real rival for the Beach Boys' surf throne was a duo called Jan and Dean, also from the South Bay, who beat them to a surf music number one record in 1963 with 'Surf City'. Jan and Dean were hugely successful through the early 1960s, but when surf and hot rod began to wane as fads, they could not reinvent themselves over and over in the way of the Beach Boys, who had the great fortune to be led by a musical genius (albeit an unbalanced one) in Brian Wilson.

In Australia, which by now had fallen into a product lead-time of about two years behind California for all things surf-related, local surf music first appeared with the release of a single called 'Surfside', by The Denvermen, in 1963. Although principally famous as the backing band for a diminutive and very un-surf rocker named Digger Revell, The Denvermen were led by guitarist and composer Les Green, who, while not a surfer, captured perfectly the soundtrack of the coastal life in this mellow instrumental. Within months, however, the more raucous sound of The Atlantics had taken over, and their first single, 'Bombora', went to number one. The Atlantics didn't surf either, but they sure could rock.

As in California, surf songs were better sellers than surf instrumentals, and veteran vocal quartet The Delltones stepped up with 'Hangin' Five' in 1963. 'Little Pattie' Amphlett was an actual surfer (or at least a teenage 'femlin') who rode out of suburban anonymity with a song about her home beach, 'Stompin' at Maroubra', backed by 'He's My Blond-Headed Stompie-Wompie Real Gone Surfer Boy'. As surf got bigger, the vocal efforts seemed to get worse, with talent-deprived TV hosts and the like trying to cash in or revive ailing careers by warbling about beach balls and bikinis. Fortunately for all concerned, including ballet legend Sir Robert Helpmann (the last totally inappropriate famous person to record a surf tune), surf music in Australia was killed stone-dead by the arrival of The Beatles and the Merseybeat and, when it encored years later, only the good stuff was remembered, and it was treated with the love and respect it deserved.

By 1963 the surf craze (for that was what it had become) had conquered both coasts of the US and its new state of Hawaii, and most other places that had a developing surf culture, such as Australia, New Zealand, South Africa, France and Great Britain. The inane beach movies, the often tuneless, twanging music and the antics of the surfers themselves, who were like 1950s surfers on steroids, were all a bit much for some sections of the community, particularly the rockers and the bikers, who felt usurped as society's leading youthful rebels, and civic leaders, who saw their monuments, halls and auditoriums endangered by these rampaging mobs of 'surfies', who stomped all over everything, including authority.

Compared with the race-related gang wars of later decades, the 'wars' between rockers and surfies were fairly harmless, with only minor injuries reported as gangs of oily-haired youths descended on Sydney's northern beach suburbs throughout the summer of 1963–64, determined to put the surfies in their place. There were a few scuffles, particularly outside Manly's many pubs, and a few arrests, but the only people who got really excited about it were the excitable Sydney media. For a time, the hugely popular Sunday papers vied to produce the biggest coverage of brawls that no one else remembered.

Meanwhile, as the estimated number of surfboards in use in Australia topped 20,000, officialdom started to crack down on surfie behaviour. After the Anzac House 'atrocities', surf movie venues had been restricted, and by 1964 many dance halls had banned the stomp, for fear of floorboard damage. Closer to the bone, that summer some Sydney councils introduced surfboard registration fees, with the surf clubs authorised to police the system, impounding boards that did not display a current registration sticker. Surfers saw this as an alliance of the establishment against them, and they were partly right.

While the dramatic growth of surfing, particularly on the many beaches of Australia's most populous city, gave government legitimate concerns about the safety of bathers, factions within the Surf Life Saving Association were still resentful of what they saw as the hedonism of surfboard riders, many of them their former members, who preferred riding waves to saving lives. After nearly sixty years of service to the community, the SLSAA had thoroughly deserved clout at all levels of government, so the new laws were enforced to the fullest extent. In the United States, where lifeguarding was a paid profession from the beginning, surfers and lifeguards were often the same people, and their cultures overlapped, but in Australia petty resentments created a wall between 'surfies' and 'clubbies' for more than a generation.

When Lee Cross bowed out of the surf publishing game after just two issues of *Australian Surfer*, one might have expected others to be a little wary of entering the same market, but in fact, even as Cross was shutting down the presses, two new surf magazines were preparing to publish. Photographer Jack Eden was first to hit the newsstands with the quarterly *Surfabout* in August 1962. The magazine was subtitled 'Australasian Surfer' but the masthead should have read more like 'Cronulla Surfer'. Not only was editor/publisher Eden the guy who had put the southern Sydney surf zone on the map, but Cronulla surfers Gary Birdsall and Bob Weeks were cartoonist and chief photographer respectively, and Cronulla surfer Bobby Brown was the subject of the centrefold poster. Most of the photo features were of Cronulla, although one was on south coast surf spot Bellambi, the favoured weekend getaway of the Cronulla gang. Despite its obvious parochialism, *Surfabout* captured the times and was well received by surfers. Most of its editorial was in the form of explanation of surfing photos, but editor Jack Eden did manage to editorialise against the 'decadent types' who were defying authority by surfing outside their designated area.

Three weeks after the appearance of *Surfabout*, entrepreneur Bob Evans made his long-anticipated move into publishing with *Surfing World Monthly*, a publication that not only boasted superior editorial content but appeared to have the support of a much broader advertising base. Like Severson before him, Evans used the magazine to promote a film – his debut feature *Surf Trek to Hawaii* – but there was also a wealth of material from all over Australia and beyond. The two magazines were to have a six-year battle for supremacy, but from the very first issue, it was clear which would ultimately win.

Surfing World's first issue carried advertisements for beachwear in its two most prominent ad pages, back cover and inside front. The back cover featured the Speedo corporation's 'Beachniks' board shorts, in what was possibly the first print use of the term 'board shorts', as opposed to the American 'surf trunks'. The ad announced that the tight nylon shorts were 'cut for on-the-board comfort', with 'some really swinging patterns'. A little too swinging, as it turned out, and the iconic Australian swimwear company, founded in 1914 and justly famous for introducing the 'budgie smuggler' brief in 1961, missed out on the surf market. It would be another forty years before surfers would entertain the idea of body-hugging shorts, this time in lycra. Speedo also dominated the inside front cover ad for Anthony Horderns beachwear department, with equally unlikely matching shirt and shorts combos, while inside the magazine, Hollywood Beachwear focused on fashions for femlins, Cedar Wood toiletries displayed their full range of deodorants and aftershave over a full page, and Philips advertised the 'Ultraphil' tanning lamp, apparently believing that surfers only surfed in summer: 'Be this brown on your first day out.'

Bob Evans, as previously noted, was a player at the 'big end of town' and no doubt had connections in the garment industry through his work for the Hickory lingerie company, and quite possibly leaned on a few friends in marketing departments for a small slice of their ad spend, but the advertising content of his first issue was a clear departure from anything that had gone before. Suddenly it seemed that big business would take the surfing market seriously. Conversely, some of the surfboard manufacturers were beginning to take big business seriously. Alongside ads for Joe Larkin (now moved to Queensland), Bill Wallace, Scott Dillon, Greg McDonagh, Denny Keyo, southsiders Jackson and Cansdell and Gordon Woods, *Surfing World* also subtly introduced the department store surfboard, a Norm Casey available from Anthony Horderns for £44.10, or a 'Jamieson Malibu' at just £36. Within a few months a whole range of department store 'pop-out', or mass-produced, surfboards had emerged. Some, like Ron Surfboards, at least had the credibility of having been shaped by surfer/shapers (usually moonlighting from their day jobs with the big names), while others, like South Pacific's epoxy boards and South Coaster's polystyrene and aluminium stringer jobs, had no credibility at all.

As surfing began to boom in Australia, a surf culture also emerged in Europe. Surfboard riding had been introduced to Biarritz, on the south-west Atlantic coast of France, by film director Richard Zanuck and screenwriter Peter Viertel, who passed through in 1956 on their way to Pamplona, Spain, for the shooting of Hemingway's *The Sun Also Rises*. Zanuck, a Malibu regular, had brought his Velzy-Jacobs pig and was delighted to find excellent waves along the Basque coast. But it was Viertel, a learner, who fell in love with Biarritz, made it a second home and became mentor to the local surfing community. Parisian student Joel de Rosnay, who learned to ride on Viertel's board, became France's first surfing champion in 1960, while Viertel's wife, the actress Deborah Kerr, became patron of France's first surfing club, the Waikiki Surf Club, in 1962.

In that same year, a group of Australian lifeguards introduced surfboard riding to the beaches of Cornwall, England. Bob Head and his friends, from the Avalon Surf Life Saving Club, brought their Scott Dillon malibus with them when they arrived for summer contract jobs at Newquay. Despite the cold water, they became regular fixtures in Cornwall, introducing more Aussies each season. Head became the

UK's first surfboard builder, but he was soon followed by Bilbo, a local brand that soon became the biggest player in the British market. With only primitive wetsuits available, surfing in Cornwall was not for the faint-hearted, but the sport flourished, and by 1966 Britain could claim a finalist in the world titles, even though fifth-placer Rodney Sumpter had grown up in Avalon, Sydney.

Meanwhile, in California, surf trunks (as opposed to board shorts) were becoming a hot item. Not only were the mainstream swimwear brands like Jantzen, Balboa, Catalina, Sandcomber and MacGregor offering their versions, but core brands Katin and Birdwell had been joined by another authentic surf company, Hang Ten, which was to become surfwear's first breakthrough brand.

In 1960 former marine and footballer Francis 'Duke' Boyd was attending Long Beach City College on a service scholarship and fooling around the periphery of the nascent surf industry in advertising and design. His first 'big idea', he told the author in 2005, was to design a long, fleecy jacket for after-surf wear, and for sleeping on the beach when required. Boyd did some sketches and took them to a woman named Doris Moore, who was starting to hit it big with Dickie's girls' tops. Boyd was hoping Doris would finesse his pattern and help him sell it to Jantzen. Said Boyd:

> I wore the prototype around to her studio over my surf trunks, hoping to impress her, but she said, 'Never mind the dumb jacket idea, what about those trunks?' I went back to my sewing lady, Grace West, got her to knock up some trunks in different styles, then I returned to see Doris. She was right down to business. She says, 'Okay, we're gonna sell these for three seventy-five and they'll retail at seven bucks.' Wow, that was two bucks more than Catalina and Jantzen, but she was adamant.

The unlikely duo of Duke Boyd and Doris Moore went into the surf trunks business. She kept the books and called the shots, he drove up and down the coast with an order book. Says Boyd:

Most of the surf shops sold boards and wax, that was about it. I knocked on Dewey Weber's door twenty times before he'd talk to me, then he goes, 'Okay, I'll take them, but only in white and only in my size, in case they don't sell.' Then one day I had a coffee with the guy at Hobie's and I told him my trunks would make him forty per cent of the sale price. I asked him how much he made off of a surfboard sale. It was half that, and the boards were taking up all the space! He got that, and soon all the guys started to realise that trunks would pay the rent.

Business was brisk, if not yet booming, when someone pointed out that 'Doris Moore of California' was not a very sexy name for a surf trunks company. Doris and Duke brainstormed it. 'What's the big deal in surfing?' asked the older woman. 'You know, like a hole in one in golf?' Duke told her the big deal was to hang ten toes over the nose. (It was 1961.) Says Boyd: 'Hell, it was corny even then, but we both liked it and we had a feeling it would work in the commercial world.' It did. The embroidered logo featured two golden feet against a background that could have been either sand or the deck of a surfboard. It was the great promise of the surfing lifestyle in one little square – barefoot and free.

In its early days Hang Ten used canvas and cotton twill, and its trunks were not much different from Katin's, but by 1963 the brand had moved exclusively to fast-drying nylon and aligned itself with the emergence of competitive surfing through the ubiquitous 'competition stripe' on just about all its designs. Duke Boyd opened up markets in Hawaii and Florida – 'Never mind the groovy California shit, that was where the money was' – and in 1964 Moore and Boyd licensed the brand to the Don Rancho Corporation in the San Fernando Valley, who applied the barefoot logo to a broad range of nylon beachwear garments. At that point, Hang Ten was the most popular surf brand in America (read the world), but, unbeknown to the principals, they had reached the stage of corporate expansion where growth can kill. They had become the first surf company in the world to face the axiom that would later become known as 'Big is the enemy of cool'.

As Hang Ten made its ascent, only one brand emerged to rival it for authenticity and immediate popularity with the opinion-makers in the sport, and it was completely out of left field. In 1963 a highly regarded surfer, sailor and adventurer named Dave Rochlen chucked in his job with the Rand Corporation to live and surf in Hawaii. With fellow Californian surfer Dick Metz, he opened a surf shop in Waikiki called Surfline Hawaii. Rochlen's Hawaiian wife made some colourful aloha print drawstring trunks or 'baggies' that came down to the knees. She called them 'jams', for pyjamas, which they resembled. Rochlen tested the waters by wearing them to the Makaha International surf meet, where he was one of the judges. Top surfer and Hang Ten trunks model Mike Doyle was one of the first to notice them. In his 1993 memoir, *Morning Glass*, Doyle recalled:

> I liked them right away, so I called out to him, 'Dave, what the hell are you wearing?' He said they were his new jams … I'd never heard the word before, but I said they were really cool. Dave stripped them off right there – he had some briefs on underneath – and handed them to me. 'Here, they're yours.' I wore Rochlen's jams for a long time. They were so wild they made an anti-fashion statement, which I believe was the beginning of surf fashion.

Jams may have been a bold anti-fashion statement, but after Surfline Hawaii's print surfwear made the pages of *Life* magazine in 1965, they were no longer anti-establishment. Within six months every major department store in the US stocked Jams, and their popularity had transcended surfing. 'Surfline went from two million turnover to ten million in one year,' big wave pioneer and fabric guru Walter Hoffman told the author in a 2005 interview. 'They were on fire, and so were we.'

'We' was Hoffman California Fabrics, a company founded by Walter's father in Los Angeles in 1924 and taken over by Walter and older brother Philip ('Flippy') in the 1950s. Both the Hoffman brothers spent each winter in Hawaii surfing Makaha, and later the North Shore, and they brought the flavour of the islands back to their Californian business, creating beautiful prints. In 1955 they were hired by Balboa Originals to design and make print trunks. (The first Balboa catalogue featured a surfing photo of Walter on its cover.) Later, they supplied fabric for Laguna Sportswear, but with the rise of Hang Ten and the solid colour trunks of the early sixties, their surf business dried up. And then along came Rochlen's Jams. Hawaiian prints never really went out of fashion again for more than a season or two, and the Hoffman brothers subsequently worked with just about every surfwear start-up, and still do.

With the surf industry firmly established in California by the end of 1962, if nowhere else, the boosters decided it was time to do what every other industry did – have a trade show. Surfing's first trade show was sponsored by *Surf Guide* magazine and Los Angeles radio station KRLA. In fact, *Surf Guide* was not yet a magazine, and its first issue was a newsprint program for the Los Angeles Surf Fair, held at the Santa Monica Civic Auditorium just before Christmas. By the few accounts available, the Surf Fair was a modest affair, with most of its space given over to the major surfboard manufacturers, their leading lights looking distinctly uncomfortable as they stood around their booths dressed in ties, slacks and blazers. But the event survived to try again at Christmas 1963, by which time *Surf Guide* was a real magazine and Surf Fair had some real entertainment, including a bikini contest, a skateboard contest, an art show and live performances by the Beach Boys and the Surfaris. Again, there is scant record of what business went down at the fair, but the following year's Surf Fair (by now also known as 'Surf-o-Rama' and enjoying its last hurrah) is thumbnail-sketched beautifully by surf historian Matt Warshaw in his 1997 book *Surfriders*:

A few hundred surfers had filed through the Civic turnstiles on Surf Fair weekend, most of them dressed in Levis and Keds, with white competition T-shirts underneath wool Pendletons. Their general mood wandered from indifference to mildly stoked. They directed smirks towards the two kooks in ties and cardigan sweaters who sat at the Salt Creek Surfing Society booth, next to a sign that declared them 'dedicated to the exchange of ideas in regard to the formation and mechanics of surfing clubs'. On the other hand, everyone thought the Jacobs Surfboards booth was totally boss. Surfer Mike Doyle wasn't actually there, but his board was ... Tucked off the main thoroughfare, on the far side of the hall, [Greg Noll Surfboards'] booth featured three surfboards, a few scattered boxes, a plain metal fold-out table and two fold-out chairs. A hand-lettered banner was tacked to the wall, along with a pair of surf trunks and a droopy length of nylon fishing net. It looked like a 20-minute installation job ... Then the display strategy was made clear as Noll himself stepped into the ten-by-twenty foot area ... He was the real exhibit, and suddenly the entire Surf Fair seemed to tilt in his direction.

Almost half a century on, big Greg Noll was still sitting on a fold-up chair at every surf show in America, happily being his own exhibit, talking story to old friends and maybe selling a board or two, while all around him the surf industry's sales and marketing whiz-kids bro'd down, drank beer and talked in weird codes inside their half-million dollar monuments to Big Dick Syndrome. This writer has actually heard a pimply Master of the Surfing Universe with four inches of Gotcha boxers hanging over his stovepipes, scooter up to his pals and ask, 'Who's the old dude with the big crowd around him?' It makes you want to pull his jeans up until they hurt, shake him by the shoulders and scream: 'Dude, where were you in '62?'

6 MIDGET MANIA

You go into oblivion. Suddenly, all your life is there in this long, long,
stretched-out wave – nothing matters any longer but you and the board and
this instant of time ... I sometimes wonder whether this feeling's a healthy
thing, and it's not really what I'm after in surfing ... I'm like a drug
addict then – everything seems simple; everything seems to fit into place.
Midget Farrelly, *This Surfing Life*, 1964

By 1963 Bob 'Evo' Evans was the most influential person in Australian
surfing, but he wasn't its biggest star. That distinction was held by a
slightly built and socially awkward young man from Manly named
Bernard Farrelly, who had been nicknamed 'Midget' since his early
surfing days, when he would drag a sixteen-foot toothpick board down
to the water with great difficulty.

By 1960 Farrelly had emerged as the most promising young
surfer in Sydney, mentored first by Joe Larkin, then by Bob Evans,
who took him along on the first group tour of surfers who sailed
on the *Orsova* to compete in Hawaii at the Makaha International in
1961. It was a bad winter season in Hawaii, the contest was postponed
several times while the organisers waited for good waves, and the

Aussies finally caught their ship home without competing in the final rounds. This didn't stop Evans from putting together his first movie, *Surf Trek to Hawaii*, which was not in the league of Bud Browne or John Severson's work, but it was Australian, and that was enough for it to show to packed houses late that summer.

Evo, the 'king of contra', organised free Pan American Airways tickets for himself, Farrelly and big wave rider Dave Jackman to travel back to Makaha for the 1962 event. Again the waves were slow to come, and the 1962 Makaha International was finalised on 2 January 1963. While this has confused the statisticians and historians ever since, there was no confusion about the result. With the finals held in small, difficult conditions, Farrelly stuck to the inside section directly in front of the judges and put together a commanding hotdog performance, riding thirty waves in the one-hour heat. The points he missed for length of ride he more than made up for with the strength of his surfing, whipping fast turns and flamboyantly walking the board through the treacherous Makaha backwash.

The Makaha International was not an official world title, but that mattered little to Evans or to the Australian media, who went nuts over 'Australia's first surfing world champion'. Evo rushed out a short film, *The Midget Goes Hawaiian*, and took it on the road as a double bill with his new feature, *Surfing the Southern Cross*, which also featured Farrelly, just as 'Midget mania' swept Australia.

It was the summer the whole deal gelled – surfboards, bikinis, peroxide-blond hair, surf music, surf movies, the stomp, surf magazines, even surf columns in the Sunday papers! Midget Farrelly was tanned, blond and muscular. He fitted the bill as Australia's first surf idol, even though he was shy, awkward and serious. Of course, there was a fun side to Midget, but only his mates saw it. His public persona was brooding and mysterious from the start, which helped fuel public interest in the weird surf cult that was recruiting teenagers at a ferocious rate, with a 1963 estimate of more than 100,000 surfers in Australia, up from 1500 in 1959.

While pushing the Midget bandwagon was a major task for Bob Evans throughout 1963, it was by no means his only one. Evo had a dream of hosting a legitimate world title event in Sydney, which he fully expected would be won by Farrelly. As he editorialised in the February 1963 issue of *Surfing World*: 'I honestly can't see any obstacle in staging the 1964 World Boardriding Championships in Australia.' But from an organisational perspective, Australian surfing was still a mess, so Evans took it upon himself to organise and sponsor the first 'Interstate Surf Meet' which he promised would be run under 'international conditions', with world champion Midget Farrelly as head judge. About a thousand spectators turned up for the two-day event held at Avalon at the end of April, and Evans used the occasion to rally the competing clubs behind the establishment of the Australian Surfriders Association (ASA), with Farrelly becoming founding president, and surfers Ross Kelly, Ray Young and John Witzig on the committee.

With a formal structure now in place, Evo and the ASA organised another national event, this time called the 'Australian Invitational Surfing Championships', held at Bondi in November 1963. Evo pulled out all the stops for this one, attracting sponsorship from Ampol Petroleum and the *Sunday Telegraph* newspaper, and offering the open men's winner (fifteen-year-old Nat Young) a first class airline ticket to Hawaii and California. And Evo's *pièce de resistance* was in getting Duke Kahanamoku, now elderly, to make the trip back to Australia to present the awards. At the end of it, no one was left in doubt – Australian surfing was organised and Evo knew how to put on a show.

There was still no world governing body of competitive surfing, but Bob Evans was not one to get bogged down in the detail. Ampol backed up for another surfing sponsorship, Sydney's Channel Seven agreed to televise it, Evo's friends in the cocktail bars of the Clubs Waikiki of France and Peru, and the Outrigger Canoe Club of Honolulu all agreed to come, and the first 'official' world championships of surfing was set for May 1964, at Manly, just around the point from where Duke had first introduced boardriding half a century earlier.

The 1964 World Surfing Championships were held over three perfect autumn days from 15 to 17 May at North Steyne, in adequately contestable surf, in front of a crowd that at one point was claimed to be 65,000, while another several hundred thousand watched the live telecast on black and white television. The leading riders from every established centre of surfing competed, including Mike Doyle and LJ Richards from California, Joey Cabell from Hawaii, John McDermott from New Zealand, Max Wetteland from South Africa, Gordon Burgis from Guernsey but representing Great Britain and Joel de Rosnay from France. As Bob Evans had envisaged, Midget Farrelly emerged victorious and his Makaha victory was vindicated. By any account, this was a major coup for Evo and his various enterprises, establishing surfing as a serious competitive sport and Australia as its leader.

To the surfing world at large, however, the 1964 world titles at Manly meant very little. Evo had jumped the gun on its official sanction, for a start, and on top of that something else was stirring the hearts of surfers around the world, and it was at the other end of the spectrum from contests.

Film-maker Bruce Brown had first arrived in Australia a month after John Severson at the end of 1961, at the invitation of young surf promoter Paul Witzig. Brown arrived in Sydney with three of his movies to show, and California surf star Phil Edwards in tow. While they completed the Witzig roadshow tour up and down Australia's east coast, Edwards surfed and Brown filmed him. This was not exactly a novel act – Bud Browne, Greg Noll and John Severson had all done it before him – but Brown had more of a feel for the surf travelogue, conveying simply but effectively the thrill of discovery through his naive narration and bad visual jokes. To the surfers who watched his films, Brown seemed more like one of them.

A year later Brown returned to Australia, this time accompanied by Californian surfers Mike Hynson and Robert August. While their major mission was to roadshow the new Brown movie, *Surfing Hollow Days*, this was also the first stop on a world tour for Brown's next project, an ambitious travel/surf film tentatively titled *The Endless Summer*. The Australian shoot proved to be somewhat anticlimactic, with the surf in the summer doldrums, but Brown shot a comedy sequence at Palm Beach with his two stars and 1963 women's champion Pearl Turton, 'topped and tailed' a Paul Witzig segment of juniors Nat Young and Rodney Sumpter surfing at Bells Beach (a recent big wave discovery in Victoria), and flew home reasonably satisfied that his round-world adventure was off to a good start.

Next, Brown put together a compilation of all his previous films, called it *Water-Logged*, put a narration soundtrack on for the first time, and gave the print to some surfer friends to roadshow over the summer and keep the cash rolling in, while he, Hynson and August took off on the adventure he had already tagged as 'two surfers travel the world in search of the perfect wave'. With the exception of an immaculate day at Cape St Francis in South Africa, Brown and his crew never really found the perfect wave, more often arriving out of season, as they had done in Australia, or making some other elementary mistake that today's sophisticated surf adventurers would find laughable. But none of this mattered in 1963. Brown shot good-looking, fun guys surfing waves no one knew existed, then he spent more than a year in the editing suite, ensuring that this film had higher production values than any that preceded it.

The Endless Summer opened to packed houses and rave reviews in 1964 and soon became the biggest grossing surf movie of all time. But this was only the start. In 1965 Brown experimented in Middle America, showing his film to audiences in frosty Wichita, Kansas, and flying in a Columbia Pictures executive to see the reaction. Columbia took the bait, bought the movie and blew it up to 35 mm and released it nationally in summer 1966. It eventually took more than US$30 million. Influential *New York Times* film critic Vincent Canby wrote of the film's 'hypnotic beauty and almost continuous excitement', while *Time* magazine recommended it to those 'surf-bored by the dry run of Hollywood's beach party musicals'. Brown resisted producing a sequel for almost thirty years (and probably wishes he hadn't relented then) but the original movie, while certainly dated and sixties quaint in many ways, still holds up as a wonderful surfing experience today, its theme tune by The Sandals as refreshing as a trade wind blowing through the coconut palms. The surf genre's one true classic, it still sells more DVD copies per year than any other surf movie.

Meanwhile, the beach party movies scoffed at by the critics in the mid-sixties were nevertheless playing their part in bringing surf to the mainstream market, even though surfers were generally depicted as lame when portrayed by lame actors, such as former Mouseketeer Annette Funicello and crooner Frankie Avalon. It didn't matter: they were young people having fun on the beach, and they inspired other young people to do the same. The act of riding waves rarely got a look-in with typical fare, such as *Beach Blanket Bingo* and *Muscle Beach Party*, but 1964's *Ride the Wild Surf* attempted to tell a story about the ethos of big wave riding. It failed, of course, and instead told a familiar morality tale about jobs and family responsibility taking higher priority than the hedonistic thrill of surfing. But the film did give work to leading big wave surfers Miki Dora, Greg Noll and Mike Hynson, who worked as stunt doubles.

Over the two or three years of surfing's first commercial boom, surfboard sales went through the roof in the US and Australia. In southern California, unquestionably the heart and home of the industry, most of the big-name manufacturers, such as Bing, Hobie, Greg Noll, Jacobs, Gordon & Smith, Hansen and Con were producing more than 3000 units a year. With boards selling for between US$150 and $180 at retail, several manufacturers were turning over close to half a million dollars with their combination of wholesale and retail sales – good money for the period. In a conversation with the author in July 2009, Greg Noll recalled that in 1965 and '66, he would normally have 'one hundred sets of sawhorses for boards to be glassed and another hundred for sanding'. In Australia the market wasn't as big, but industry leaders like Gordon Woods, Bill Wallace,

Scott Dillon, Barry Bennett and Keyo were doing the best numbers of their careers.

Despite the good business, the surfboard industry in the US was always looking for new ways to grow it (even when they had backlogs of custom orders), and in 1965 they introduced the concept of the 'signature model' to capitalise on surfing's new star system, a by-product of surf's expanding media and the formalisation of surfing competition. While professional surfing was still a whacky dream, an increasing number of surfers were able to eke out a living through sponsorship and royalties from their signature models. The most famous of these arrangements was Miki Dora's 'Da Cat' model, produced by Greg Noll.

Miklos Sandor Dora, born in Budapest, Hungary, in 1934, was surfing's 'rebel without a cause'. The handsome, brooding star of dozens of surf films and Hollywood beach party epics (Dora was still receiving Screen Actors' Guild royalty cheques when he died in 2002), Dora was a brilliant and beautiful surfer whose feline grace led to his nickname, but he was also a strange and mysterious individual who constantly rubbished the commercialism he lived off. The more he railed against the surfing establishment, the more popular he became. When he teamed up with the hugely popular Greg Noll, it was a marriage made in heaven, particularly when surf marketing guru Duke Boyd created a typically off-the-wall advertising campaign to announce the arrival of Da Cat. One full-pager tastefully showed Dora nailed to a cross of two surfboards. Some people were shocked, others raced to their nearest surf shop to order one. It didn't hurt, either, that the boards were beautifully crafted pieces that rode like limousines (and are today among the most prized of surfboard collectibles).

Other popular signature models included Hap Jacobs's Lance Carson Model, the Dewey Weber Performer (the designer was also the star, which was good for the books) and Hobie's Gary Propper Model, brought out to capture the fast-growing East Coast market by using the best of their local talent. In Australia, Midget Farrelly had a model with Keyo before going into production of his own boards, and Gordon Woods brought out a Nat Young Model.

At the same time, Farrelly, Phil Edwards, Dewey Weber and other surf stars of the early to mid-1960s also lent their names to skateboard models. The skateboard began life as the home-made 'roller board', a plank attached to rollerskate wheels which on surfless days offered sidewalk thrills and gravel rash in about equal measure. By 1963 there were about half a dozen manufacturers of skateboards (now with purpose-built wheels and turning trucks) in the US, while in Australia film-maker Paul Witzig and his university student brother John had gone into production with the Midget Farrelly Skateboard. Then the surf boom took off, and while surfboards always had to fight for a national market, skateboards knew no geographic or cultural restraints to sales. One industry report claimed a total of fifty million skateboard sales in the US by the end of 1965.

Another of the best-selling signature model surfboards in California in the mid-sixties was the Bing Lightweight David Nuuhiwa Noserider. Originally intended as a small subset of the popular Lightweight, the Nuuhiwa Noserider rode a wave of success with the angular, more cat-like than Dora, California-based Hawaiian who could plant a foot over the nose of his board and seemingly stay there forever. Soon, virtually all the big manufacturers had a noserider in their stables, some of them in conflict with surfboard aesthetics (like the 'Con Ugly') as they tried any design or hydrodynamics trick to afford the rider longer time on the tip.

Dale Velzy is usually credited with pioneering the 'sport within a sport' of noseriding at Manhattan Beach in the early 1950s. By the end of the decade 'hanging five' or 'hanging ten' toes over the nose was regarded as the ultimate 'hotdogging' trick, usually restricted to small wave riding, although tiny seventeen-year-old Jeff Hakman was to ride to fame when he performed an amazing 'cheater five' noseride on a big wave at Sunset Beach to take out the first Duke Kahanamoku Invitational contest in December 1965. Earlier that year, eccentric surfboard designer Tom Morey had staged the first specialist noseriding contest, the Tom Morey Invitational, with America's best noseriders competing for US$1500 cash. Not only was surfing for cash a first, the event utilised a new system of judging in which competitors were timed for their noserides in front of a tape placed across their boards, rather than judged subjectively on their performance. In a tight final Mickey Munoz edged out Mike Hynson.

The noseriding craze continued through 1966, with sales of specialist boards going berserk and David Nuuhiwa, now widely recognised as being in a class of his own on the nose, expected to dominate the world championships, to be held in San Diego in October. But at the same time a new school of waveriding technique was being developed at the quality point breaks of Australia's east coast. From Crescent Head to Noosa Heads, a small group of Australian surfers and board designers (and one notable expat American) was experimenting with a style of surfing they described as 'riding the wave, rather than the board'. This was a direct reaction to the Californian hotdogging approach, which was built around tricks, such as noseriding, and its guru was a small, energetic surfer/shaper named Bob McTavish.

Originally from Queensland, McTavish had moved south in 1962 and sought work in Sydney's northside surfboard factories. He became notorious a year later when, after being sacked by Scott Dillon for taking too much time off to surf, he and another surfer stowed away on the *Orsova*, bound for Hawaii. McTavish spent five weeks surfing the North Shore before being arrested and deported. Disappointed by the surfboard designs he saw in Hawaii, McTavish decided to develop his own ideas about 'functional' surfing on the north coast point breaks between Byron Bay and Noosa. Here he ran into George Greenough, a surfer from Santa Barbara, California, who shared McTavish's vagabond lifestyle and his radical ideas about surfboard design.

Greenough rode a flex-tail kneeboard with a deep, tuna-inspired fin, but his design principles could be applied to any kind of surfboard, and he and McTavish began refining the traditional Malibu shape by thinning the rails and contouring the bottom. In the Australian winter of 1966 they were joined in Noosa by Nat Young, who had finished second in the 1965 world championships in Peru, and was now being touted as a future champion. The three men used Noosa Heads as their laboratory while they experimented with designs and Young prepared himself for the San Diego world contest, shaping a thin and relatively lightweight board to McTavish and Greenough's designs. He called the board 'Sam', and claimed it came back to him when he whistled for it in the surf at Noosa.

In San Diego, Young planted his huge feet on Sam's deck and the board responded with massive snap turns that were way beyond the surfing of other contenders, including David Nuuhiwa, who dazzled the crowd with a ten-second noseride but couldn't match Young in all-round surfing. Three days into the week-long event, Young couldn't be beaten and surfing had a new hero.

The surfing public of Australia seemed to have matured in the two and a half years since 'Midget mania' took hold, and Australia's second men's world surfing champion wasn't subjected to the same kind of adulation and media attention, but the impact of his win on the Australian surf industry was far greater than Farrelly's victory had been. Midget had ridden a board much the same as the Americans and surfed much like the Americans, only better. Nat rode a distinctly Australian board and rode it in a manner that would quickly be identified as distinctly Australian power surfing. In early 1967 virtually every surfboard factory in Sydney was churning out boards that looked a lot like Sam. But Bob McTavish felt that the refinements of surfboard design that had led to Sam were merely the first chapter in quite a big book. He had much more radical plans, as he explained to this writer, during the production of a film about the era, *Going Vertical* in 2009:

> I'd had a dream, not long after I got back from the stowaway trip to Hawaii, and in it I was riding a shorter, wider surfboard and I was turning it straight up the face of the wave, then off the top and back down to the bottom. I'd broken the straight line and I was going vertical on the face of the wave. But I knew that there was no surfboard known to man that would do that. That became my passion – to design a board that would go vertical – and by early 1967, I knew I was getting close.

7 HOT KID RIP BOARD

The sea taught me to love
And I love the sea
But it does not control me
We control each other
You and me
We are free
To feel the energy
Of the sea
Ted Spencer, White Kite ad for Shane Surfboards, 1969

The 'Summer of Love' is generally defined as that period between about May and September 1967, when the northern hemisphere exploded in a youth revolution of free love, loud music and mind-expanding drugs. Conventional wisdom has it that the revolution started in San Francisco (specifically the Haight-Ashbury district west of the city), and spread like wildfire to the youth capitals of the world – Los Angeles, New York, Amsterdam, London and even distant Sydney, the R & R centre of the Vietnam War. Few accounts of this interesting moment in the social history of the world note that surfing played its part, but in fact surfers were among the early adopters of the drug culture, and by 1967 there were stoners on every beach from Doheny to Durban, and psychedelic imagery and coded drug references had become part of even the straightest surf advertising.

In Australia this cultural shift could be seen in the pages of the debut issue of *Surf International*, edited by John Witzig. On the inside front cover an advertisement for Gordon Woods Surfboards shows Gordon himself, resplendent in bermuda shorts and long socks (the country club attire of the day), with his production team looking wholesome in competition tees and cord shorts. Turn the page and we have Bob McTavish and Kevin Platt looking a little more trippy in bright shirts and paisley neckerchiefs, photographed with their Keyo boards in a forest. But on the back page, an ad for Shane Surfboards goes several steps further, showing Russell Hughes posed in front of another tree (trees had become visual code for getting stoned – go figure!) wearing a Sergeant Pepper/Maharishi–inspired shirt and matching belt, above a copy line: 'Look up through a crystal vessel and get nailed to the wall'.

Within a few months even Bill Wallace – a straight-up, old school wood surfboard craftsman if ever there was one – had succumbed. At the bottom of a full-page, flower power collage, he wrote: 'The observer is the third part of a creative triangle. Any comment on a work of art is also a comment on the observer and the participation of the observer in the creative act is the last stage in its effectiveness ...' And so on and on, finishing with the invitation: 'My studio is always open to the surfer.' Studio, Bill? Whatever happened to building boards in the back shed?

Not everyone was stoned, of course, but adoption of the look, language and demeanour of the drug culture was considered cool. If you didn't want to align yourself with the grim realities of drug dependency, you just called it a 'search for enlightenment', a phase you were passing through in the journey of life. Slap bang in the middle of all this was Bob McTavish and his growing crew of acolytes who, to the casual observer (or reader between the lines of surf magazines), seemed to spend most of their time surfing perfect waves between Byron and Noosa, when not tripping on acid or gold-top mushies in the rainforests behind the beaches. The March 1967 issue of *Surfing World* broke from the tradition of a surf photo on the cover to feature instead McTavish and friends – new era trendoids Russell Hughes and John Witzig among them – pictured in the Noosa National Park rainforest wearing their antipodean version of Haight-Ashbury hippie gear. It was a little bit try-hard, but so was the era.

Bob McTavish has since admitted to this writer, and to many other interrogators, that yes, he experimented and yes, he inhaled, but his real mission was much more serious. By the winter of 1967, while working for Hayden Kenny at Alexandra Headland, south of Noosa, McTavish felt that he had chipped away at the template of the breakthrough surfboard for long enough. One night over a campfire at Noosa's Main Beach, he confided to a group of surfers that included Doug Warbrick, a goofy-foot from Victoria who had recently established the Bells Beach Surf Shop in Torquay: 'I'm going down to Sydney and I'm going to get one of the factories to back me while I design a new board that will change the face of surfing.' On his way home to Torquay a month or so later, Warbrick looked up McTavish at the Keyo factory in Brookvale. 'He took me out to the back of the factory and showed me the work in progress, and I went, whoa … this is a bit different.'

Indeed it was. McTavish's prototype board (later dubbed 'Plastic Machine' by film-maker Paul Witzig) was eight feet long and two feet wide, with a deep V-bottom, like the transom of a boat, at its rear. While surfboards as short as six feet long had been ridden occasionally through the 1950s and 1960s, the conventional Malibu board was between nine and ten feet long, with a flat or rolled bottom. The Plastic Machine looked like nothing that had come before it, and in early test drives McTavish and Nat Young both hailed the new design as 'breaking the straight line'. At the same time, Midget Farrelly was also experimenting with new, lightweight surfboards with no centre-strip or 'stringer', previously held as essential for the strength of the board. Farrelly's stringerless boards were a major innovation, but they had to wait their turn for recognition. Australia had gone crazy for the Plastic Machine.

In October 1967 a visit to Australia by California's Windansea Surf Club (accompanied by a Hollywood film crew, trying to emulate the success of Bruce Brown's *Endless Summer*) served to demonstrate the difference between the two surf cultures. The Californians rode the traditional longboards that had changed very little in five years, and were thrashed in competition by Australians riding the McTavish-inspired 'shortboards'. Film producer Eric Blum was so shocked by the equipment advantage of the Australians that he abandoned his surf travelogue, focused on McTavish, Young and the new designs, and renamed his film *The Fantastic Plastic Machine*.

In December, McTavish and Nat Young took the Plastic Machines to Hawaii. It was a bold move. Even though they 'blew up' their eight-foot boards to a more appropriate nine foot plus, the wide-tailed, V-bottom boards had not been tested in bigger waves, and their plan shapes flew in the face of conventional wisdom about what was required to ride the North Shore waves, particularly Sunset Beach's powerful peaks. But McTavish had been invited to compete in the Duke Kahanamoku Invitational, and he was quietly determined to put his design to the ultimate test, with the entire surfing world watching.

The Duke contest, in just its third year, was a fairly low-key event, over in one day and attracting only a small crowd, but it was televised by the American Broadcasting Corporation's *Wide World of Sports* program and was regarded as the most prestigious surfing event of its time. When McTavish appeared on the beach at Sunset for his heat, nervously checking out the eight- to ten-foot west peaks breaking way outside, Californian surfer and design guru Mike Hynson sidled up to him, looked disparagingly at his Plastic Machine, and said, 'Dude, you don't want to go out there on that thing right now.'

But McTavish did go out, taking off on several large waves, then watching powerless as the wide tail spun out on the steep face. He took three long swims to the beach and scored the derision of many,

Tom Blake and Duke
Kahanamoku, Waikiki, 1920s.
Photo: Spencer Croul Collection

Above: Chubby Mitchell,
vintage Hawaiian trunks,
Malibu, 1962. *Photo: Leroy
Grannis*

Left: Surfers at San Onofre,
California, early 1960s.
*Photo: courtesy
Rose Harrison*

Above: All aboard at Fairy Bower, 1959, as the surf craze takes off.

Left: Debut issue of Surfing World, 1962.

Queensland titles winners, 1965.

Above: Dale Velzy, 2003. *Photo: Maurice Rebeix*

Left: Greg Noll surfshop, 1963.
Photo: Leroy Grannis

Miki Dora, Malibu, 1964. *Photo: Leroy Grannis*

Above: The Noosa laboratory, 1966. *Photo: John Witzig*

Right: Summer of Love in Noosa, 1967.

Left: George Greenough with flexi spoons, 1969. *Photo: Frank Pithers*

Below: Bob McTavish on the Plastic Machine at Honolua, 1967. *Photo: John Witzig*

Above: Rip Curl co-founder Doug Warbrick, around 1970. *Photo: Art Brewer*

Right: Curl's first factory, Boston Rd, Torquay. *Photo: Rip Curl Archives*

Finalists, Bells Beach Easter contest, 1967. *Photo: Rennie Ellis Archive*

Above: Greeny's 21st birthday car. Noosa North Shore, 1967. *Photo: Robert Ashton*

Left: Alan Green surfs Noosa, 1967. *Photo: Robert Ashton*

Right: Sparra Pyburne cuts the first Rip Curl wetsuit, 1969.
Photo: Rip Curl Archives

Below: Friday 'beer o'clock' for the Torquay surf industry, 1976.
Photo: Stephen Cooney

Above: Early ad, *Breakway Magazine*, 1974.

Right: First Quiksilver logo, 1970. *Photo: Quiksilver Archives*

Alan Green, Torquay, 1975. *Photo: Stephen Cooney*

Gordon Merchant, Kirra, 1973 (the year he founded Billabong).
Photo: Frank Pithers

Peter Townend, first
world pro champ,
in Quiks, Coolie
shorebreak, 1975.
Photo: Martin Tullemans

but others, including several photographers recording the action, saw what he was trying to do. On one wave in particular, McTavish turned hard off the bottom, setting the board on its rail. The board responded by driving vertically back up the face, before gravity sent the rider hurtling off. By anyone's reckoning it was a wipeout and McTavish was swimming for the shore, but he had a huge grin on his face even as he was pounded into the reef by wave after wave. The Plastic Machine had gone vertical at Sunset. The straight line had been broken.

Following the Duke contest, McTavish, Young and other Australian surfers spent time on Maui, the neighbouring island that had recently become home to Dick Brewer, the most advanced surf-board shaper in America at the time. While McTavish had created a shorter, more responsive surfboard by simply lopping feet off the length of a standard board, Brewer had been trimming his pintail designs into thinner, narrower, sleeker speed machines. The American was initially disdainful of McTavish's approach, but after seeing Young and McTavish surfing brilliantly on the Plastic Machines during a big swell at Honolua Bay, he changed his tune a little. Likewise, McTavish started to rethink the wide tail, influenced by Brewer's 'pocket rockets'.

There was a fierce rivalry between the two designers, and neither would admit for many years that what happened next was down to advances they had both made, but by early 1968, Brewer was building pintails as short as seven feet, while McTavish had gone on to California to test a narrower, rounded tail version of his shortboard. The phenomenon that would become known as the 'Shortboard Revolution' had begun, and in time it would be recognised as one of the most important benchmarks in the history of the surfboard, but in the northern spring of 1968, it was greeted with horror by America's biggest manufacturers, sitting on huge stock inventories of summer boards – all of them over nine feet long and yesterday's news. Some of the factories even threatened to pull their advertising from the national surfing magazines if they editorialised about the shortboard. But it was too late, the horse had bolted. As journalist Paul Gross observed in a *Surfer's Journal* article in 1999: 'In an abrupt, eighteen month span between 1967 and 1969, virtually one hundred per cent of the active, worldwide surfing community abandoned longboarding in favour of the shortboard.'

This period later became known among surfboard collectors as the 'transition period', because so many different designs and different lengths were tried (and many discarded) before the single-fin shortboard settled into a standard shape, by about 1970. Constant change meant good business for the manufacturers in the US, who soon forgot about their longboard inventory write-downs. (If only they'd had the foresight to put those boards in storage for twenty years, they would have made a fortune!) Many of the longboard heroes adjusted quickly to the changes and emerged as mouthpieces for the new production model shortboards, but the flavour of 1968 and '69 was definitely Australian, with leading Australian surfers and designers much in demand.

Nat Young, *Surfer Magazine's* Surfer Poll winner for 1968, despite the fact that he hadn't won a big contest for over two years, signed with Dewey Webber Surfboards and immediately came out with 'Nat's Ski', a big nose-lift, rounded pintail that supposedly was inspired by Young's latest passion, snow skiing. McTavish joined Morey-Pope to produce his signature 'Tracker', Midget Farrelly produced his lightweight stringerless for Gordon & Smith, and the lesser known but highly respected Keith Paull joined Dick Brewer at Bing Surfboards. Only junior sensation Wayne Lynch held off on an American contract, and in so doing became the underground leader of the Aussie push in the US.

Meanwhile, in Australia, the summer of 1967–68 proved to be the biggest in the twelve-year history of the modern surfboard. Within weeks of the prototype Plastic Machines rolling out at the Keyo factory in Brookvale, most of the big Sydney manufacturers had their own version in production. Doug Warbrick, who had enjoyed a box seat for the birth of the shortboard revolution, prevailed upon Keyo owner Denny Keogh to give Bells Beach Surf Shop the

Victorian agency so that they could take advantage of the summer boom. 'Claw' Warbrick managed to secure Plastic Machine #4 for his protégé Wayne Lynch, commonly regarded as the most exciting young surfer in Australia, and a board numbered in the twenties for himself, but there was already a long waiting list and he had to return to Victoria and wait for delivery. Warbrick recalls: 'When our boards finally arrived everyone was blown away. Within two days we had a hundred orders for them but Keyo couldn't supply for months. It was a ridiculous situation. My partners, Brian Singer and Terry Wall, and I had a discussion and decided we'd have to go to the knock-off blokes. Brian drove to Sydney the next day to cut a deal.'

Singer, who when he wasn't running a surf shop was teaching at Lorne High (or more likely missing class to surf with his star pupil, Wayne Lynch), contracted veteran shaper Bill Wallace to produce a version of the Plastic Machine, but Wallace was also suffering from a backlog of summer orders, and ultimately Singer was forced to go to the relatively untried Shane Surfboards. Shane Stedman had started out a couple of years earlier in landlocked Eastwood, building decidedly uncool surfboards for the mass market. But the affable Stedman was a competent craftsman and a great marketer, and when he finally made the move to 'surfboards central' at Brookvale, he went after the market, signing big names, playing the psychedelic game and creating a big enough production facility to take on the surfboard establishment. Singer shook hands with him on a deal to supply boards for the Victorian market.

In Noosa in the winter of 1967, Claw Warbrick had been fascinated by one of the Hayden boards that McTavish had built as he edged closer to defining his new concept. The board was certainly shorter and wider than most, but it was still a standard longboard, a fact that McTavish had attempted to disguise by getting a local artist to design a logo in the drug-haze style of Sydney artist Martin Sharp's *Disraeli Gears* album cover for the super-group Cream. (If the shape wasn't quite there, at least the graphics would be!) Under the logo, McTavish had placed the words 'Hot Kid Rip Board', a kind of obscure shorthand combination of words that might be seen as the free-flowing verbiage of someone tripping on LSD … or so McTavish hoped. In fact, the slogan went nowhere, but Warbrick remembered it, and when he took delivery of his own personal Plastic Machine, he had Torquay artist Simon Buttonshaw paint a flower power emblem on the deck. All hippie art needed words, so Warbrick and Buttonshaw brainstormed and came up with a slogan in homage to the McTavish original – 'Rip Curl Hot Dog'.

When Brian Singer returned to Torquay with the news of his contract surfboard deal with Shane, the partners had to hurriedly decide on a graphic logo and a slogan that could be sent to the Brookvale decal guru, Jim the Printer, before the first boards were glassed. Simon Buttonshaw came up with a mushroom cloud logo that all agreed looked great, but, recalls Warbrick: 'The original words from my board didn't fit, and we kind of felt they were too American anyway. So we dispensed with the 'hot dog' part, and that left us with 'rip curl'. None of us thought it was that brilliant, but you've got to remember, there was a lot of shit going around at the time, so it wasn't that bad either.'

Rip Curl Surfboards were manufactured under licence by Shane Surfboards until late 1968, when the Torquay partners went into production for themselves, using Singer's garage as their first factory. But a dozen years since the American lifeguards had introduced the balsa Malibu board, this was far from Torquay's first surf industry start-up. Although surfboat builder Bill Klimer built a few plywood okinuis in 1957, the first company to regularly service the Victorian market was T-Boards, a partnership between former toothpick surfers Peter Troy and Vic Tantau, who located a supply of short-length balsa, step-joined the pieces to make blanks and went into business in a shed behind Tantau's father-in-law's house.

One day in the summer of 1957, Arch Warbrick, a boxing champion and all-round athlete who had just moved to Victoria from Queensland, brought his young son, Doug, down to Torquay to try out a hollow, balsa veneer board that he had given him for his fourteenth birthday. Rather than send the boy out alone, Arch borrowed a T-Board, snapping the step-joined board on his first wave. 'That was Torquay's introduction to the Warbricks,' Doug Warbrick recalled. T-Boards eventually sourced proper balsa blanks and remained a viable business for several years, establishing the Bells Beach Surf Carnival to promote their brand in January 1962. T-Boards went, but the Bells Beach event, moved to Easter the following year, stayed, eventually went pro and is now the world's longest-running surf contest.

Through the early sixties, several surf-related businesses opened and closed in Torquay, their owners unable to withstand the seasonality caused by the long, harsh winters. But there was an ever-increasing group of Melbourne-based surfers and shapers who began to divide their time between city and beach. After T-Boards, Vic Tantau produced boards in both places, while George Rice stayed mainly in Melbourne. In 1966, Fred Pyke set up Torquay's first serious surfboard factory, capable of producing thirty to forty boards a week, and Doug Warbrick was one of his first hires.

After moving from Queensland, Warbrick's parents had relocated to Melbourne in the 1950s and Doug had learned to surf as a 'Brighton Stormrider', riding the choppy waves created by local storms on Port Phillip Bay. It was in Brighton that Claw started his first surf business in 1962, the grandly titled Bayside Surf Centre, which was a glorified broom closet on Railway Walk. Claw sold surfboards and wax and little else, but the venture gave him the confidence to open a surf shop next to a beatnik coffee lounge in Torquay the following year. By the end of the summer, surfers and beatniks being in equally poor supply, both businesses folded, but Torquay remained a passion for Claw, and for his Stormrider mates, Pat Morgan and Rod Brooks.

In the summer of 1964, Claw Warbrick moved permanently to Torquay, and went into business with a student he'd met around a campfire at Bells Beach the previous winter. The student, Brian Singer, recalled the meeting in an interview with the author in 1997: 'One morning we got out of the surf and were warming ourselves by the fire and this guy in a dressing gown comes over and starts cooking a can of baked beans in the ashes. A dressing gown! That was Claw.'

Totally different characters, Warbrick and Singer shared the same passion for riding waves and taking a chance in business, so they opened a summer-only surf shop under the Cumberland Hotel in Lorne. They made no money but they met a lot of girls, and in February, the summer fun over, Singer went back to uni. The Bells Beach Surf Shop was a more serious part-time endeavour for the two, but neither really felt that a retail store was the way to make a go of it in business. They were more interested in accumulating state-wide agencies for surf products they could sell to the ever-increasing number of surf shops up and down the coast.

One such agency, which Warbrick had acquired in late 1966, was for White Stag Wetsuits, an American company that had made serious inroads on the markets of pioneer wetsuit companies O'Neill and Body Glove. In chilly Victoria, this seemed like a money-spinner, but just as he began to get serious orders, Warbrick learned that new world champion Nat Young had returned from California with a big trophy and an Australia-wide licence to sell White Stag. Devastated (at least momentarily), Warbrick quit Fred Pyke and headed north for the winter warmth of Noosa, planning to look for new surfboard agencies in Queensland and in Sydney, when he wasn't surfing. When he got back to Torquay six months later, the loss of White Stag was just a distant memory. The Bells Beach Surf Shop partners had bigger fish to fry.

By 1968 there were surf shops all around the Australian coast, even in places where there was little or no prospect of surfing (Cairns, Darwin) or where weather conditions made it strictly seasonal (Tasmania). They all had the same problem – how to pay the rent while their customers were deliberating over the big-ticket purchase of a new or second-hand surfboard. Surfboard wax sold regularly, but it was not enough. Surfing magazines sold well, too, but most had by now gone into newsagent distribution channels. Surf-styled apparel was the obvious answer, with clothing display racks taking up little of the designated surfboard space. The only problem was that it didn't really exist.

In the absence of good quality manufactured board shorts in Australia, a cottage industry had built up around the mums. It seemed that in almost every surf locale, a top surfer's mother had sewn him a cool pair of boardies, all his acolytes had wanted a pair the same, and hey presto, there's your market. In the case of this writer, the surfer was Kevin Parkinson (a national junior champion who sadly succumbed to heroin in later years), whose mum produced excellent high-waisted, long-legged cotton shorts with a single stripe down one leg. But Mrs Parkinson was by no means the first surf star mum to turn it into a business.

As early as 1963, surfer/shaper Kevin Platt's mother had started producing good quality board shorts that soon became the favoured style between Manly and Dee Why. By 1965, Jean Platt had been joined in the business by husband Lance, and Platt's 'Surfrider' board shorts and 'Sandhopper' walk shorts were being sold in surf and menswear stores all over Australia, and their own retail store at Dee Why followed. The Adler family was not far behind, offering nylon board shorts they happily claimed were 'the most expensive in Australia'. Continuing the reverse psychology, they offered only two colour choices and underlined their advertising with the motto 'No Gimmicks'.

There were plenty of gimmicks in the heavy-handed attempts of major corporations to capture the surf market, starting with the 1965–68 Philishave Cordless campaign featuring Midget Farrelly attacking his stubble below the immortal headline 'Avoca, 5am & No Cord'. What a relief for all those surfers who wouldn't dream of going for an early surf unshaven! Nat Young also scored some early endorsement deals, first for Kennard Roof Racks, to which he was shown strapping his board while dressed for an apparent court appearance in suit and tie. Young was also the face of Bumpers, by Dunlop, an Australian version of the immensely popular American Keds sneakers. By 1967 he had also scored an apparel contract, with Speedo introducing the 'Nat Young Surf Shorts by Speedo'.

Speedo's attack on the surfwear market was short-lived, but it was reasonably well-targeted, with fashionable and functional shorts paraded by surfing's biggest star. Swimwear rival Casben was less astute with its 1968 attempt to capture the mood of the market. A campaign called 'The Great Casben Happening' claimed that their appalling product range of bermuda shorts and matching long socks, and crotch-strangling surf shorts was 'Super Cool. Ultra-hip. Wilder Than Wild.' Not.

Smaller players continued to pop up in the marketplace with surfwear offerings they hoped would emulate Hang Ten's success in the US. In Brookvale, just around the corner from the surfboard manufacturers, Jay Walker tried to overcome its lame name with a reasonable range of shorts and tees, while Baronwear tried to capitalise on a little-known surfboard brand with a range that included board shorts, corduroy walk shorts and bikinis. But the first brand to even get close to resonating with the surfwear market was Kream, established in 1968 by Tommy Moses, a surfer who had the advantage of coming from a Sydney garment family. Kream's designs – high-waisted, snap-closing fronts, thick cords, flower power prints – had nothing specifically to do with surfing, but they captured the Summer of Love feeling that all aspects of youth culture were suddenly blending. And, precisely because of that, they were big sellers at surf's new retail phenomenon, the city surf shop.

The first generation of surf shops, in Australia and elsewhere, were tiny showrooms for surfboards, usually in the front room of the factory, and never more than a few hundred metres from the beach. The second, true retail stores in shopping precincts, was pioneered by Ken Wiles with his Surf Shop in the Brisbane central business district and followed in 1963 by the arrival of Surf, Dive & Ski in central Sydney.

Surf, Dive & Ski, which opened in George Street, Sydney, and later in the heart of Melbourne, was a collaboration between two of the Australian surf industry's original thinkers – Greg McDonagh and Barry Bennett. McDonagh had pioneered the use of foam and fibreglass as construction materials for surfboards, while Bennett could see that the local industry could never make enough margin on surfboard sales while importing foam blanks from America, and determined to do something about it. He flew to California in 1963 and checked out the operations and blank 'blowing' techniques of foam kings Clark and Walker, before establishing Dion Chemicals to supply the local surfboard industry. Bennett soon cornered the market for raw materials in Australia, and looked at expanding his surf industry empire in other areas.

When the surf boom took hold, pop-out surfboards began appearing in the sporting departments of retail giants like Nock and Kirby's, at a price far less than the genuine manufacturers could consider. Bennett and McDonagh, along with Greg's brother Denis, decided to fight fire with fire. Not knowing how they were going to pay the astronomical rent, they opened downtown.

The name Surf, Dive & Ski (SDS) was a fairly blatant rip-off of a surf shop Bennett had seen on his California travels, the Meistrell brothers' Dive 'n' Surf, and like the original, the SDS partners relied on the subsidiary markets of scuba diving and water and snow skiing to see them through the first year. But SDS took off, and after the Melbourne shop was also successful, the McDonaghs (Bennett took a back seat on operations) opened a new shop each year for more than a decade, pioneering the concept of a surf retail chain. But SDS did not have the market alone. Other chains began to appear, and by 1966 Surf 'n' Gear (oh, please) had nine outlets in suburban Sydney, while the Dee Why Surf Shop had morphed into four shops, three of them nowhere near Dee Why.

Meanwhile, in Adelaide, travelling surfer John Arnold used his family's footwear business as a base from which to build the John Arnold Surf Centre. Although he had spent most of the early sixties surf exploring around the globe, Arnold, like McDonagh and Bennett in Sydney and the Bells Beach Surf Shop partners in Victoria, was someone who could think outside the square. From his retail base in Adelaide, many miles from anything that looked like surf, he hired

Wayne Lynch out from under the watchful but uncomprehending gaze of a nest of Victorian mentors, and created the Wayne Lynch Involvement surfboard, which soon became one of the top-selling models of the transition era.

Arnold, a consummate industry networker (before the term was known), had struck up a relationship with Barry Bennett at precisely the time the foam blanks baron was seeking to expand his interests. On Arnold's instigation, he and Bennett flew to California and jointly acquired the Australian licence for O'Neill Wetsuits, relying on Bennett's friendship with Clark Foam guru Gordon 'Grubby' Clark to open the negotiating door with Jack O'Neill. They shipped in a few hundred suits and quickly launched multicoloured 'short johns' on an Australian market desperate for a decent surfing wetsuit. Within a year, Arnold had sourced the neoprene, set up a factory in Adelaide and was producing his own O'Neill Wetsuit for the Australasian market.

In the late 1960s, John Arnold, a surf lifesaver few 'real surfers' had even met, had come from left field and caught the cool dudes napping.

8 CREATIVE SOUP

Big business and custom producers will find their particular level, and a man's business will be as successful as his ability to create an image for his product. Merchandising will become far more important, and an integral part of the business, and greater share of the consumer market will be available.
Bob Evans, *Surfing World* editorial, 1970

A couple of years after the Don Rancho Corporation was awarded the licence to produce and sell Hang Ten garments, the company's two principals, Bob McAlister and Scott Thompson, took Duke Boyd out for a drink and told him: 'Duke, we love Hang Ten and it's making good money, but we want a brand of our own.' Duke took a quick pull of his beer and offered Hang Ten to them for a quarter of a million dollars. Says Boyd: 'The bastards laughed at me. Okay, move on.'

The Hang Ten brand was then at the height of its power, with surfers like Mike Doyle and Phil Edwards endorsing it and the chubby feet logo reaching iconic status. When Boyd did finally sell, in 1970 to the Rattner Corporation of San Diego, they paid three million dollars for a brand that had passed its use-by date, so the Don Rancho amigos had missed out on one hell of a deal, but what the hey, they were all friends, and Boyd started thinking about a new brand for Don Rancho.

At this point in his career, Duke Boyd became surfing's first 'Mr Ten Per Cent'. There was nothing he didn't have a piece of. He'd become friends with another surfer of creative mindset, Dick Graham, and the two of them ran a boutique advertising agency for the surf industry, while at the same time publishing *Surfing* magazine, which was fast becoming a legitimate competitor for Severson's *Surfer*. In 1967, the duo had come up with an advertising campaign for Bing Surfboards to loosely associate the established brand with the new, freewheeling hippie spirit in surfing. They called the campaign, 'The Golden Breed', and it was promptly knocked off by film-maker Dale Davis as the title of his next feature.

But Boyd thought there was still plenty of life in the concept, so he and Graham (both ex-marines and unlikely hippies) sketched some ideas for a Golden Breed brand to pitch to Don Rancho. In an interview with the author in Honolulu in 2006, Boyd recalled: 'We got some designer back east to fuck around with the gender symbols and come up with a logo, while Graham and I fooled around with the brand story with weird, angel-winged guys, all sorts of shit. Man, it was a wonderful time. Everyone was running around with long hair, buff naked and screwing each other. That's why the winged guy worked!' The Don Rancho Corporation loved it.

Golden Breed backed its out-there imagery with a commitment to supporting the sport's leading athletes in a softly-softly way that typified the innovative marketing approach of Boyd and Dick Graham. As the 1960s closed, Duke signed a deal with emerging super surfer Jeff Hakman to become Golden Breed's brand ambassador. This was a deft stroke, since not only was Hakman revered as a diminutive teenage big wave rider who had won the first Duke Kahanamoku Invitational at sixteen, but he had just emerged from a drugs importation trial and was considered an undesirable by most of surfing's hierarchy. Ergo, Hakman was cool and he was cheap! And soon he was the leading pro surfer in the world. While Hang Ten continued to play to the cleancut college surf buff (while expanding its imagery into other action sports as well), Golden Breed took the edgy territory of cool.

Back in Australia, John Arnold had become a mini-mogul almost overnight, and soon he was looking to expand into apparel. Again funded by Barry Bennett, he flew to California to secure a licence for the biggest surfwear brand in the world, Hang Ten. Arnold had several meetings with Duke Boyd and Dick Graham at their Total Concept Advertising offices in Los Angeles, where it became apparent that a Hang Ten licensing deal was off the table. However, the ex-marines explained, Golden Breed was a better prospect anyway, what with the hippie surfers running around naked and screwing each other. What happened next is in dispute. Duke and Dick say John Arnold taught them an invaluable lesson in trademark protection. Arnold has always maintained he was granted a licence to manufacture, market and sell Golden Breed in Australia and New Zealand. In an interview with the author for *Tracks* magazine back in 1976, Barry Bennett said: 'All I know is it was going to be Hang Ten but there was a dispute over the name, so we took up the Golden Breed name instead.'

However it went down, Arnold took the Golden Breed brand to Australia and used his Midas touch to launch it through the vast network of surf shops that he and Bennett had cobbled together. Initially, Arnold concentrated on boldly coloured striped T-shirts, very much in the mould of Hang Ten's American range, but by 1970 Golden Breed had added surf and walk shorts to the range and was challenging the market leaders Platt's, Adler's and Kream in all states. Not only was the Breed's apparel range expanding quickly, but Arnold also announced that Golden Breed Surfboards' 'Jeff Hickman Model' was 'coming soon'. Hakman may have been the leading surfer in the world at the time, but apparently he wasn't fully on John Arnold's radar yet.

Rip Curl Surfboards was launched on the back of the Plastic Machine, but by the summer of 1968–69, Doug Warbrick and Brian Singer had settled into creating their own designs in the garage of

Singer's new home in Jan Juc, with the assistance of travelling South African surfer/shaper Andy Spangler. In a 1998 interview with the author, Singer recalled:

> Claw had quite a bit of shaping experience, but our first boards were pretty rough. I graduated from fin sanding to glassing, but we didn't have a room clean enough for finish coating, so we used marine varnish and told everyone it was the new thing. We started off doing four boards a week. Claw would start shaping on Monday and we'd have them finished by Friday night. As we got more orders we outgrew my shed and moved into the old Torquay bakery in Boston Road.

Ensconced in a real factory, albeit an extremely primitive one, the Rip Curl partners felt emboldened to announce themselves to the world in a full-page ad in *Surfing World* in winter 1969. The headline, 'The dawning of Rip Curl Surfboards', appeared over a moody Barrie Sutherland photo of the sun rising over Winki Pop (sister break to Bells Beach) and the accompanying text announced: 'Rip Curl Surfboards were born on the Bells reefs last winter ... We know what we are doing and we will be around for a long time.'

And so it was to prove, but well before the ad appeared, even before the move to the Boston Road bakery, the future direction of the Rip Curl brand had been ordained not through some dramatic new surfboard design, but through a visit to Brian Singer's shed-cum-factory by a determined young accountant from Melbourne. Alan Green was twenty-one years old in the late summer of 1968–69, when he pulled up outside the house in Jan Juc and dragged a bulging bag of patterns and samples off the back seat of the 1953 Ford Customline that had been given to him as a coming-of-age present by his grandmother just a few weeks earlier.

Born in 1947 at Pascoe Vale, in the working-class suburbs of Melbourne's north, Green learned as a boy to use his fists. When a teacher slogged him from behind for some alleged insolence, 'Greeny', as he was known to all, turned around and 'king hit' the unfortunate fellow. Expelled from school over the pleas of his parents, Greeny got a job at Ansett Airlines, first in the mailroom and then as the personal gofer for Sir Reginald Ansett, the airline's founder and one of Australia's most dynamic and ruthless businessmen. Ansett liked the boy's spirit, but he advised him to go back and finish school. A friend was about to enrol at Footscray Technical College to study accounting, so Greeny tagged along, lied about his high school graduation and was accepted for the course.

While still at school, Greeny had hitchhiked on summer weekends down to the coast at Ocean Grove, where he learned to surf on the old boards stored in the surf club. As soon as he was old enough to drive, he started borrowing his mother's Mini Minor and taking his Pascoe Vale friends along. One of them, Robert Ashton, recalls: 'He was a bit of a bad-ass. He'd go into a shop and order a toasted cheese sandwich, and while they were out the back making it, he'd help himself to a carton of smokes. He was bold and brave and he always seemed to get away with it.'

The Pascoe Vale punks took a road trip to Cactus, a recently discovered series of breaks off the remote desert of the Great Australian Bight. Once their Ford Falcon station wagon hit the desert back roads, Greeny perched on the hood and fired his .22 calibre rifle at anything that moved and much that didn't. With fifteen-year-old Ashton at the wheel, the vehicle crested a hill and collided head-on with another car, as Greeny dived into the brush to save his life. They camped out for three days waiting for replacement parts.

Later, when Grandma bestowed the Customline, Greeny put the old team back together, made sure they had enough money to cover the fuel bills and headed for Noosa, a two-day drive north. While the older guys slept, Ashton, still too young for a driving licence, drove through the night. But the passengers woke up quickly when he smashed the birthday car into a guard-rail. Ashton recalls: 'Greeny inspected the damage, abused me a bit and then went back to sleep while someone else drove. But the next morning he walked around the car, made a note of every dent and scratch it had ever taken and told me I'd have to pay to have them all fixed.'

With most of his classes at Footscray Tech at night, Greeny took a day job as a trainee accountant at a winery, and then as book-keeper at a company called Australian Divers in North Melbourne. With a steady job and a time-consuming passion for surfing, Greeny dropped his accountancy course without a diploma.

Australian Divers was the creation of 'Commander' Batterham, a former career naval officer who had worked with the famed undersea expert, Jacques Cousteau, during World War II. After the war, Cousteau became a major investor in Batterham's enterprise. By the time Green became their book-keeper, Australian Divers made or imported everything a recreational or professional diver needed, including neoprene wetsuits. When Greeny pressured his boss to diversify into surfing wetsuits, Batterham told him: 'You should leave and do it yourself. I'll even sell you the materials at cost to get you started.' Greeny borrowed $1500 from his father and set out to give the wheels of industry a spin.

By the time Alan Green came to see them, the Rip Curl partners were starting to realise that the slim profit margin on surfboards would take them only so far. Even as they penned their 'We know what we're doing and we'll be around for a long time' slogan, Brian Singer and Doug Warbrick wondered how true this would be if they didn't diversify. Greeny convinced the partners that he knew how to make wetsuits, which was a lie that they wanted to believe. Warbrick had seen the potential market for White Stag a couple of years earlier, and even now, with O'Neill suits being produced in Adelaide and Ron Harding's Surf 'n' Dive expanding into surfing wetsuits in Sydney, he believed the market was still wide open for an authentic surfer's wetsuit. So the three young men shook hands, cleared a space at the back of the shed and tacked up a 'Rip Curl Wetsuits' shingle.

'The first ones were a complete fucking disaster,' Greeny recalled in an interview with the author in 2005. 'John "Sparra" Pyburne was a hot young local surfer on the way up, so I decided to make the prototype for him. He'd stand there while I cut and glued the panels around him, but it was such a mess that he got the shits and took over as the cutter. He's still cutting rubber at Rip Curl today.'

Greeny sourced a vintage cutting machine which was first shuffled between his own flat and Warbrick's, then moved into the 'wetsuit factory' when Rip Curl moved to the Boston Road bakery. Another local surfer, Maurice Cole, joined the team as a gluer, and Greeny hired women with industrial sewing machines to sew the seams. The first 'short johns' and long-sleeved vests hit surf shops in the autumn of 1969 to an enthusiastic reception, although any profits in those early days went towards replacing suits that fell apart. 'Long johns' followed soon after, once Green and Singer had found a long arm Singer sewing machine in Melbourne. This put them on a par with O'Neill, giving them the capability to produce the state-of-the-art cold water protection of the time – a combination of 3-mm long johns and a 3-mm long-sleeved vest. Warbrick recalls: 'It was effectively a 6-mm steamer, so the cold water protection was good, even if your movement was restricted somewhat. Everyone in Victoria had to have one, and we started to do very good business.'

It was a promising beginning, but the Rip Curl partners had less than a year to fine-tune their wetsuit act if they were to exploit a heaven-sent global marketing platform at the 1970 world surfing championships, to be held at Bells Beach in May. Singer and Warbrick took that task very seriously, perhaps at the expense of their developing surfboard business, but Alan Green's nature (like quicksilver, his girlfriend, Barbara, often said) meant that he had already moved on in search of new challenges. The first of these was the 'ug boot', a fleece-lined sheepskin boot that is often claimed as a surfer invention. In fact, according to evidence filed in American courts in 2004 in a trademark case over the many variations on a similar theme, the boot was first worn by World War I fighter pilots, and was given its name by the Blue Mountains Ugg Boot Company in 1933. In the surf context, John Arnold was the first to introduce the ug in 1969, but Greeny's Rip Curl ug was not far behind, and he circumvented any problems over use of the name by registering a company called Ug Manufacturing. Coming into the winter of 1970, it was this that occupied much of his time, rather than the marketing possibilities of the world titles.

In the event, Rip Curl Wetsuits came off a poor second when the Americans arrived with their superior 'closed cell' Rubatex neoprene suits. Warbrick remembers that he and Singer were able to get many of the other visiting surfers into their suits, including South Africa's youngest competitors, cousins Shaun and Michael Tomson, but that the Rubatex O'Neills worn by the eventual winner, Rolf Aurness, and most of the Americans, were vastly superior. Within six months, Rip Curl was using Rubatex too.

The world titles (which almost didn't happen due to lack of sponsorship, but were bailed out financially by the Victorian government) put the spotlight on a growing cultural divide within the surfing community of Torquay. As pioneer surfer Joe Sweeney recalled in an interview with the author in 1998: 'The event began with a big march through the streets of Lorne. It was a very big deal and the Americans, the Japanese, the South Africans and all the rest dressed nicely in their team uniforms, but the Aussies … oh, mate, they were a bloody disgrace. Jesus, they were scruffy. Full-on hippies.'

This was to become a burning issue for Torquay. While the town had felt totally at ease with the boozy antics of the Boot Hill Gang and the subsequent larrikinism of the boardriders, the marijuana-fuelled flower power era outraged their sensibilities, and it wasn't until the surfers held economic sway in the town that they were fully accepted again. Champion surfer Rod Brooks, who moved permanently to Torquay just after the world titles, remembers that the divide fell right across the cottage surf industry, with Singer, Warbrick and Green representing the free spirit lifestyle, and boardbuilder Fred Pyke representing the traditional work ethic.

In the southern summer of 1969–70, Alan Green spent some time on the road, selling wetsuits in the warmer states of New South Wales and Queensland. Whenever he took time out to surf, he studied the shorts that people were wearing. In his view the surf trunk, or board short, screamed for innovation. The dominant Australian brands, Platt and Adler, were a bulky fit and the heavyweight fabric often caused rashes and chafing on the upper legs. The few imports, usually canvas or nylon, were not much better. Greeny wasn't the first to think along these lines. A couple of Torquay surfers, Tim Davis and Nigel Coote, had begun tinkering with new designs – part of a general process that Claw Warbrick called the 'creative soup' of the surf-mad town at that time. The Davis/Coote shorts (they had no name) utilised a semi-yoke pattern to create a more body-hugging fit, and a high waistband because it was fashionable. They were selling a few to the growing number of surf shops around coastal Victoria, but the business was going nowhere. Greeny decided to see if he could do any better.

The wetsuits manufactured at Australian Divers in Melbourne had incorporated a shoulder entry, secured by a velcro strip with a metal snap at each end, and Greeny had brought this design feature (and a huge supply of snaps and strips) with him to Rip Curl. Now, as he fitted the snaps into the neoprene and tested the closure, it occurred to him that the same system could replace buttons and flies on board shorts. One night in the Torquay flat he shared with his schoolteacher girlfriend, Barb, he sketched some designs on a pad, focusing on fit. Making use of wetsuit parts, Greeny developed the first technical board short. He drew a yoked waistband, higher at the back than the front, with scalloped legs to ensure ample movement. The next morning he delivered two bolts of cotton in contrasting colours and his sketches to one of his wetsuit sewers. He said: 'Do us a little favour, would you, love?'

In 1970, with no room left at the Boston Road bakery, Greeny's Rip Curl board shorts division operated out of a series of rented flats and shopfronts around Torquay. His sewer, Carol McDonald, turned out twenty to thirty pairs a day while Greeny added the snaps. The

Rip Curl partners had already decided on a separate branding for the board shorts, but it was left to Greeny to come up with a name. Barbara Green recalled many years later that she had looked up the definition of the word 'quicksilver', just to make sure it really did match elements of her boyfriend's 'elusive, mercurial' personality before suggesting it. It helped, too, that a favourite album on the couple's turntable was by the San Francisco psychedelic band Quicksilver Messenger Service. So Quicksilver it was.

At Cash's, a Melbourne labelling company, Greeny flipped through volumes of logo designs and selected a swan, or a 'duck' as he preferred to think of it. But then he began to have second thoughts about the rights to the name 'Quicksilver'. Maybe the band would sue! Without the money to do a trademark search, he decided to play it safe, changing the name to 'Kwiksilver'. He even designed the lettering, but then McDonald pointed out that a 'k' next to a 'w' was an embroiderer's nightmare. Finally he settled on 'Quiksilver', thus ensuring that the fledgling brand's name would forever be misspelled.

Meanwhile, Rip Curl Wetsuits had gone into full production with the long johns, an event Brian Singer recalls as 'the defining moment. We had one hundred orders to meet one week with ten bucks profit in every suit. I suddenly thought, shit, we could make a bit of money out of this.' Says Warbrick: 'It was becoming pretty clear that we had to divide to conquer. There were too many dominant bosses in a small space for all of us to work on all the projects. For me and Brian, the focus was definitely Rip Curl, and for Alan, it was the development of new brands, but we were still one company, and for years when you went out selling, you sold surfboards, wetsuits, board shorts and ug boots out of the same van.'

Quiksilver's first customer, in the spring of 1970, was the Klemm-Bell Surf Shop in the Melbourne suburb of Gardenvale. Greeny had offered Terry Klemm and Reg Bell a partnership in the wetsuits before he took the idea to Rip Curl, and since they had turned him down then, they felt obliged now to stock his board shorts. But the designs sold well and Klemm-Bell ordered more, and when they opened a shop and surfboard factory in Torquay in November, manager Rod Brooks remembers that Quiksilvers were his first stock purchase. 'Greeny delivered them himself, walked in with a box and plonked it on the counter. They were one of many projects buzzing in Torquay at the time, but they were well made and our customers liked them. To be honest, I didn't think he had much hope of making money out of board shorts, but as the product evolved, I began to change my mind.'

Other clients that first season included Speaky's Surf Shop in Torquay and Tony Olsen's Melbourne Surf Shop, next to McDonagh and Bennett's Surf, Dive & Ski, the biggest surf retailer in the city. By Christmas, the 'duck' Quiksilvers had sold out, but Greeny was too busy with next season's wetsuits to oversee another production run in time to catch the last of the summer business.

Quiksilver soon moved into a shop next to the post office on Pearl Street, Torquay, and Greeny hung up a shingle. With plans for a wider range of board shorts, he needed fabric at a good wholesale price and, through a friend of his father's, he was introduced to a German immigrant rag trader. Joe Ronic had contacts behind the Iron Curtain in East Germany, where excess stock piled up in the wake of another unrealistic Soviet five-year plan. Though he specialised in dress fabric, Ronic also had access to a double-twisted cotton poplin, which was used mainly for raincoats. Greeny asked Ronic how they might structure a deal. The older man must have liked the kid, because he said: 'You tell me how much you want and what colours, I dye it for you and you pay me when you sell your range.' This generous arrangement, which remained in place for several seasons, put Quiksilver on a footing for future profit. It was a kick-start that Alan Green never forgot.

But if Quiksilver board shorts were going to take on the world, the duck had to go. Greeny again pulled out his sketch pad and began playing with the shape of a wave. He drew the outline of a breaking wave with a few droplets of foam hovering around the lip. Then, for good measure, and for balance, he added a tiny snowcapped mountain underneath it. Though unconnected, or at least not joined at the hip as they are today, Greeny felt that surf and snow represented nature's A-list for the adventure sportsman. He took his sketches back to Cash's where designers refined them into a square patch with QUIKSILVER in capital letters across the bottom. It was a difficult and expensive logo, but by the time it went into production, Greeny was convinced that the little mountain and wave on the bottom of the left leg made a profound statement about the new brand's commitment to its cultural roots.

The world titles of 1970, ultimately decided in mediocre waves at Johanna, two hours' drive from Torquay, in front of an audience of three men and two cows, wasn't quite the death knell of the event – this was to come two years later in San Diego in a snowstorm of cocaine abuse and widespread apathy – but its failure to ignite the general public was further evidence that surfing was much more than the sum of its contests. The world titles of 1964 (Australia) and 1966 (California) had captured the imagination of the surfing public around the world, and made heroes of their respective champions, but by 1968 (Puerto Rico), the concept of a world amateur event already appeared dated (the start of each heat was signalled when an official shimmied up a coconut palm and fired a gun) and its champion, the Caucasian-Hawaiian Fred Hemmings, did not become a household name, although he did become a politician. The 1970 champion, Californian Rolf Aurness (the son of *Gunsmoke* television star James Arness), took a bow and then left surfing to become a pianist.

Since the youth revolution of the late 1960s and a shift of values away from the commercial and back to nature, many surfers at or near the top of the pile, in Australia and America, had given up on competition completely in favour of 'free surfing' and living the healthy lifestyle in places like Byron Bay, the north shore of Kauai, or Baja California. Bob McTavish, who'd never been a regular competitor anyway, was one of them. Nat Young, formerly the most competitive animal in surfing, was now sharing the brown rice and the waves around Byron with acolytes Russell Hughes and Ted Spencer. In California, Mike Doyle had swapped a contest jersey for an Indian headdress, while Mike Hynson had become a disciple of Timothy Leary and was mindless on LSD every day. In Hawaii, Rusty Miller had taken up residence at Elizabeth Taylor's brother's hippie colony in the wilds of Kauai. Shaper Dick Brewer would soon end up in Taylor Camp too, spending hours sitting in the lotus position.

Meanwhile, the surf media embraced alternative surfing lifestyles wholeheartedly, and publications like *Surf International* and later *Tracks* in Australia either ignored contests or presented them with a disparaging slant. Film-maker Bruce Brown had never featured a surf contest in any of his films, but by the late 1960s and early '70s, new wave cinematographers like Paul Witzig and Albert Falzon were making strong cultural statements about free surfing in films like *Evolution* and *Morning of the Earth*. Both films featured original soundtrack music by the leading hippie rock bands of the time, no narration and no divulging the whereabouts of the exotic surfing locations they showed. The balance would shift back to contests, of course, and the alternative surfers would come running from their geodesic domes at the smell of real money, but for the moment, the surf industry's fiscal health depended on how well it could pretend it wasn't about the money.

9 SURFING FOR MONEY

The road to Utopia is fraught with sorrow. Introspection shows it to be paved with the bleached bones of the uncourageous and unenlightened.
Miki Dora, *Surfer* magazine, 1974

During the autumn of 1970, Duke Boyd phoned pro surfer Jeff Hakman in Hawaii and invited him to spend a few days at his recently acquired ranch behind San Juan Capistrano, California. Dick Graham would be there too, Duke said, and some of the California surfers. They wanted to run a few ideas past him about a new kind of surfing contest. Hakman was not in a position to say no. He had just avoided jail when acquitted of serious drug charges on a legal technicality (the United States Postal Service had illegally opened the package of dope he'd mailed to himself), but he was persona non grata for most of the surf industry. Golden Breed saw it differently. Looking to buy instant credibility as a surf brand, they had thrown him a lifeline.

Jackie Baxter and Gary Chapman were among the surfers who turned up at Duke's ranch for the meetings, but Boyd and Graham were clearly looking for Hakman's approval of their bold idea. 'Traditional surfing contests are out of fashion,' Duke opened. 'What we want to do is align the brand with a new kind of event that provides a focus for surfing performance, but is not a contest. No winners or losers, just performances.'

'An expression session,' said Hakman. All eyes in the room fell on the small, muscular 22-year-old, who was to play a significant role in the surf industry in the decades ahead, but had already been written off by some as a 'drug-fucked loser'. Duke Boyd was a better judge of character. He smiled at Jeff and took some notes.

The Golden Breed Expression Session was the opening event of the Hawaiian season, ahead of the Duke Kahanamoku and the Smirnoff Pro, both of which offered small cash purses as the professional era dawned in surfing. Golden Breed offered its twenty invitees (a list secretly put together by Hakman, and meant to represent the best surfers in the world, competing or non-competing) a $200 appearance fee. Since you wouldn't get anywhere near that unless you were a semifinalist in the other events, and since you could spend an entire winter on the North Shore for less than two hundred bucks (excluding dope), the new event was warmly received by the leading surfers.

In keeping with the informal, folksy and soulful nature of the Expression Session, Boyd and Graham decided to forego the usual formalities and launch the event with a beach barbecue at Hakman's rented digs overlooking Pipeline. Duke sprung for the beers and burgers, Dick put on the chef's apron and the 'Good Karma Party' was under way. One of the first arrivals was Bob McAlister, president of the Don Rancho Corporation and owner of the Golden Breed brand, a slight man in late middle age who felt more at home in a country club environment, but had accepted Duke's advice that he needed to 'touch base with the market'.

'It was loose,' Hakman recalled in a 1996 interview with the author. 'I was just boppin' around, making sure everyone was having fun, and they were.' The pickup truck pulled off Kam Highway just on dark and rumbled straight up the lane to Hakman's house. It was a big truck and it was carrying a big load. Locals. Jeff looked out the kitchen window and saw the Aikau brothers, Eddie and Clyde and, behind them, Butch Van Artsdalen, the one-time king of Pipeline who had recently been usurped by the new kings, Gerry Lopez and Jock Sutherland, both invitees. Behind Butch and the Aikaus were another half-dozen large men. They swayed as they walked, and there were empty beer cans all over the flatbed, but none of them looked happy. It would emerge later that they had spent the previous six hours at the Seaview Inn in Haleiwa, lamenting the fact that 'Mr Pipeline' hadn't been invited to the Expression Session.

Hakman went to the door to head them off. 'Hi, Clyde, what's happening?'

'Aloha, Jeff. We want to talk to Mr Graham.'

The Aikaus were akin to Hawaiian royalty, respected and respectful … until maybe a little too much lamenting had gone down. Hakman was only too happy to get out of the firing line, and no-nonsense former marine Dick Graham was only too happy to put himself in it. Soon the punches were flying as Graham defended the door and the Hawaiians stormed it. Duke Boyd recalls: 'You gotta remember, Graham was one tough motherfucker back in those days, so it was really on. Dick's got Clyde nailed against a wall and bodies are flying out windows, someone knocks over Jeff's aquarium and fish are floppin' all over the floor. I was running to hide in the broom closet, and I suddenly go, oh shit, where's Bob McAlister?'

Hakman and Gary Chapman were way ahead of him. They had shouldered McAlister and run him out onto the beach where a neighbour kept a dinghy upturned in the sand. They pushed the chief executive under it and told him to wait there until the fuss was over. *Surfer* correspondent Drew Kampion arrived as the heat went out of the fight. 'Outside is a pickup truck. Six or seven Hawaiians are in the open bed, drinking Primo and singing very sad, very nostalgic Hawaiian songs. Other Hawaiians and a few *haoles* stand around, some joining in, tentatively.'

Slowly, the party was reborn inside the wreckage of the house, with a boozy brethren swaying to the old songs, arm in arm. Clyde was sorry, Eddie was sorry, Butch was passed out somewhere. Dick

Graham nursed some broken ribs, but he was sorry too. Everything was okay again in the small world that was the North Shore. Nothing too bad had happened, the Golden Breed honchos couldn't be too upset. Oh, shit! Hakman looked at Gary Chapman and they both ran out past the lanai onto the beach. Bob McAlister had been under the dinghy for almost two hours, but he seemed relaxed enough. 'Bob, let's get you a drink,' said Hakman. 'Good idea,' McAlister grunted.

After the Good Karma Party, the Golden Breed Expression Session itself was something of an anticlimax. The surfers, given the vote on when to stage it, outsmarted themselves and, with the waiting time running out, had to settle for a mediocre day at Rocky Point. And since it wasn't really a contest, none of the recreational surfers came out of the water, and the casual observer had no idea what was going on. The same applied to the television crew filming it, and with nowhere near enough footage in the can, the session was eventually finished on Maui, but with a much-diminished cast.

Despite (or perhaps because of) the groundbreaking spirit of the Expression Session, Golden Breed failed to rack up huge numbers in the US, particularly after the 1972 arrival of another aspirant to the Hang Ten crown, Ocean Pacific. Jim Jenks was a salesman for Hansen Surfboards in San Diego before starting his own sales agency in 1968, representing Hansen, Surfboards Hawaii and a few offbeat surf companies like Mike Doyle's Surf Research, which manufactured wax and other accessories.

Like other salesmen on the road, Jenks saw what sold and what didn't, and was well positioned to spot an opportunity in the market. Unlike most, he moved on it, and started to develop a performance board short. In search of a name with surf credibility, he began looking through the register of surfboard brands. When his first choice, Sunset, wasn't available, he settled on Ocean Pacific, a brand that had been passed around in San Diego, eventually ending up with Don Hansen. The thing that Jenks liked most about the brand was the simplicity of the two-letter 'Op' logo, which he immediately saw embroidered on a pair of trunks.

Jenks found a backer, again through Don Hansen, and brought out an initial line of three trunks and two walk shorts. Op clicked almost immediately, for a variety of reasons. Jenks was authentic. He had salt on the face, but at the same time, he had an apparel industry pro's feel for product and market positioning. In short, he was a smart operator who surrounded himself with smart operators, and there were few smarter than Walter and Flippy Hoffman, at Hoffman California Fabrics. Noting a rekindled interest in the classic aloha shirt, Jenks went to the Hoffmans and asked them to come up with a new approach to an old theme. The Op 'silky' was born, and, along with the later Op cord shorts, it was to position the brand at the cutting edge of the surfwear market for the rest of the decade.

While the brand struggled a little in the US, in Australia Golden Breed paralleled Ocean Pacific's growth, soon selling more than all of its competitors put together. There was nothing original about its product – the T-shirts were straight out of the Hang Ten catalogue, the silkies out of Op's – but John Arnold's marketing was breaking new ground. Duke Boyd and Dick Graham had created the brand's ethereal imagery, but in avant garde artist Peter Ledger, Arnold found the perfect translation for the Australian market. Vivid Ledger centerfold posters became prized tear-outs in every issue of trendy new surf mag *Tracks*, and Golden Breed borrowed again from the Boyd and Graham creative team in taking the brand imagery beyond surfing. In the early 1970s, Dick Graham was largely responsible for taking the Hang Ten brand into extreme sports such as skiing, dirt-biking and motocross. Teaming with Sydney advertising agency Harris Robinson Courtenay's dynamic young creative team, Arnold did the same for Golden Breed, a decade or more before most surf companies broadened their focus from surfing to all board sports. Arnold also followed Hang Ten's lead in creating dual distribution channels into surf shops and department stores.

While John Arnold was busily putting his surfwear into every store that mattered, Gordon Merchant and his wife Rena were just as busily cutting out board shorts on the kitchen table of a rented flat in Coolangatta, so they could offer their product to a few surf shops on Friday and sell the remainder at flea markets over the weekend. It wasn't much of a living, but they both had other incomes. Gordon was a shaper at Joe Larkin Surfboards and Rena crocheted bikinis. They didn't really need to do the shorts, but Gordon had a strong feeling about what surfers wanted to wear, and Rena knew how to translate that into patterns and products. If only they had a name for them ...

Born in Sydney in 1943, Gordon Merchant had spent his early years on a mixed farm on the western outskirts of Sydney, in what is now high density suburbia. He helped his parents feed the chickens, and rode a horse to school. He might have ended up a jockey or a rodeo rider, but the family gave up the land and moved to beachside Maroubra where, slowly and painfully, the undersized lad who couldn't swim gained acceptance into the beach culture.

Gordon's mother sewed for Anthony Squires, Sydney's leading men's tailor, and afternoons after school he would sometimes sit on a pew at the factory and wait for her to finish. But she took more and more time off work, and one day he came home from school to learn she had suicided. Merchant was later to tell writer Tim Baker, in one of the rare interviews he has given, that the shock of losing his mother helped harden him against the world, and made him a hard taskmaster of himself and of others. But this wasn't evident in his first job in the surfboard industry, sanding boards for Scott Dillon. He was just a young guy, goofing off with fellow employees like Bob McTavish, experimenting with booze and drugs and planning 'the big surf trip'.

In the late 1960s Merchant, by now a respected shaper, turned up at Jeffreys Bay, South Africa,where he developed a lifelong obsession with that perfect wave, and an overwhelming ambition to develop a surfboard that matched its moods. By 1970, now living on the Gold Coast, he experimented with down-rail speed machines and felt he was getting closer to a real design breakthrough, but surfboard production was starting to play havoc with his health. He had met the girl he was to marry, the two of them wanted to play house, and he was looking for career options.

Although the prospect of working in the apparel industry, like his late mother, had never appealed, on the Gold Coast in the early 1970s Merchant reflected on the booming career of a friend from Maroubra, Tommy Moses. Moses was an apprentice tailor, contemplating throwing it in to go surfing, when Merchant urged him to make clothes for surfers. Moses started Kream in 1968, shortly after the Eric Clapton super-group Cream hit the top of the charts, and for half a dozen years it successfully exploited the surf and rock youth market. Now, Gordon and Rena Merchant were ready to do their own Kream ... if only they had a name.

'Cabbage' was a young dogsbody at Joe Larkin's factory, learning the art of sanding from Merchant, when the subject of a good name for board shorts came up. 'Why don't you call them "Billabong"?' Cabbage suggested. Gordon drew an arch and framed the words around it. For good measure, he wrote 'Since 1973' underneath. Billabong was an Aboriginal word for a waterhole. It didn't make much sense, but then what was a quicksilver or a rip curl? At least it was Australian, and that was becoming a very good thing to be in the world of surf.

At the end of the week he took the first Billabong board shorts to the Brothers Neilsen surfshop in Surfers Paradise. Manager Kim Lomas looked the product up and down, his eyes finally settling on the 'Since 1973' on the logo. Lomas drew conspiratorially close to Merchant across the counter. 'Gordon,' he whispered, 'this *is* 1973!'

The idea of a world tour of professional surfing had been kicked around since the introduction of money contests in California and Hawaii in the late 1960s, and at various times there was a very small group of elite surfers – Nat Young, Mike Doyle, Gerry Lopez and Jeff Hakman among them – who travelled from California to Hawaii to Peru to South Africa to compete for even smaller purses. But by the early 1970s, a three-event Hawaiian pro season was becoming a reality, with Smirnoff Vodka and Hang Ten among the sponsors, and more than a few Australian surfers, despondent about the future of amateur surfing after the lacklustre world championships in San Diego in October 1972, were eager to add an Australian tour.

Rip Curl's Doug Warbrick was one of the biggest of the Australian tour boosters, particularly after he saw first-hand the innovative objective judging system developed by surfing pioneer George Downing for the 1972 Hang Ten Pro. Downing's system was the first to put a points value on known manoeuvres and surfing skills, thus allowing surfers to build a score, rather than rely on a sympathetic subjective score from judges who liked the 'style'. It was rough, and frequently arbitrary, but those who saw Jeff Hakman take out the inaugural Hang Ten felt that the best surfer had won.

Nevertheless, the Downing system had its share of critics, and the concept of the objectification of surfing was satirised beautifully (and presciently) by surfing's original anarchist, Miki Dora, in *Surfer* magazine in 1974. Announcing a mythical $50,000, winner-take-all event, Dora outlined his judging system:

An entirely automated and computerised system will be employed to prevent all human error and personality factors, a pair of buoys will be set off the second point at Malibu, forming a gate, while a second pair will be placed past the first point. Photo-electric devices are mounted on each buoy, creating a light beam. The riders passing through the first gate (breaking the beam) activate the timing device on shore, and, traversing the second gate, stop it … the only variation on the IBM pure visual scan scoring will be a universal difficulty factor to allow for wave speed change, due to changes in tide. Simplicity is the key to this endeavour, speed is the essence.

Back in Victoria, Warbrick convinced his partners to spend about ten times their marketing budget for the year on taking the Bells Beach Easter Contest professional in 1973. It was a bold move, aligning the new brand with competitive surfing well before the pendulum had swung back from the preoccupation with the 'country soul' movement, and Alan Green, for one, was unconvinced. But Claw's arguments were persuasive, and the first Rip Curl Pro (men only, the women would have to wait a few more years for the money), for $2500 prize money, was a huge hit, with a large crowd on the cliffs to watch Queensland's Michael Peterson notch his first money win, and impressive coverage in the surf magazines and on ABC television.

More than any advertising they had done to this point, the Rip Curl Pro firmly positioned the brand as the 'surfer's wetsuit', giving back so soon after its inception, to ensure the future development of the sport for all. It was a position that neither of its neoprene competitors – Arnold's O'Neill franchise and Fred Pyke's new Dive 'n' Surf brand – could emulate because Warbrick was fast becoming simultaneously the voice of Rip Curl and the voice of Australian pro surfing. But the bottom line was that for most foreign surfers, Australia was a long way to come for one $2500 contest. The mission for Warbrick and the others boosting a pro tour was to get some more major sponsors interested in expanding the tour to make it financially worthwhile. A precedent of sorts had been set when jeans manufacturers Amco came in late as presenting sponsor of the Rip Curl Pro. If the surf industry itself couldn't finance a tour, maybe there was youth marketing money in the bigger business world.

Sydney finance journalist and surfer Graham Cassidy knew a bit about that, and soon after the success of the Rip Curl Pro, he approached the cashed-up, Sydney-based distributors of Coca Cola to sponsor 'the world's biggest surf contest'. A lot of Coke's Sydney ad spend went to the top-rating pop radio station, 2SM, so it wasn't much of an arm twist for Coke to pull them in as co-sponsor, and the 2SM–Coca Cola Bottlers Surfabout was born. (Sadly for 2SM, only the signage and their disc jockeys ever called it this. The event was known to all as the 'Coke contest'.)

Making its debut in May 1974, the Surfabout was an immediate hit, with a major contingent of top surfers coming from Hawaii, California, South Africa, New Zealand, Japan, Brazil and even Europe, big, challenging waves at Fairy Bower providing spectacular photos and news footage, and the media bonus of Nat Young controversially donating his third place prize money (all of $600) to Gough Whitlam's embattled Labor government. The event also signalled the arrival of a new superstar in world surfing. Winner Michael Peterson, a nervy, taciturn natural footer from Queensland, won every major event in Australia in 1974, following up from his 1973 victory in the inaugural Rip Curl Pro. Sponsored by Rip Curl, he was to prove unbeatable in Australia for the next five years, before tragically disappearing from the scene to fight a long battle with the demons of schizophrenia.

In the wake of the successful launch of the Rip Curl Pro, Rip Curl had a clear strategy for the growth of its wetsuits business. Quiksilver did not. Warbrick and Singer were taking on market leader O'Neill with the weapon of surfer credibility, while accountant Butch Barr had been brought in to keep the business running smoothly. Meanwhile, all Alan Green knew for sure was that he had a good product and there was a huge market for surf shorts out there in the warm water world beyond icy Bells Beach, but it was going to take a full-time effort to deliver it. The writing was on the wall for a split, but it was not going to happen in a hurry. 'The bottom line is we didn't have enough capital to expand both brands at the same time,' Greeny told the author in a 1998 interview. By 1973, Green had taken on a minority partner in Brewster Everett, an artistically minded local surfer, had trademarked the Quiksilver name and its mountain and wave logo, and moved the operation into new premises, an old house at 29 Pride Street, Torquay. The living room became the production line while the boss took over the master bedroom, installing a rough desk and some movie and concert posters to cover the holes in the walls.

The following year, Greeny registered the business name of Ug Manufacturing Co Pty Ltd as the owner of Quiksilver, but the company remained a division of Rip Curl as it ploughed through its first market mistakes. As he explained to the author in a February 1976 interview at his Pride Street office: 'We're not in the big league like Platt's and them, but Quiksilver's got a certain vibe about it that guarantees success at the level we want it. A year or two ago we got into shirts and ug boots, the whole junky surf trip, and we did our arses to the tune of nine grand. So we decided to stick to doing what we could do well.'

For years to come, the Quiksilver mantra would be 'board shorts, board shorts, board shorts', and its major marketing tool would be Greeny's 'flow program', in which the leading surfers and opinion-makers around the world would find themselves gifted with a couple of pairs of beautifully tailored, two-tone, scallop-legged, velcro-flied, snap-fastened Aussie board shorts. It was the most basic word-of-mouth marketing program imaginable, and it worked.

As both Rip Curl and Quiksilver developed as brands, the founders worked inexorably toward severing the umbilical cord. This was made even more complex than it might have been by the fact that the partners had invested in some property speculation, including almost fifty acres of grazing land at Bells Beach. But while they debated the split, Alan Green had already chosen his new partner. As Brewster Everett began to take a back seat to attempt to work through personal and drug problems that would eventually claim his life, Greeny approached young local surfer John Law.

'Lawro', as he was known, had been a junior league 'Brighton Stormrider' while at school in Melbourne, then a champion skate-boarder and junior surfer, reaching the pinnacle of his competitive career with a third place in the Rip Curl Pro in 1974. Smart, business savvy and good-looking, Lawro flirted briefly with a career as a stock-broker, then turned his attention to the growing Torquay surf industry and went to work for entrepreneur Fred Pyke's expanding empire, which by then included Pyke Surfwear, Pyke Surfboards and Surf Skis, and the Australian licence for Body Glove Wetsuits. Lawro cut rubber at the start, but soon progressed to designing and overseeing production of board shorts for the Pyke range.

Although there was widespread respect for Lawro as a talented surfer and a coming force in the surf industry, there was no love lost between the Quiksilver/Rip Curl crowd and his employer, Fred Pyke.

Pyke was seen as an authoritarian figure who harked back to an earlier era, when work was a man's pride and joy and leisure was for sissies. For his part, Pyke regarded the new cool crew in Torquay as nothing more than hippies and druggies. When Alan Green started making ug boots in opposition to Pyke's, Fred retaliated by making board shorts. Just as he snared the Body Glove licence for wetsuits, the Rip Curl partners registered the name in Australia, which forced him to revert to the less popular 'Dive 'n' Surf' brand. And so it went. Nothing would have given Alan Green greater pleasure than to poach John Law out from under Fred Pyke, but Lawro had already quit to marry his childhood sweetheart, Geraldine, and spend an extended honeymoon in Europe. He had just got out of the surf in Hossegor, France, in October 1975, when Greeny phoned to make him an offer.

The deal that finally split Rip Curl and Quiksilver into two companies involved John Law buying Doug Warbrick's shareholding in Ug Manufacturing for $13,000, while Alan Green swapped his share of the Bells Beach land for Brian Singer's shareholding. The 30 June 1976 tax filing for Ug Manufacturing recorded the distribution of company shares as Alan Green (2890), Barbara Green (1418), John Law (2871) and Brewster Everett (1436). Gross revenues for the year were slightly more than $300,000.

While Rip Curl and Quiksilver positioned themselves to grow, the first of Australia's surf empires was poised to crash and burn. The John Arnold Group employed more than four hundred people by 1975 and had seven production facilities around Adelaide, including a purpose-built factory at Lonsdale. But during 1976, John Arnold began to falter. Interviewed by the author at a Sydney hotel late at night, the normally smooth entrepreneur looked like a broken man. He had flown in from Los Angeles in the morning, spent all day working on new advertising campaigns with his advertising men, Mike Robinson and Vince Tesorerio, then hosted a dinner for retailers. The interview with *Tracks* magazine was his last engagement for the day. He poured himself a whisky from the mini-bar, took off his tinted aviator specs, stretched and let out a cry of deep anguish. 'Sorry,' he said, trying to soften the moment with a laugh. 'Sometimes you've just got to let it out.'

O'Neill Wetsuits were still the Australian market leader, Golden Breed was the best-selling surfwear and he had even begun exporting it back to the US. But Arnold had had to look beyond Barry Bennett for funding, and he was now hocked to the max to the South Australian government. The company posted a $1.2 million loss in 1977 and was placed into receivership, but Arnold blundered on, forming a partnership with the American Richton Corporation and the South Australian Development Corporation. There were wholesale sackings to cut costs, but the brands were dead in the water and Arnold himself was shattered. In 1980 the South Australian government finally walked away from the business, vowing never again to expose itself to the surf industry.

10 EAT THE DOILY

Sorry about the delay in getting this stuff to you guys, but here are the patterns, the samples (poplin, snaps, logo, velcro) and the agreement on royalties. Good luck, and if you need any advice, see Walter Hoffman.
Alan Green, letter to his new US Quiksilver licensees, 1976

While Golden Breed was crashing and burning in Australia, in America it was just quietly fading away. Dick Graham was busy overseeing Hang Ten's speedway and motocross directional shift, but he was over it, and Duke Boyd was just kind of bored with the angel-winged guy and all of Golden Breed's hippie trippie stuff. He was way more interested in a simple, pure, branding exercise that was starting to set Hawaii alight.

Back in 1969, Gerry Lopez, just beginning to create a cult around his smooth tube-riding at Pipeline, started using a brightly coloured lightning bolt decal on his surfboards. It was the perfect symbol of speed for a man whose surfing was defined by it, and the bolt decal followed him briefly to Hansen Surfboards in 1970, then back to Hawaii when he and Jack Shipley, his former colleague at Surf Line Hawaii, decided to open their own surf shop in Honolulu. Lightning

Bolt Surfboards opened in the former Hobie showroom on Kapiolani Boulevard in the summer of 1972, and soon became the hub of surfboard design in Hawaii.

The reason for this was twofold. First, Jack Shipley was an old-school salesman with good surfing credibility through years of judging amateur events. He knew how to make a shop work, and he knew how to exploit Gerry Lopez. Second, Lopez was not only the most exciting new talent in surfing, but he also oozed charisma. He was becoming a good shaper in his own right, but every leading surfboard craftsman in Hawaii (and several from the mainland) was suddenly beating a path to Shipley's door to work for Lightning Bolt. The business was run as a co-op, with leading shapers like Bill Barnfield, Tom Parrish, Barry Kaniaupuni and Reno Abellira making their boards in home factories and bringing the finished products into the Bolt showroom to sell, thus saving Bolt the factory maintenance costs.

By 1974 Bolt's sales were enough to justify opening a second store on Maui (where Lopez had built a home), and Jack Shipley had begun his own 'flow' program, one far more dramatic than Alan Green's, flowing free surfboards to the world's leading surfers as they arrived for the North Shore winter season. It was an expensive program, but excellent marketing, and the Lightning Bolt team soon included not only Hawaiians like Rory Russell, Abellira and Jeff Hakman, but also upcoming Australians Mark Richards, Ian Cairns, Rabbit Bartholomew and Peter Townend, and South Africans Michael and Shaun Tomson. Just as the North Shore became the focal point of the growing global surf media, there was nowhere you could point a camera and not shoot a Bolt. For a period of three or four years, claimed Matt Warshaw's *Encyclopedia of Surfing*, 'no board-making label before or since has dominated the surf media the way Bolt did'.

Shipley's flow program hit only one hurdle. After friction between Hawaiians and Australians on the North Shore in 1975, the following season Shipley was told in no uncertain terms to stop supplying free boards to the Aussies. Confronted on the issue at his office on Kapiolani by pro surfer Peter Townend and the author, Shipley wriggled a little in his chair and said: 'Hey, I don't like to treat you guys this way, but I gotta live here.' The Aussies paid two hundred bucks for their boards in 1976, but the next season the flow program was back to normal.

It didn't take long for an astute marketer to see the potency of the brand. 'Man, it was everywhere,' Duke Boyd recalled. 'And not only that, it was very, very cool. I knew that from the moment I saw their first advertisement, with the line, "a pure source". That came from the best cocaine supply in the Islands, a group of guys on Maui, but only the cool people knew that.'

After initially protesting that they already had too many surf brands, Hang Ten proprietors, the Rattner Corporation, dispatched Boyd to Hawaii to negotiate on their behalf. He offered Lopez and Shipley $3000 for the name (there was some dispute over its ownership at this point) and a percentage point each in the new company, plus they kept surfboards and accessories. The Bolt guys weren't buying it. Dick Graham flew over to help put the screws on, and slowly a deal was cut. In the end Lopez and Shipley split fifteen per cent, Boyd and Graham thirty per cent, and The Bolt Corporation registered its trademarks around the world and went to work on its portfolio.

'Worst deal I ever made in my life,' Duke Boyd remembers. 'It was my idea and I should have had the power to implement my vision. Instead we cut the cake and divided the authority.'

'It was the biggest ride of my life,' Dick Graham says. 'We went from zero to thirty million in the first year, and to $125 million in three. It was just insane. We didn't have to create a brand. That work had been done for us. We just had to make product that lived up to it.' And that was where many felt The Bolt Corporation failed, despite its slick advertising and its massive distribution. The best loved and most recognisable surf brand in the world started lending its name to middle-of-the-road sportswear, beach towels, backpacks, even cheap jewellery. By 1980, brand icon Lopez had had enough and sold his stake.

Back at the beginning of Lightning Bolt's bull run, Duke Boyd had pulled Jeff Hakman off his Golden Breed sponsorship and put him on the Bolt Sportswear team, hoping to use not only his marketing appeal but also his canny feel for surfwear. When the first ads for Bolt board shorts appeared, it was no coincidence that they looked remarkably like Quiksilver's. In 1974, right after the initial Coke Surfabout contest in Sydney, the visiting pro surfers scored the best surf of their visit when an unseasonably warm offshore breeze caressed a solid groundswell. Hakman arrived at Whale Beach on the tip of the northern beaches peninsula on an absolutely perfect morning with only a wetsuit. Fellow pro Mark Warren lent him a pair of Quiksilvers, and Hakman slipped into them under his towel in the car park. 'Wow, these feel good,' he said. He surfed for three hours, drove to the airport and flew to Bali. Warren never saw his shorts again.

In Bali, Gerry Lopez had been equally impressed, and the following year he and Shipley, in Australia on judging duties, made a deal to buy a hundred pairs for their store, making Lightning Bolt Quiksilver's first offshore customer. Not wanting to pay duty, Shipley taped the shorts to the inside of his prototype board bag. He recalled in a 2006 interview with the author: 'Man, they just disappeared. We sold out in two weeks, so I got organised with a customs clearance agent and all that shit, but we could never get enough. As soon as Greeny made them, they sold.'

In the early summer of 1966, twelve-year-old Robert Buchner McKnight Jr cut a photo out of *Surfer* magazine and tacked it to the wall beside his bed. The photo showed seventeen-year-old Jeff Hakman, who had just won the Duke Kahanamoku Invitational, crouched on the nose of his board, driving hard through the inside section of a Sunset Beach wave that seemed five times taller than him. Bob wanted to ride waves like that, and as he lay in bed, waiting for sleep, he imagined himself doing so on his new Harbour Surfboards Banana Model that stood in a corner of the room where he could watch over it.

The McKnights lived in leafy San Marino, in the shadow of the San Gabriel Mountains, their large and comfortable home a testament to the business success of Robert Sr, who had been a navy fighter pilot during the war and later used his contacts in Tokyo to establish a flourishing import business. Bob and his older sister, Kathie, grew up in suburban utopia, with a neighbourhood full of kids around them and active parents who took them hiking, fishing, diving and camping. After his father sold the import business and bought a second house in Newport Beach, Bob discovered surfing.

By his middle teens, Bob McKnight was an accomplished surfer, but he had also developed a passion for film, shooting every surf trip with a state-of-the-art Sony Super-8 his dad had brought back from Japan. In his final years of high school, and into his college years at the University of Southern California, Bob made pocket money showing his surf films to eager student audiences. Majoring in business but minoring in cinema, Bob seemed to have his working life mapped out, his options for the future covering his parents' wishes and his own. But then his parents gave him a semester travelling through the East with World Campus Afloat (a co-ed deal known to Bob and other freshmen as 'World Butt Afloat'), and Bob discovered Bali. Since the construction of the Ngurah Rai international airport in 1969, Bali had passed from being a well-kept secret of the lotus-eaters to becoming a cool hideaway for hippies and surfers, with gorgeous beaches, cheap food and lodgings and plentiful drugs. And, for serious surfers, the 1972 release of Albert Falzon's *Morning of the Earth* had revealed the island's enormous reef break potential, away from the topless stretch of Kuta.

After his brief introduction on Butts Afloat, Bob McKnight couldn't wait to get back, and despite the fact that a stock exchange rout of his father's investments meant he could expect no family assistance, he picked up some change roadshowing his surf movies, scammed a free Pan Am ticket as a tour leader, and flew out of LAX with a bunch of Californian surfers as soon as school broke for the summer of '74.

McKnight and his group set up home in a simple guesthouse, or *losmen*, in the heart of Kuta, a village about ten minutes by *bemo* bus from the airport. Today, it is difficult to explain how mellow Kuta was, just as it had been impossible for 1930s tourists like Charlie Chaplin to adequately describe the sylvan setting they had found. In the early seventies, cows grazed in paddocks between the *losmens*, and after dark, people carried torches to navigate their way home along muddy tracks. The smell of fruit, flowers and clove cigarettes hung in the air, and, in the distance, a gamelan orchestra always seemed to be playing. And the waves poured in, day after day.

McKnight's tour group eventually faded away, leaving him with new-found surfing friends, among them Australian surfboard shaper Phil Byrne and photographer Dick Hoole. The trio had many surfing adventures, and some others to boot. One night they shared a chocolate hashish cake with some surfers. McKnight enjoyed the experience for a while, and then spun out, hallucinating so badly he fled for home. When he eventually found his bed, he lay awake for hours, shivering, seeing visions and believing death was imminent. Then he blacked out. He was later to claim that his career as a druggie ended right there.

One afternoon while McKnight and Byrne unloaded their boards after a surf trip, Dick Hoole cruised by on his motorbike and called, 'Hey, McKnight, Hakman's back, hope you got plenty of film.' Even in super-cool Bali, the arrival of a superstar was an event. There was a buzz in the bars that night. Who's with him? Is Lopez back? What boards did he bring? In fact Jeff Hakman, who'd made his first trip to Bali with Gerry Lopez earlier in the year, had returned on a cheap charter flight through Guam with a couple of unknown buddies from the North Shore, hoping to lie low and surf plenty until the start of the winter season in Hawaii.

At twenty-five, Hakman was arguably the best competitive surfer in the world. Arguably because Michael Peterson had just dominated the Australian season, but Hakman, with a decade in top company, two Dukes, two Pipeline Masters titles and the Hang Ten Pro under his belt, was generally regarded as the man for all seasons. Born in Redondo Beach, California, in 1948, Hakman had moved with his family to Hawaii in 1960 and within two years was surfing huge North Shore waves with his father, Harry. His surfing education continued at Punahou School in Honolulu, where the faculty included big wave surfers Fred Van Dyke and Peter Cole, and his classmates included Fred Hemmings and Gerry Lopez.

After his victory in the inaugural Duke contest, Hakman had followed the routine path of sixties surf stars, with all the accoutrements of fame except money. He returned to the mainland for college, but Hakman had already decided to join so many other top surfers in an occupation that offered travel, money and plenty of time to surf. He became a drug smuggler, first doing a hashish run in Lebanon, and then a big league marijuana deal in Thailand, which led to his arrest as he picked up the goods from Haleiwa Post Office. Perhaps, in some worlds, none of the above would look good in a resume, but in the weird little world of surf, it actually made Hakman more bankable. Duke Boyd had seen that. Jeff was flawed, sure, but he was likeable, sincere and smart. And in 1974 he was the biggest star in surfing.

Dick Hoole introduced his friends to Jeff Hakman at a juice bar and they all shared a *bemo* to the surf at Ulu Watu. Bob McKnight was totally in awe, a pimply college kid, surfing with his hero. Hakman liked the kid's enthusiasm. One day he noticed Bob sitting very wide in the line-up, seemingly waiting for a bigger set than was likely to appear. It reminded him of big wave pioneer Buzzy Trent, who would sit for hours out there, and eventually catch the wave of the day. 'Hey, Buzz,' Hakman called, 'what are you doing way over there?' A few days later McKnight was in Hakman's room when he noticed a letter addressed to 'Jeff Hakman Esq.'. The 'q' was written with a flourish. 'What's this "Q" hangin' off your name?' McKnight joked. 'I dunno. I guess some people call me Jeff Hakman, Q,' Hakman answered.Buzz and Q. No one else would ever call them that, but it was their code from that day on. They were two young men from totally different worlds, but their worlds had collided in Bali, and they formed a bond that would see them through good times and bad.

When Bob McKnight went back to school at USC in September 1974, he was a different person. Not only was he grappling with psychotic flashbacks from his chocolate hash cake experience, plus the residual effects of a tapeworm he had picked up in Bali, but his head was full of dreams. Meeting Jeff Hakman had rocked his world. Before Bali and Hakman, he felt he had everything in perspective – a career path in business and film that would afford him the time and the money to travel the world and surf exotic breaks once or twice a year. Now he wasn't so sure that was enough. In Bob's mind there had been a clear division between career and surf, and the former had to come first if it was going to fund the latter. But in Bali, surrounded by young people who made their living from the surfing lifestyle, one way or another, he began to feel that his passion for the sport was becoming more important than his career plan.

Bob's confusion wasn't helped when Hakman phoned just before Christmas and invited him to join Phil Byrne as a guest at Jeff's A-frame on the North Shore. He found his friend in a buoyant mood, having continued his good form of the previous year into the Hawaiian winter season, winning the Hang Ten Pro and finishing a close second in the Smirnoff Pro, held at Waimea Bay in the largest waves ever contested, just a couple of weeks before Bob's arrival. McKnight recalled in interviews with the author in 2005: 'I was like a kid in a candy store. All this momentous stuff was going down and there I was, right in the thick of it.'

The 1974–75 North Shore season was momentous because its three events, held in good to excellent conditions and generating maximum publicity, created a launching pad for the emergence of a world pro surfing tour, and also because it heralded a changing of the guard in world surfing, with teenage prodigies like Wayne 'Rabbit' Bartholomew from Australia and Shaun Tomson from South Africa leading a performance push that dominated the surf media. Jeff Hakman, who had posted his first tournament win almost a decade earlier, was an elder statesman in this company, but he was held in awe by the new guard, both for his ability and his humility. Bruce Raymond, an exciting young Sydney surfer then spending his first winter in Hawaii, recalls:

On my first day on the North Shore, Sunset Beach was perfect. I surfed all day and went home to our rented house, exhausted. I was sprawled on a bed when there was a knock on the door, and this voice goes, 'Hi, I'm Jeff Hakman. Does Bruce Raymond live here?' It was *the* Jeff Hakman! Can you imagine? He told me he'd watched me surfing and really liked the way my board worked. He wanted to have a look at it. That was how I met Jeff Hakman. I couldn't believe it.

McKnight too was in awe of Hakman, but the friendship soon went much deeper than hero worship. While Hakman toured the world again in 1975, including another summer sojourn in Bali, Bob waited tables on weekends at The Cannery in Newport Beach, knuckled down to his studies at USC and graduated with a diploma in business administration in January 1976. With a long break ahead before graduate school, he once again headed for Hakman's A-frame in Hawaii.

He found his pal as friendly and effusive as ever, but also somewhat distracted. 'He kept going on about swimsuits, for Christ's sake!' says Bob. 'Jeff was always passionate about something – surfboards, Valiant cars, and now it was these Australian surf trunks that he'd had in Bali when we first met, how they could change the world. At first I just listened to be polite, but then he started making some sense.'

'You know, Buzz, if we were to get a licence for Quiksilver in the US, we could start our own little company, hang out and surf together, maybe make a few bucks,' Hakman told his friend. It was ironic that, even as he spoke, Hakman was featured in a back page ad in the surf magazines for Lightning Bolt's new, Quiksilver-inspired board shorts. McKnight humoured him. 'Whatever you say, Q, with you all the way.' Enlisted to house-sit for Hakman and his girlfriend, Joey, while they did the Australian tour, McKnight settled back, surrounded by his friend's surfboards and trophies, and waited to see where all this would lead.

Prior to departing for Australia, Jeff Hakman ordered two new surfboards from his Lightning Bolt shaper, Tom Parrish, requesting thicker than normal fibreglass fins, hollowed out in the middle 'to keep the weight down'. Before the fins were attached, Hakman took them home, to examine their hydrodynamic qualities, he told Parrish. And while he was at it, he jammed three ounces of cocaine into the centres, before sealing them. 'Looking good,' he told Parrish, handing them back to be glassed onto the boards.

Hakman had no love for cocaine, but he knew it would fetch a good price in Australia, where, coincidentally, heroin was relatively cheap. As physically fit as he had ever been, surfing at the peak of his powers and fired up to start a surf business with his new friend McKnight, Hakman was also in the grip of a dangerous flirtation with heroin that had begun the previous year in Bali. He wasn't yet ready to call it an addiction, he simply wanted to have access to heroin wherever he was in the world. He landed in Sydney and drove straight to the Central Coast headquarters of Geoff McCoy Surfboards, unwrapped his Parrish boards and recoiled in mock horror as the fat fins were unveiled. 'Oh, Jesus, Parrish! What have you done? These have got to go.'

Hakman set up the boards on sawhorses, sawed the fins off and deposited them in his bag. McCoy team rider and ding fixer Bruce Raymond was commandeered to glass in new fins, and as soon as the work was done and he'd picked up some new McCoy boards, Jeff was on his way back to the airport. A few hours later, the trade having been made in a beachside car park on Queensland's Gold Coast, Hakman was loaded on heroin and had slipped into a fitful sleep in a grungy motel bed. So began the campaign that would see him become the first non-Australian to win an Australian professional surfing title and, more importantly, deliver him the American licence for Quiksilver.

The 1976 Bells Beach Pro, sponsored by Rip Curl with a qualifying trials event sponsored by Quiksilver, was an interminable affair, postponed for days at a time due to lack of surf. Frequently in a drug-induced haze, Jeff nevertheless remained focused on his business objective, to secure the Quiksilver licence. Exactly what this would mean, he was not sure. Would he and Bob import the Australian product or manufacture it themselves? Would they buy their stock or pay a royalty on the pairs that they sold? All he really knew was that he had to convince Alan Green that he and his new partner were the right people to take the brand into America, and so he used every moment of down-time from the contest – every moment he was straight enough to leave the rented house – to quiz Greeny about his ambitions for Quiksilver.

For his part, Alan Green had reservations about doing a deal with Hakman. He liked the guy – everyone did – and had great respect for his ability as a surfer, but the fact was that Quiksilver was beginning to build a small portfolio of export clients. In addition to the growing business with Lightning Bolt in Hawaii, he had opened up a retail account in New Jersey and had another on the way in California. He recalls: 'I really needed to be convinced that giving a licence to a couple of untried blokes in America made commercial sense.'

In the end, it was Greeny's sense of fun rather than his business acumen that sealed the deal. Having led through the early rounds of the contest, Jeff finally won the Bells title, even though his performance in the latter stages was patchy. At a celebratory dinner at the Sovereign Hotel in Torquay, after many bottles of wine had been consumed, he leaned over the table and said to Greeny: 'Alan, I'm totally committed to getting this Quiksilver licence. What do I have to do to show that to you?'

Greeny blew a thoughtful cloud of cigarette smoke into the air while he traced circles on the paper doily at the centre of the table. Finally, he looked Hakman in the eye, pushed the table decoration towards the American and said: 'Eat the doily.' Hakman didn't hesitate. He grabbed the doily and started ripping it apart with his teeth and chewing it into semi-digestible lumps, almost gagging as he swallowed each one, then washing it down with wine. Rolling on the floor with laughter, Alan Green gave up. 'Okay, Hakman,' he wept, 'you've got a fucking licence!'

The phone woke Bob McKnight from a deep sleep. He looked at his bedside clock before answering. It was four in the morning in Hawaii. 'Buzz, Buzz, we got it, we got it!' McKnight recalls: 'It was ten minutes or more before I could get a word in. Jeff was so excited it was scary. When I eventually got him to hang up, I lay awake in bed thinking, oh my god, what have we gotten ourselves into?!'

Even when Jeff returned to Hawaii, Bob remained none the wiser for several days while Hakman and his girlfriend stayed in their room, coming down from their long heroin binge. Perhaps a more doubting soul would have wondered about this behaviour, but McKnight remained blissfully unaware of his partner's dark side. When Jeff finally emerged, pale, drawn and sniffly, he sat down to explain the deal to Bob. As he talked about Quiksilver, a veil seemed to lift from him and he grew in enthusiasm. 'It didn't take long before he was so excited he couldn't stand it,' says McKnight. 'He had two pairs of Quiksilver shorts now, and he said that in a few weeks Greeny would send us everything we needed to get started. That was it! That was the deal! I'm like, oh really? Don't we have a contract or something? But Jeff's stoke was so sincere it was infectious. After a while I just joined in. Yeah, let's get started!'

By 1977 the Australian surf industry seemed to be on the edge of something big, although no one could quite tell how this would manifest itself. But the portents were good. The surfboard companies had survived a few summers of moulded pop-outs eating into their sales and had settled into steady production levels, with old schoolers like Woods, Bennett, Farrelly and Shane having been joined by Hot Buttered, Energy, McCoy, McGrigor, Morning Star, Van Straalen,

Harmony and Hot Stuff. Surfboard design was being refined constantly by innovators like Midget Farrelly, Terry Fitzgerald and Simon Anderson, pushing consumers into a new board purchase each year, while some surfers were even emulating their heroes and developing multi-board 'quivers' to cope with all conditions. Even so, business could have been better. Indexed against the rising cost of living, surfboards had become cheaper since the mid-sixties, and the margins for manufacturers were so lean that some, like Shane Stedman, had gone into tangential production deals with such oddities as bathroom vanity basins or, even worse, the new ski/kayak hybrid known to surfers as 'goat boats'.

Some surfboard companies, realising that surfboard production was an image-building rather than wealth-creating activity, diversified into retail and established surf shop chains, like Klemm Bell in Victoria and Brothers Neilsen in Queensland. Meanwhile, the surf media had grown to four monthly publications, all trying to transcend the meagre ad spend of the core industry, while mainstream media paid greater attention to surfing trends and to the newly established International Professional Surfers (IPS) World Tour, won in its first year by Queenslander Peter Townend, who had immediately packaged himself into a marketing troupe with fellow surfers Ian Cairns and Mark Warren, with a plan to license their surfing image around the world. As ambitious as Townend's 'Bronzed Aussies' business plan was, it seemed to fit the mood of the times.

Torquay had by now made a genuine claim to be considered Australia's surf industry capital, as both Quiksilver and Rip Curl reached out from their cottage industry roots to attract world markets, and Fred Pyke's grab-bag of brands was consolidated as Dive 'n' Surf (later Piping Hot) under the astute management of Rod Brooks. At the mass market end of surfwear, as the John Arnold/Golden Breed empire began to look shaky, many apparel companies cast avaricious eyes over the surfing sector and waited for an opportunity. One of these was the Brisbane-based Edward Fletcher & Co, justly famous as the originators of 'Stubbies' shorts, hard-wearing, stain-resistant and worn almost exclusively in Australia by road workers, prisoners and wife beaters.

During winter 1976, Edward Fletcher public relations and marketing hacks threw a party at a Gold Coast hotel to announce their grand plan for a revolutionary international surfing contest to be held at Burleigh Heads the following March. As surprising as it was to most present that the manufacturers of the uniform of the Aussie battler would be interested in surfing, it was even more surprising that they had chosen unpredictable surfer Peter Drouyn to run it. One of the more flamboyant surfers to compete in the shadow of Farrelly and Young in the 1960s, Drouyn had made the change to shortboards with ease, and with the coming of the pro era, he had emerged as a strong competitor again. But he was not exactly a team player.

As the contest drew closer, Drouyn revealed bits and pieces of his bold vision. It was to be a 'gladiatorial contest', pitting 'the best against the best, man on man'. It was the man-on-man bit that got everyone sucked in. The inaugural Stubbies Pro was to be a no-holds-barred battle with only two surfers competing, as opposed to the then norm of six. It was a radical concept, but many surfers relished the idea of being judged in such specific circumstances, where there was less chance of confusion.

Six weeks before the event, Drouyn consented to an interview with the author at the Surfers Paradise Beer Garden, on a hot and thirsty afternoon. Over beers, he explained his man-on-man vision: 'We're looking for a bit of bloody flair. We're sick and tired of getting out there year after year and trying to impress a small group of people to win a contest. We want something concrete, some physical and mental contact where we can vibrate off each other ... We want to be able to touch the other guy. Let him look at me and say, "Well, fuck you" or "I love you" or "Let's fight it out to the end". Let's have some contact going!'

But surely you're not suggesting that surfing is a contact sport?

'It can be. I feel it's the only way surfing is going to reach into the big money. A blow must be thrown.'

Thirty years later, when Peter Drouyn made his first public appearance as an attractive middle-aged woman called 'Westerly' and announced his intention to seek gender reassignment, some things from the murky past became a lot clearer, but at the 1977 Stubbies Pro, Drouyn's gladiatorial vision never materialised. However, over a week of perfect waves and blazing sun at Burleigh Heads, competitive surfing was changed forever. The man-on-man format opened up a sport that was often difficult to understand, to the general media, as a clash of styles or temperaments. The final of that event, Michael Peterson versus Mark Richards, might have been Nastase versus Borg, White Knight v Black Knight, Good v Evil. He might have been massively difficult to deal with, and the blockheads at Stubbies might have discovered that fairly quickly, but Drouyn had set the new agenda, and pro surfing was never to look back.

11 IF YA CAN'T ROCK AND ROLL ...

From nine to five I have to spend my time at work
The job is very boring, I'm an office clerk
The only thing that helps me pass the time away
Is knowing I'll be back at Echo Beach some day.
'Echo Beach', Martha and the Muffins, 1980

Although it was Shaun Tomson who first came to international attention – a spindly little guy with a Spiderman stance on a too-short board, filmed by Albert Falzon for Bob Evans's 1968 film *The Way We Like It* – it was his cousin, Michael Tomson, who initially made the greater competitive impact, finishing seventh overall at the 1970 world titles at Bells Beach. He was just fifteen years old, making his first trip outside South Africa, travelling with Shaun and his dad Ernie, a judge at the event.

Six months later the two cousins spent their first North Shore season without parental supervision, sharing a caravan at Haleiwa. Michael loved Sunset from his first encounter, but Sunset did not love him in equal measure. He free-fell down the face, got pitched, smashed and held down. In a 2005 interview with the author, he recalled: 'I've made a career out of trying to surf that place and sometimes I still feel like a complete idiot out there. I remember being caught inside three times before I stood up on a wave.'

He also made a big hit with the locals. 'I was sitting in the line-up at Haleiwa and this guy paddles up to me and says, "You gotta go in." I said something like, "No thanks, I'm fine," and boom! The guy that clouted me later got religion and became a friend, but that day I had no idea what was going on.'

The Tomsons were fast learners. They kept their heads down, showed respect to their elders and got out of the way when fat old guys on elephant guns came careening down the face. Michael got a start in the Smirnoff that first season but flipped out in big Sunset waves and bombed in his heat. He made a mental note to watch the waves and think more about strategy. Most importantly, the Tomsons stayed longer than most of the surfers, and slowly gained an acceptance that the two-week tourists could not. Says Michael: 'Almost from the very start, Hawaii seemed like a second home to me. As soon as I could, I bought a house there and these days I think of it as my first home.'

Coming of age in South Africa in the early 1970s was a turbulent, uncertain experience for most young men. For a start, the apartheid regime was coming apart at its tawdry seams under the pressure of international sporting boycotts and economic sanctions. It seemed the best careers were the ones that got you out of the country. Then there was the military. At eighteen all young men who could not claim educational deferment were compelled to spend a year in the service – a threatened white minority preparing to defend its birthright. The leading surfers at Durban's Bay of Plenty were not exceptions: the Tomsons, followed by Mike Larmont, Bruce Jackson and Paul Naude, were all called up, and each faced his sentence in his own way.

Shaun, by now the best known surfer in the country and a public figure, quietly made plans to avoid the draft, while for Michael an economics degree course at Natal University offered a reprieve from both military service and taking up a position at his father's side in the auto business, both of them extremely distasteful prospects. As he finished his degree at Natal, Michael, who had been an excellent student despite his growing preoccupation with surfing, was offered a post-graduate position at Harvard and thus another deferment, but by this point the wheels had begun to move faster. Michael now had two aspirations. One was to be a writer; the other was to be a professional surfer, if such a profession were to become viable. As it turned out, both careers blossomed simultaneously. By the time he was twenty-five, Michael had been the fifth-ranked surfer in the world, published his own magazine and written for the *New York Times*.

There were more beautiful surfers to watch in the mid-1970s – his cousin for one – but few were more effective than Michael Tomson when the going got tough. In and out of the water, Michael meant business, a surfer's surfer, a man who read the wave and responded to it. In the momentous North Shore season of '75 and the years that followed, he was the unsung hero of the much-mythologised 'Backside Attack' on Pipeline, a new and gutsy approach to riding the most dangerous wave in the world that became known as 'bustin' down the door'. Says Tomson: 'It was what you had to do. Pipe was a great wave, of course, particularly that season. But the thing was that you had to surf down there – Pipe, Backdoor, Rocky Point – to get the photographs. And then this thing just started to happen. I clearly remember the first wave. It was the afternoon of the second or third day of a swell, and I pulled in too late and too far back. There was only one way to go – through it.'

The first thing people noticed was the attitude, but the Tomsons and their acolytes backed up attitude with a superior technical approach to backside tube riding that changed it forever. Frontsiders like Gerry Lopez, Rory Russell, Jackie Dunne and Mike Armstrong had long set the standard at Pipe, but now the backsiders were pushed to the fore, and what the Tomsons and Rabbit Bartholomew were doing in December '75 became the backside standard the following season, with surfers like Simon Anderson, Bruce Raymond and Mark Richards taking off deep and flying the high line.

But the charge at Pipe extracted a price from Michael Tomson. He went over the falls and caught his board between his legs, opening up his scrotum and causing his testicles to swell so badly he couldn't walk for a week. He bounced off the reef on numerous occasions, but managed to avoid any career-threatening injuries. And by the end of '75 he was widely recognised by his peers as the leading charger of the season. But it was cousin Shaun who won the Pipe Masters that year and it was Shaun who emerged as the matinee idol of the Free Ride Generation. Michael finished second to Rory Russell in the Lightning Bolt event in 1976, but already he seemed to have another agenda.

That year, after Michael competed in the Australian pro events, Quiksilver founder Alan Green flowed him some board shorts and put him on the team. (Greeny remembers it as a product-only sponsorship, Michael recalls a $300 cheque each month.) The following year, Quiksilver's US founders, Bob McKnight and Jeff Hakman, approached him in Hawaii on Greeny's behalf and offered him a licence for Quiksilver in South Africa. Tomson had been a house guest of Hakman's during the past two winters and had witnessed his friend's growing obsession with the Quiksilver brand. Says Michael: 'The shorts were gems, man! And Hakman had this crazy enthusiasm that was quite electrifying. [Lightning Bolt shaper] Tom Parrish was going to be involved, there was a whole crew. When they made me an offer I was like, I'm in!'

Michael went back to Durban and discussed the proposal with college friend Joel Cooper, whose father was in the rag trade. Cooper's reaction was: 'Why do we need them? Why don't we start our own brand?' If the proverbial light didn't immediately begin flashing in Tomson's head, the conversation at least got him thinking. He knew a bit about fit, function and fashion. He mightn't have won a world title, but he was a big name in the surfing world and, like Hakman, he was passionate about the possibilities of an authentic surfwear industry. 'I knew that I could walk into a surf shop and they would try my product because it was me selling it,' he recalls. 'That's a big help when you're getting started.'

So, instead of becoming Quiksilver licensees, in 1978 Tomson and Cooper founded Gotcha, with a line of credit from Michael's dad, Sonny, to fund a sample production run at Cooper's dad's factory. After selling in the limited range of board and walk shorts in South Africa, Michael flew to California and pounded the surf shop beat. The market liked Gotcha's 'New Wave' music culture style, and Michael set up a base in a house at Laguna Beach and rented space at a shipping company warehouse for the ranges as they arrived from Durban. It was an unwieldy way to start an American business, but the exchange rate worked in the partners' favour and they were able to fund expanded ranges in 1979 and 1980.

Gotcha was built on fashion and attitude – the fashion sensibility supplied by Michael himself, whose personal style had moved from surf casual to edgy rock star. The attitude came from the brand's in-your-face advertising style, best exemplified by the infamous, 'If you don't surf, don't start' campaign. Gotcha's first team rider was Cheyne Horan, at the time probably the second-best surfer in the world, but destined never to emerge from Mark Richards' shadow. Says Tomson: 'I've always leaned towards the mavericks, but Cheyne's weirdness irritated me a bit. It wasn't part of the package I wanted. It pissed me off when he wouldn't ride a twin fin because the guy had so much talent it was ridiculous. Then he got on the winged keel board, which was madness. But I sponsored him until I didn't have a brand, and it was the right thing to do.'

Michael was also impressed by the surfing of a pugnacious twelve-year-old in the line-up at the Bay of Plenty, and he befriended a young Martin Potter, watching him develop into the agro super-grom known as 'Pottz', at which point he took over from Horan as the Gotcha brand icon. By the early 1980s the brand had taken off, but growth was outstripping cash flow and the company soon reached a financial crisis point. Ever the networker, Michael visited magazine publisher Clyde Packer, for whom he'd briefly worked, who helped Tomson find a $50,000 lifeboat in the New York investment community. 'It saved the company,' says Tomson, 'but it also made the investor five million bucks when we bought him out a few years later.'

In their third season, the Gotcha partners introduced long bermuda shorts to their range. It was an in-joke between Tomson and designer friend Sean Stussy, to see if kids would respond to the brand satirising the country club lifestyles of their fathers. They did, big time. Says Tomson: 'We were laughed at in the beginning, but it's not an exaggeration to say that Gotcha was built on bermudas and madras.'

Just nudging thirty, Tomson was having the time of his life. He had a rock and roll surf company and a lifestyle to match. Michael on the catwalk with a bevy of gorgeous models at some outrageous trade show party, Michael hanging out in Hollywood with Johnny Rotten, Michael and his buddy Stussy on the hip Laguna art beat – Michael spinning way too fast ... As sales soared towards the $100 million mark, rumours abounded that the founder was strung out on drugs and that Gotcha was haemorrhaging internally. Says Michael:

> Yes, there were drugs. If you're asking was I one of the ten people in the surf industry who never experimented with drugs, no, I was not. I was partying with the other ten thousand. Was I a special case? No, I don't think so. People have absurdly overstated the drugs factor at Gotcha, but yes, drugs did get in the way. They're detrimental to your performance and that was a sobering experience for me. But you have to see this in perspective. There were other issues coming to the fore at Gotcha. What screwed us was success itself.

In the late summer of 1976, it didn't take Bob McKnight long to realise that his one-page Quiksilver licence agreement was not a licence to print money. He and Jeff Hakman spent a lot of time scratching their heads and wondering what Greeny's next move would be, if he were them. But somehow, despite their misgivings, the partners found enough materials to get them started, and a team of seamstresses who would make the shorts at a small-time bikini house, Summer Girl by Sandi, in Encinitas. Despite the fact that Quiksilver USA only managed to dribble out a small number of pairs in the late fall of 1976, the arrival of the 'board shorts from Down Under' created quite a stir in the surfing community. Hobie's Surf Center in Dana Point put up a sign on the sidewalk on busy Pacific Coast Highway: 'Quiksilvers are coming!' When McKnight and Hakman made their first delivery in Bob's battered VW bus, the sign was changed to: 'They're here!' They sold out in a matter of hours.

While their meagre working capital dwindled and they searched for a third partner to help them finance production, McKnight and Hakman took Greeny's advice and went to see Walter Hoffman at Hoffman California Fabrics, supplier of fabric to brands such as Hang Ten, Hobie and Ocean Pacific. After they had revealed their 'getting started kit' of patterns and velcro and fabric samples, the fabric guru's first words echoed an earlier reaction of Bob's father: 'You guys are out of your freakin' minds!' But later Hoffman provided them with industry contacts, while McKnight Sr put them in touch with investment brokers Jim Beazley and Steve Kleeman, who agreed to bankroll Quiksilver USA's production runs for a thirty per cent stake in the company.

Now they were getting serious. McKnight, who had somehow imagined that the business would be like a summer fling before getting back to a real career, realised just how serious when he found himself freezing in snowy New York City just before Christmas, learning about warp and weft from a helpful salesman at the headquarters of fabric giant Milliken's. Fortunately for the surfers turned garmentos, in Milliken's Christopher Glenn they found an ally, just as Alan Green had found one in Joe Ronic. The colours weren't perfect, and unlike the Australians, who used 100 per cent cotton, they were priced down to a sixty-five per cent polyester blend – causing some retailers, like Jack Shipley at Lightning Bolt in Hawaii, to refuse to deal with them and continue to buy direct from Australia – but they had a regular fabric supply, and soon they moved into their first factory, a Quonset hut in the backblocks of Costa Mesa.

In the spring of 1977, Quiksilver began its first advertising campaign, a series of full-page, full-colour ads in *Surfing* magazine. Since they still could not meet demand, the ads were an indulgence, but Hakman was determined to reinforce their market positioning as 'real board shorts' by identifying the brand with the leading surfers who wore them. The first ad featured an action shot of recently crowned world champion Peter Townend and the lines, 'A Sense of Style! The Quiksilver look: often copied but never matched'.

But as Quiksilver USA geared up for summer '77 production, the partners ran out of money again. Asked for a new round of funding, Beazley and Kleeman demanded another thirty per cent. McKnight knew that it would be fatal to surrender control, so he looked for another solution, and found it in Pete Wilson, a San Marino surfer and USC fraternity brother who had organised the rental deal for the factory in Costa Mesa. An architecture graduate, Wilson had made some money renovating and selling houses, and this he used to buy some of the Beazley–Kleeman stake. Although he hadn't made a formal study of it, Wilson had a natural flair for business, and with the help of his father he organised a bank line of credit to fund production, and moved into the role of general manager of the young company. By the end of the summer, Quiksilver USA had overtaken the sales of its Australian parent company. Realising that the trial period seemed to be over, Greeny had a proper licensing contract drawn up, giving the American partners five years with an option for another five.

In September 1980, Quiksilver in Australia introduced a radical new range of board shorts and T-shirts in outlandish colours and patterns, featuring bold harlequin stars and polka dots. 'Echo Beach', the creation of Alan Green and artist Simon Buttonshaw, was actually based on the style of clothing worn by jockeys (horse-racing being another passion of Green's) but the theme also carried with it the rock and roll feel of a new decade and a new generation, a feeling best summed up by a catch-phrase doing the rounds at the time and quickly adopted by Quiksilver: 'If ya can't rock and roll, don't fucking come.' The Echo Beach name was taken from a 1980 hit by Canadian band Martha and the Muffins, but Quiksilver's Echo Beach proved to be more enduring than the band.

Buttonshaw was a hippie surfer who had strong views about art and life. He and Alan Green had enjoyed a volatile relationship since the 1960s, as Buttonshaw told the author in a 2006 interview:

> Greeny was a clubbie from Ocean Grove and he kept dropping in on everyone at Bells, so I came up behind him, grabbed him by the hair and pulled him backwards over the falls on an eight-foot wave. He waited on the beach for two hours to beat me up. I didn't even have a wetsuit on but, on [surfboard shaper] Pat Morgan's advice, I stayed out in the water until he'd left the car park. That's how our relationship started and it pretty much went on in that vein.

Nevertheless, as soon as Quiksilver grew big enough to afford a fabric designer, Greeny's first call was to Simon:

> The deal was, Alan would do the patterns and I'd design the fabrics. Up to this point, it was all just solids and prints from the Hoffmans in California. Even the theme, Quiksilver Country, was just an in-house name for Hoffman prints. But I was completely art-driven, didn't have an ounce of commercial art training. So Walter Hoffman came out from California to share the trade secrets of print-making with Greeny, because he liked him I suppose, and Greeny dragged me along to a lunch at the Southern Cross Hotel in Melbourne to learn the skills from the great man. Walter and Alan got shit-faced drunk all afternoon, to the point where they couldn't sit up, and I was a healthy hippie so I just watched. During this process, Walter somehow gave me my only formal lesson in fabric printing,

all the technical stuff. I took notes all afternoon and got a rudimentary understanding over this alcoholic bender. There was a lot of cross-pollination between the Hoffmans and us as we went on, but that was the starting point.

The working relationship was unique from the beginning. Alan had a very astute and creative design brain that was kind of married to his intuitive business sense. That made Quiksilver different. Plenty of people came along with one or the other, but not many integrated them. Where his design sense was focused was on the cut and design of the shorts. Soon after we started working together we started doing engineered prints that blended the cut and the fabric. Walter had taught me how to do an overall print and repeat it, and what Alan and I introduced was the engineering sensibility.

Quiksilver was creating its own prints, but, much to Buttonshaw's frustration, there was nothing very original about them:

We did flowering gums, things like that. I wanted to do distinctly Australian things but Alan was always very Polynesian in his thinking. It was successful, so you couldn't knock it, but naturally we fought about it. I remember one day I went into Alan's office and thumped the table and said, 'If I have to paint one more fucking hibiscus I'm out of here.' To my surprise, he agreed, he'd had enough. A few days later he brought in a bunch of pictures of jockeys in their bright colours and patterns. Alan grew up by the race track in Moonee Ponds, and that's a big part of his life. So he drops these pictures on the table and says, 'Why can't we do something like that?' There were a lot of other influences, of course, one of them being the harlequin stage clothes of rock band Split Enz, who'd come out of the same generation of art school I was in. In America Devo was wearing similar stuff.

Despite the fact that it had a cool name and a cool new look, Greeny was nervous about how the Australian retailers would react to Echo Beach, so he didn't tell them. Whatever they ordered that spring, Quiksilver shipped them Echo Beach. Having much greater faith in the customer than the shop, he manned the phone when the outraged calls came through. He recalls: 'I just told them, "Don't be as fucking boring as all the other retailers who just buy what they sold last season. Stick them out there where the kids can see them and they'll buy them."'

John Law was the one who had to deal with the serious issues, like the company's biggest account, the General Pants jeanery chain, sending their entire stock back, but Echo Beach survived the initial shock. Simon Buttonshaw:

> Alan is by nature provocative, so the idea of sending the new stuff to the shops without them having seen it was all his. The company wouldn't have the guts to do that now. Lawro was more conservative by nature, so it was pretty much a conspiracy on the part of Alan and me. It was designed to maximise the impact, and it was one of the high points in our working relationship. It was fun. We expected it to have great shock value but we didn't expect surfing to embrace it so much. We thought it would be perceived as a reaction against the standard surfwear prints, not as the successor to them.

In California, the big kahuna of Echo Beach was Danny Kwock, the diminutive goofy-footer and shorts thief who had by now risen to the position of marketing manager at Quiksilver. Kwock, still a teenager, was the king of the peak at what the surf magazines had begun to call 'the hottest hundred yards', the stretch of beach between 54th and 56th streets at Newport, and photos of him and his posse wearing the bright new Quiksilvers soon dominated the surf media. A design enthusiast himself, Danny and his friends actually modified their shorts, adding patches here, a daub of colour there. In an interview with the author in 2005, Kwock recalled: 'We launched the theme with the Echo Beach Pro-Am Surf Challenge at 54th Street, and photographer Jack McCoy shot an ad campaign that featured Tom Carroll, Preston Murray, Craig Brazda and myself lying on silver tanning blankets wearing wrap-around shades. Whoa!'

While Gotcha's crazy bermuda shorts were putting their brand on the map, Echo Beach planted not just Quiksilver's flag, but flags for the whole Australian beach culture. The Echo Beach kids teamed their polka dot and harlequin shorts with brightly coloured Rip Curl wetsuit vests, and most of them rode the hot new McCoy boards from Australia, being heavily promoted in the US by shaper Geoff McCoy and team rider Bruce Raymond, who was also a rising executive star at Quiksilver. Suddenly, Australia was flavour of the month, and marketing troupe The Bronzed Aussies, led by former Quiksilver team rider Peter Townend, joined in and launched their own beachwear brand.

Hakman and McKnight had never intended to ride the brand's Australian roots into the American market, but that was the way it happened. The Australia fad was destined to be short-lived, and other brands – Rip Curl, for example – would find that cracking the American market was a long and pot-holed road, but it gave Quiksilver the jump-start it needed. The second Californian surf boom had begun, and Quiksilver USA's sales soon shot through the three million dollar mark, more than trebling Australia's.

But if it was blue skies all round for Quiksilver USA, storm clouds were gathering around the company's charismatic co-founder, Jeff Hakman. Quiksilver's small management team had been through something of a 'revolving door' period, as the brand grew rapidly and its founders grappled with the many complex business issues to be faced, including the suitability of partners. But Bob McKnight was reasonably well equipped to handle it, especially since the new blood in the company was almost exclusively from his own San Marino/ USC social circle. Hakman clearly was not, and as he felt the pressure of being a surfer out of water, he turned more and more to heroin.

It took McKnight a long time to catch on, but his once-revered partner was becoming an industry joke, selling blocks of his Quiksilver shareholding to finance his habit. Although few of his colleagues would admit to it today, they and several colourful characters in surfing bought into the company at bargain prices in this way. Among them was North Shore big wave rider and adventurer Mike Miller, whose eventual conviction as part of a major international drug ring would bring Quiksilver closer to the dark side than McKnight had ever wanted to go. Bob McKnight recalled in a 2005 interview with the author: 'Jeff would always show up to get his pay cheque, and there'd be a line-up of cars waiting for him to go pay his drug debts. I was starting to get the picture, but I really didn't want to know. He didn't contribute much to the company, but by now I had a good team around me, and I guess I just cut him too much slack.'

In October 1982, Hakman and his Australian girlfriend, Cherie, had their first child, Ryan. It should have been a happy time but Jeff was constantly loaded. Danny Kwock, who'd tried to play minder to his friend and mentor, remembers: 'Jeff was nodding off all the time, and Cherie wasn't coping. I had to help with the diapers and stuff, then drag Jeff off to meetings where he'd be straight into the bathroom, and come out this sweating monster. Everyone knew. It was just sad.'

Later in the winter, Hakman contracted hepatitis from sharing a needle. He disappeared for a month and when he emerged he was a shell of the champion surfer everyone knew and loved. He'd sold his car for drugs and took buses when a ride wasn't available, sometimes forgetting where he was going and riding to the end of the line. McKnight: 'It was out in the open now. You could see it was killing him and, frankly, I didn't know what to do. There were no interventions back then.'

In the end it was McKnight's new partners, the Crowe brothers, Larry and Charles, and their friend Randy Hunt, who forced the issue. They were rich kids from San Marino and, although Hunt was a boozer who'd been on the wrong side of the law briefly as a student, drug addiction had no part in their lives. They didn't understand it and didn't want to. Hakman simply had to go. More than twenty years later, sitting in the stateroom of a boat off the coast of Sumatra with McKnight and the author, Jeff Hakman's eyes clouded as he remembered the moment he was sacked from the company he founded: 'In all fairness to Bob and the others, I was just too far gone to have around. Bob and I knew that, and I think he handled what had to be done with dignity. Larry Crowe just wanted to kick me around the block. That hurt.'

Hakman walked out of Quiksilver with nothing. No shares, no cash. His friends threw a benefit night at The Cannery in Newport Beach and raised $400 to help the young family resettle in Australia. And then they were gone.

12 LE SURF

At the Hôtel Au Bon Coin, three hundred yards from the main drag, we got a room with two double beds for six and ninepence a day. We settled in and made our way to the Côte des Basques ... where Philippe Gerard introduced us to the Waikiki Surf Club. In the club rooms, to my great surprise, I found Peter Troy, my old surfing mate from Torquay ... We loaded boards on the wagon and with the local gremmies, headed north to La Barre.
Rennie Ellis, *Odyssey of a Surfer*, 1965

In 1979, Australia's Mark Richards won what was to be the first of four consecutive world professional titles, winning four of the ten events on the International Professional Surfers' Association World Tour. It was an impressive victory, even though he only just kept out fellow Australian Cheyne Horan by winning the last event in Hawaii, because for most of the tour Richards rode boards that had previously been considered as toys to be used in near-flat conditions.

The twin-finned surfboard made its first appearance in the late 1940s, when pioneer board designer Bob Simmons experimented with two tiny fins on his concave-bottom, balsa ten-footers. In the early

1970s, several Californians played with the idea again, but the designer who actually took it somewhere was San Diego's Steve Lis, whose 1971 'fish' used two fins with a wide, split tail. The following year, Jim Blears and David Nuuhiwa finished first and second respectively in the amateur world championships, riding twins in marginal conditions in San Diego, but despite the good results, twin fins remained a curiosity, just another blip on a radar screen filled with flawed ideas.

Mark Richards, a keen student of design theory and a shaper from the age of fourteen, knew about the Lis fish, but he only really began to think about the possibilities of two fins after watching Hawaiian Reno Abellira ride a fish superbly in small waves at the Coke Surfabout contest in Sydney in 1977. In a 1979 interview with the author, Richards said: 'I want to make one thing perfectly clear. Reno got me back onto twin fins. I got my ideas from him. I get bummed out when I see articles where I'm supposed to have invented the thing ... Reno's five-seven fish started the ball rolling.'

Richards's desire to set the record straight is understandable. From 1978 he absolutely dominated in small to medium surf, and as his twin fin designs matured, he dominated in almost all surf. 'They can talk about Kelly [Slater] and the rest,' says Michael Tomson, 'but the difference between Mark Richards and the rest was so dramatic that even a layman could see it. The lines he was drawing were just completely different. I got on a twin fin too, and won a tour event on it, but it took most of the tour a long while to catch up.'

The one-time Quiksilver rider was by this time the pin-up boy of Duke Boyd's Lightning Bolt, and Victory Wetsuits of Japan, and his superstar status certainly helped their bottom lines, but Richards's greatest impact was on surfboard sales. It had been more than a decade since the shortboard revolution, and while sales had been consistent in all major markets for most of that time, the proliferation of brands had driven many into almost 'underground' status again, with designers building just enough boards to get by, and selling them regionally. The return of the twin fin changed all of that. Suddenly everyone wanted to swoop and fly, like 'MR'. His Superman-inspired logo was copied all over the world, but more importantly, surfboard sales shot into the stratosphere, because not only did everyone need a twin fin to surf like MR, but conventional wisdom had it that the boards did not work in all conditions. It was necessary – essential even – to have one in your three- or four-board quiver. And that was good for everyone's business.

But the twin fins' glory days were numbered, even as Richards continued to rack up world titles. The answer to the question 'What could be better than two fins?' turned out to be a no-brainer. Yes, three fins. But again, the innovator was not the originator. Master shaper Dick Brewer played around with three fins in 1970 on his boards for Reno Abellira, who briefly rode a board with a large centre fin and two tiny 'finlets' set behind. Next, brothers Malcolm and Duncan Campbell of Oxnard, California, released the 'Bonzer' in 1972, featuring keel side fins and a deeper fin in the centre. The Bonzer seemed to work, and enjoyed a brief rush of sales, but none of the big name surfers of the mid-1970s picked up on it.

Big Australian power surfer Simon Anderson finished third on the world tour of 1977, and looked certain to be a future world champion, particularly after fearless North Shore performances. But Anderson became increasingly frustrated at his own inability to master the twin fin, while the Richards juggernaut proceeded. In 1980, at his home beach of Narrabeen, he noticed local surfer Frank Williams getting a lot of firepower out of his turns. When he checked Williams's ride, he discovered that he had modified a twin fin by adding a centre fin right on the tail. Back at his Energy Surfboards factory, Anderson designed a prototype three-finned board with his fins the same size, and the side fins slightly angled in towards the nose, which was reduced in area like the 'no-nose' design unveiled by Geoff McCoy the previous year.

Anderson trialled the board in Hawaii that winter, and was so impressed by the thrust it gave him out of his turns that he christened it the 'Thruster'. The board made its competitive debut at the Stubbies Pro in Queensland in March 1981, where it failed to impress, even though other surfers, notably Tom Carroll, had their own versions of it. The pro caravan moved on to Bells Beach, and in one of the true vintage years for the famous big wave break, Anderson cut loose on his Thruster in huge waves, driving out of turns with such speed that he was able to set up long runs across the bowl section. Anderson's performance in winning Bells was sheer brilliance, and when he backed up a few weeks later and took out the Coke Surfabout in excellent two-metre waves, everyone wanted his secret weapon.

The only problem for the laconic Anderson was that his weapon was not exactly a secret. It was in his nature to share design ideas freely with friends and colleagues, particularly as he hadn't invented the tri-fin configuration, merely refined it. But it was the combination of design elements that made the Thruster unique, and it was a combination that would become universally applied. By August 1981, Gary McNabb of Nectar Surfboards in California had a licensed Thruster in production, and by the end of the year, so had everyone else. In October, *Surfer* magazine's special surfboard issue barely mentioned the Thruster, but when Anderson won his third event of the year, the Pipeline Masters, and demonstrated the design's capabilities in the most powerful waves, the tri-fin revolution was on in earnest. Within two years, the Thruster design had become the standard in performance surfboards, for all kinds of waves, and has remained so to the present day.

Simon Anderson quit the pro tour at the end of 1983 and, despite being one of the most respected designers in the industry, has made little more than a journeyman's income. The self-deprecating surfer occasionally makes jokes about his failure to capitalise on the Thruster by patenting the design, but there appears to be no bitterness, and he continues to produce cutting-edge surfboard design for the sport's leaders, including Kelly Slater.

By the early 1980s, Rip Curl and Quiksilver had emerged as the leading Australian surf brands, despite the fact that neither were doing big numbers, and neither had yet developed a brand strategy to cover the possibilities of the market. Quiksilver certainly had the edge on its parent company, with almost $20 million turnover worldwide in 1985, largely thanks to Quiksilver USA's sales contribution of almost $13 million. Rip Curl's global turnover was more like $6 million, and that was largely thanks to its recently created garments division.

Both companies had struggled with growth beyond their domestic markets, but for different reasons. Quiksilver, after initial misgivings, had embraced a licensee strategy, and after joining the company in 1976, John Law had made this his baby, establishing distributor licences for Japan and France, in addition to the first licence for Quiksilver USA. From 1982, former pro surfer Bruce Raymond took much of the responsibility for the licensing policy, using as his mantra Alan Green's edict of 'make them like us'.

Rip Curl, on the other hand, had a centrist policy of running its global affairs out of Torquay, where they felt they had established their credibility. Cracking the US market therefore proved to be difficult, despite the fact that Australian brands were in vogue in the early 1980s, and that Rip Curl wetsuits were quality products. Co-founder Brian Singer felt that the answer in the US lay in finding a highly qualified industry professional who could take the brand to the market, then create systems to deliver the product. Singer had high expectations that he had picked up from his involvement with the Young Presidents Association, a global think tank and social network for under-forty overachievers, but the reality was that no one person had ever been able to fill these roles in a surf company before, and the chosen one, Ron Grimes, didn't seem likely to either.

Grimes had cut his sports industry teeth in racquetball, which was huge in the US in the 1970s and '80s, but he knew virtually nothing about the surf industry and was thrown in at the deep end as Rip Curl opened Californian headquarters in San Clemente and simultaneously hit the American market with a range of vividly coloured wetsuits with crazy names and convoluted high tech stories on their swing tags. Backed by the endorsements of team riders like Tom Carroll and

Wayne Lynch, the Aggrolite and Dawn Patrol Rip Curls certainly made a marketing statement – they were bright and colourful while most of their competitors were black and dull – but Grimes was faced with a near-impossible task in creating operational systems in time to sell the range, and he didn't.

Rip Curl would persevere and ultimately succeed in the American market, but it was becoming clear to both Quiksilver and Rip Curl that growth of the brand meant not just geographical spread but also product diversification. Alan Green had felt the pressure on this for some time. While his view was that the brand was about 'board shorts, board shorts, board shorts', the Americans wanted to do silkies and the French underpants … or something. He wasn't interested. In any case, the issue was clouded by a gentlemen's agreement reached when both companies entered the US market. None of the protagonists has a clear memory of the details, but at some point the former partners reached an informal agreement that Rip Curl would produce wetsuits and Quiksilver would produce board shorts, and neither would encroach on the other's territory. T-shirts, however, were open season.

According to Doug Warbrick, the main intent of the arrangement was protection of the joint athlete sponsorships the brands had with surfers such as Wayne Lynch and Tom Carroll. But the landscape was changing rapidly, and by 1985 the arrangement was off. 'There was no animosity,' says Warbrick. 'The game had changed so we just ripped up the agreement and moved on.'

Rip Curl's push into surfwear and accessories was led by a ponytailed adventurer and surfer and one-time ad man named Doug Spong. Originally from Brighton Beach, the centre of bayside surfing in Melbourne, Spong first made a name for himself around the surf shops with a clothing brand called Double Dragon, which was named either for a brand of mosquito coil or for a brand of Chinese heroin, depending on the mood of the founder when asked.

Double Dragon was one of many small clothing businesses built in the seventies on the price of labour in Indonesia. As Bali became the surf tourism capital of the region, surfers soon discovered that they could finance their entire trip by bringing home a suitcase full of sarongs and batik print shirts. (Some found that they could finance next year's trip as well, by hollowing out the stringer of a surfboard and loading it with 'Thai sticks' of marijuana.) Spongy's Double Dragon succeeded because he took note of what Australian surf shops didn't have, and then supplied it. At the time, Platt's, Adler's, Golden Breed and Crystal Cylinders had the boy market covered (with Quiksilver not far behind) but no one was catering for girls. Double Dragon started producing Bali-style beachwear for girls, and within a year Spongy had four shops of his own, in addition to his wholesale client list. In search of better margins, he moved from Bali to Java and finally to India, where it all ended in tears when a manufacturing house took the money and ran.

Doug Spong returned to Australia stone-cold broke and was considering a return to advertising (he still had the ponytail) when Doug Warbrick offered him a job at Rip Curl. Claw had been watching the development of the accessories market in America, and he'd seen kids heading down the track to surf at Trestles wearing identical backpacks, with different surf brand logos emblazoned on the back. He knew they were cheaply made in Asia, and he knew Spongy knew a bit about Asian sourcing, despite coming a cropper. Spongy started at Rip Curl in 1979 as product manager of the garments division, but his brief was much wider than apparel. He did the cosmetic design for the new coloured wetsuit range for the US market, as well as a new line of windsurfer wetsuits for that fast-growing market, then designed and sourced the first Rip Curl backpacks, wallets, beach towels and T-shirts. In an interview with the author in 2005, Spong recalled:

> Garments went through the roof in the early eighties, but, Jesus, it was hard work. I had backpacks in production in Taiwan, then they got rich so I had to move somewhere else. It seemed like I spent a lot of the eighties designing on the run, scribbling on pieces of paper on plane rides, then handing them to the factory boss and flying out again. But the division was doing more than

$14 million when I left, which was sixty per cent of sales for the brand, so we all did well out of it.

Bob Hurley was shaping surfboards under his own name in a small factory and shop at Huntington Beach in 1983 when he heard that Australia's Billabong was looking for a licensee for the US. Billabong had been selling direct to a couple of retailers in Hawaii and California to test the market, and the signs were good, but it was still going to be a herculean task to wedge a foothold in a market now dominated by Ocean Pacific and Hang Ten, with dozens of smaller but fast-growing brands barking at their heels. Hurley put his hand up and, despite the fact that he had meagre cash resources to establish the brand, Billabong founder Gordon Merchant awarded him the licence. The American operation proved to be a huge drain on Billabong's resources, as Merchant told journalist Tim Baker:

> We had to subsidise the kick-off for the first eighteen months. We had no security over the stock we shipped or guarantees of cash in return. I just trusted Bob [Hurley] and his partners to do the right thing and they didn't let me down. But that business was started on less than forty thousand bucks, we really didn't know how the cash flow was going to work, and for a little bit there, we thought we were going to go down … I remember waking up in a cold sweat … terrified. [Wife] Rena was a tower of strength through those periods. She would hold it all together and we'd just keep working away.

Once the initial cash flow problems were solved, Hurley proved to be a good general for the brand, bringing on board new team riders, like future world champion Sunny Garcia, and creating the Billabong Pro Hawaii, which soon became a world tour highlight. But it was to be a pugnacious Australian teenager, one of Gordon Merchant's most unlikely signings, who would be Billabong's breakthrough brand warrior in the American market.

Mark Occhilupo first met Gordon Merchant at the age of fourteen, in the shop of his one sponsor, Cronulla Surf Design, when Merchant came in to sell his range. The owner, Mark Aprilovic, convinced Merchant to flow the up-and-comer some board shorts, but when the little guy with the tree-trunk legs made the semifinals of the Straight Talk Tyres Open a few weeks later, Merchant was on the phone to Aprilovic immediately, offering a more substantial sponsorship. Within two years, 'Occy' had become the new sensation of world surfing, a position he underlined for the US market by toppling their hero, twice world champion Tom Curren, in a thrilling final of the Op Pro at Huntington Beach in August 1985, in front of a crowd of more than fifty thousand.

Held in peak summertime at one of California's most popular beaches, the Op Pro had become surfing's biggest event by far, with more media coverage than any other. As Occhilupo told his biographer, Tim Baker, in *Occy*: 'I did this one turn where my foot slipped off the board. Everyone screamed unintentionally in the heat of the moment. I made a weird sort of recovery … and everyone started roaring. I thought, well, at least I got a cheer. It was intense. I just thought that was the way it always was in finals, but that's probably the biggest crowd I've ever surfed in front of, before or since. It was a real peak for pro surfing.'

And for Billabong. Occy: 'All of a sudden everything California had to offer just opened to me. I was staying with Gordon Merchant at Bob Hurley's house. Gordon was … working with Bob on building up the Billabong brand, so for me to win the biggest surf contest in the US, against their number one guy, was great for the brand. They were so stoked.' Seemingly overnight, Billabong made its march on the American market, while Merchant now felt confident to strike out at other markets, like Japan and Europe.

Throughout the 1960s, Europe, and most particularly France, had lain dormant in surfing terms. While the separate but interconnected surf cultures of Cornwall, France and the Channel Islands motored along happily enough, sharing their excellent waves with only the most adventurous travelling surfers, things began to change as global travel became more affordable and faster in the 1970s. The surf movies and magazines began to zero in on the beautiful Basque coast of France, which offered long, hot summers, good food and wine, beautiful girls and, most importantly, excellent reef breaks and some of the best beach breaks in the world. As visitor numbers increased, so did the market for surfing products.

In the mid-seventies, Maritxu Darrigrand, a young female surfer and skier of some repute in France, married another well-known skier and adventurer, Yves Bessas, and together they formed a company called Uhaina to distribute snow and surf films in Europe, operating out of the Darrigrand family farmhouse in the countryside behind Biarritz. They compiled a program of surf and ski footage from around the world that they called *La Nuit de la Glisse* and, after a low-key start at the Pax Cinema in Biarritz, *La Nuit* played to packed houses all over Europe.

Quiksilver partner John Law had met Bessas in Europe, and hearing of their success with surf film distribution, asked the French couple to distribute Quiksilver products in France. So Uhaina began to handle surf products too, with Rip Curl wetsuits, Lightning Bolt surfboards and California Tee Shirts soon added to the company's product range.

The two distribution businesses proved complementary, the movies promoting the lifestyle and creating a market for the clothes. And as both businesses grew, Uhaina needed partners. Bessas knew Alan Tiegen, a young American surfer who had worked in the surf film business before marrying a Biarritz girl and returning to California to finish college. Yves and Maritxu visited the Tiegens in Santa Barbara and offered them a partnership. Having just finished his business degree, Alan accepted. The Darrigrand farmhouse now became home to two couples and two businesses. The businesses thrived, but the personal chemistry did not. Finally it was resolved that Bessas would take Uhaina and do his films, the Tiegens would run the surfwear business through a new company called Surf 'n'

Sport, and Darrigrand would leave them all to it, flying to her sister in Australia.

Alan and Francoise Tiegen broadened Quiksilver's distribution throughout France, while Law tracked down distributors elsewhere in Europe. In 1979, just as windsurfing took off all over Europe, Lawro trekked through Holland, Belgium, Germany and Switzerland, finding distributors in each. These small markets for Quiksilver's limited and summer-based range collectively represented a significant market, and once Bruce Raymond took over the licensing business, he formulated a plan to create a united sales base in Europe. Surf 'n' Sport was granted a manufacturing and distribution licence for France, Spain and the UK in 1982, and the Tiegens rented a small factory in Biarritz and went into production. Alan Tiegen knew that to make inroads in Europe, the product had to be 'Europeanised', so the first garments off the Surf 'n' Sport production line were board shorts with slips or linings inside, placing them somewhere between surf culture and the promenade poseurs of Nice and Cannes.

Alan Green was outraged, but Law and Raymond convinced him to bite his tongue until they could see if Europeanisation boosted sales. It did. In 1983 Surf 'n' Sport, now with a production team of twelve, sold twenty thousand pairs of board shorts for gross sales of around a quarter of a million dollars. It was still very much a one-product, one-season business, but the Tiegens had samples of the new Echo Beach jackets and pants and had plans to steadily grow their sales base. The problem, as the Australians saw it, was that the Tiegens weren't moving fast enough. Alan Tiegen recalls: 'Quiksilver had their business plan and we had ours. There was a growing sense of frustration with our different objectives.'

In 1976 a young Australian photojournalist named Harry Hodge started working on the project of his dreams – an adventure surf film that picked up where *The Endless Summer* had left off. For his stars he chose former Australian champion Paul Neilsen, unknown Brian Cregan and two of Quiksilver's earliest team riders, Rabbit Bartholomew and Bruce Raymond. For cast, crew and investors, it became the adventure that never seemed to end. It was 1981 before Hodge's *Band on the Run* finally opened in cinemas to lukewarm reviews and low box office.

Bruised if not broken, Hodge retreated to Angourie on Australia's east coast with his French girlfriend, Brigitte Darrigrand, to work on his golf swing and a new business plan. When Bruce Raymond, now a Quiksilver executive, passed through on a surf trip, Hodge confided in him that he needed a job. Raymond promised to put in a good word, and Hodge and Darrigrand moved south to Torquay a month later, he to work in marketing, she in design.

Despite his own film's disastrous financial performance, Hodge had undoubted talents as a cinematographer and producer, and Quiksilver soon put them to use. During his time at Quiksilver USA, Raymond had put together a deal with film-maker Scott Dittrich in which Quiksilver provided two surfers (Raymond and Rabbit Bartholomew) for a shoot in Puerto Rico in return for a five-minute cut of action and product footage. Raymond gave a copy of the short (*Quiksilver Country*) to every roadshow man, and the free commercial played worldwide for more than a year. By 1983, Raymond, Green and Law had begun to talk seriously about getting Quiksilver-branded entertainment into the surfing market. Raymond recalls: 'Video was the big new thing, but the price of a tape was ridiculous. I thought that if we could keep the price down, a branded surf movie for video would work.' The project, called *The Performers* and co-produced by Raymond and Hodge, revolutionised the financing and marketing of the surf movie genre and sidelined the surf roadshow men who'd helped make it possible.

With *The Performers* in the can, Hodge and Darrigrand decided to spend the northern summer vacationing in her native France, checking out the Teigens' Surf 'n' Sport operation for their bosses while they were there. By the end of the summer they had made up their minds. France would be their new home. Back in Australia to prepare for their relocation, Hodge began to invent a freelance marketing role for himself in France, working with the Teigens, but at one of the traditional Australian Friday 'beer o'clock' drinks at Quiksilver, Green got off the phone after a long session with Alan Tiegen, fuming over Surf 'n' Sport's inability to see the bigger picture. Hodge offered some poorly timed advice and Greeny snarled: 'Well, if you're so frickin' smart, Harry, why don't you go over there and run the business?'

It was an idea conceived in a heated moment, but the more Greeny considered it, the more sense it made. Hodge and Darrigrand decided to take up the challenge. While Law and Raymond terminated the Surf 'n' Sport licence, Hodge drew up a business plan, searched for finance and pondered his team. Brigitte knew design and he was confident that he could be a leader, but a vital ingredient was missing. In surfing terminology it was known as 'the stoke', and Hodge suddenly remembered someone who had it to spare.

When Jeff Hakman, his girlfriend Cherie and baby son Ryan arrived on the Gold Coast of Queensland in May 1983, their lives had nowhere to go but up. Their departure from California had been a blur of drugs and humiliation. Only seven years after he had moved to California to start Quiksilver with Bob McKnight, Hakman had left it a tragic figure. The Hakmans rented a small apartment at Burleigh Heads and Jeff tried to regain his health by surfing every day. Cherie applied for a single mother's pension. They had no car. They walked to the store to buy what groceries they could afford. Jeff heard that the Brothers Neilsen store in Surfers Paradise was advertising for a sales assistant. He walked to the corner phone booth and called his old friend Paul Neilsen.

Few people in the surf industry had spoken out against drugs as loudly as Paul Neilsen, and Hakman's heroin addiction horrified him. The last thing he needed in his life was a disintegrating junkie behind the counter at his flagship store. But he was also a loyal friend, vulnerable to Hakman's cry for help. Jeff had a job – at $200 a week – the next day. Hakman stayed clean and sober all winter and, as the Australian summer began, he launched a surf school, giving lessons to tourists outside store hours. The business developed quickly, and he was considering devoting himself to it exclusively, when Hodge phoned. Hodge recalls: 'We were both losers on the comeback trail. We both had something to prove, both to ourselves and to our friends. And I wanted Jeff in because he'd done all this before, and he had that X-factor. He could win people over with his enthusiasm.'

By the middle of 1984, the group had a fourth partner in John Winship, a South African designer who had worked for Quiksilver in California and moved to the Gold Coast with Hakman. They also had a French base, back at the Darrigrand farmhouse, and a new company they named Na Pali, after the rugged Kauai coast. Na Pali had start-up capital of just two million French francs (approximately $230,000), a lot more than Hakman and McKnight had in 1976, but it was not nearly enough.

By the end of the summer, Na Pali had moved out of the farm and into 1000 metres of factory floor in a new industrial estate north of Saint Jean de Luz, thanks to Brigitte's family putting up property security for bank loans. Brigitte set up a cutting room and basic production facility, and Na Pali achieved five million francs turnover in its first full year of operation. The distributors elsewhere in Europe, most much wealthier than Na Pali, paid for their stock with letters of credit that provided cash flow, and the company, against all odds, flourished.

For the first year or two, Hodge and Hakman spent much of their time on the road, riding trains or driving from one end of Western Europe to the other, selling the brand. Their manufacturing presence in France significantly boosted domestic sales, but in the rest of Europe the brand was represented by distributors who had several brands in their portfolios. Getting them to focus on Quiksilver, and believe in its long-term viability, was a strategic imperative as rival brands such as O'Neill, Chiemsee and Oxbow vied for market share.

By 1988 export sales had surpassed French domestic sales and, with an increasingly Pan-European focus, Na Pali (or Quiksilver Europe, as it had been designated) was poised for major growth. It boasted good staff, good product, an aggressive marketing plan and an even more aggressive approach to selling. The ship was sailing smoothly, but Hodge spied two navigational hazards ahead. The first was that Hakman was doing heroin again. He had begun using occasionally as an escape from business pressures, then daily, then whenever he had to, which was often. By now the partners were paying themselves reasonable salaries, but not enough to support his habit, so Hakman used his company fuel card to get cash for drugs. He was stealing from his partners, and the rising tide of resentment and tension was destabilising the company.

The second problem was that Hodge's house of cards was shaky. For years he had juggled letters of credit and romanced the banks every few weeks to fund the company's staggering growth. And it was staggering – an average 175 per cent over the first few years, before levelling off to forty per cent in the late eighties. Quiksilver USA had grown from zero to $3.5 million in sales in its first five years. Quiksilver Europe had grown from zero to $13.2 million over the same period. The difference was that McKnight's grounding in business made him fiscally conservative, more interested in building a solid foundation. Hodge, ever the flamboyant entrepreneur, erected a skyscraper that could topple. He had done a brilliant job in taking the company this far without new funding, but McKnight and Hakman had needed far more than their start-up capital to support much smaller growth, and, despite his own unflagging belief that he would prevail, Hodge couldn't do it either.

13 VELCRO VALLEY

Cowabunga! Sun is out and sales are up for coastline clothing lines.
Summer may still be around the corner, but Los Angeles' legion of
beachwear manufacturers are already feeling the heat from retailers
desperate for stock.
Los Angeles Business Journal, 18 April 1988

After his stunning victory in the 1985 Op Pro, the 'Super Bowl of surfing' as its American boosters had labelled it, Mark Occhilupo backed up to win it a second time in 1986. And again, the finals were played out in front of a huge summer crowd. This time, Occy disposed of Tom Curren in the semifinals, setting up an all-Australian final against Glen Winton. The fact that California's favourite son was out of the event did not go down well with a section of the crowd that had been getting progressively drunker and rowdier as the afternoon wore on.

Occy took out the first of a three-set final, then, halfway through the second, he heard a loud explosion. He told biographer Tim Baker: 'I could hear the crowd roaring, even when no one was catching a wave, and I was thinking, what is going on? Then I heard a KA-BOOM! Like a massive explosion, and I ducked for cover. I saw something on fire, and then there was another explosion …' Apparently sparked by police asking two topless girls to cover up, a full-blown riot had broken out on the southside of Huntington Pier. Writer Matt Warshaw described the scene for *Surfer*:

> In front of the lifeguard headquarters – a hundred yards from the contest's southern grandstand – three police cars, a lifeguard Jeep, a police van, a beach ambulance and an ATC three-wheeler were burned up, smashed up, or both. Two of the cars were flipped over. Engine parts from the torched cars had been torn out and thrown through the headquarters' windows. Soot from the burned autos blackened rows and rows of cars in the parking lot north of the headquarters, and some of the cars there had been vandalised. Inside the garage there was a bullet hole in the ceiling where Marine Safety Captain Bill Richardson – the only man not to flee the headquarters when it appeared the rioters would storm in – had fired a warning shot at a group who had gained entrance.

At the end of the second set, Occy was sure he'd won the final, but contest director Ian Cairns delayed an announcement. Finally, he told Occy: 'Have you seen what's going on out there? It's out of control. You've won the contest but you have to surf the third set because we can't have people leaving the beach right now.'

Rabbit Bartholomew, who was in the commentary booth, told Tim Baker: 'Ian came in and said something like, "There are fifty thousand people on the beach, and if they go out the back, people are going to die. Tell them it's a tie and send them back out."' The surfers paddled back out. Occy recalled: 'The crowd was mosh-pitting over each other and things were on fire. I didn't want to go in.'

The Huntington riot put surfing on the front pages and on the evening news for all the wrong reasons, but there was no denying that surfing's influence in youth culture was far greater than it had ever been before. But ironically, the naming rights sponsor of the Huntington riot (not to mention the surf contest that preceded it) had already peaked as a credible surf brand, even as its revenues reached towards a 1989 peak of $370 million – way beyond any number its rivals had even dreamed of. Jim Jenks's Op had done all the right things for a growing brand. It had extended its appeal beyond surf, by embracing skateboarding and the new sport of snowboarding, not to mention motocross, windsurfing, wakeboarding and anything else with youth appeal. It had extended its product offering by licensing its name for sunglasses, hats, watches, perfumes and shoes. It had extended its distribution by selling to department stores.

Op had found a variety of ways to accumulate enormous wealth for its investors, and Wall Street saw it as the iconic surf brand of the day. But Op had lost its surfing soul, and it would soon begin to founder until it rediscovered it. This should have sent a clear message to the cool new brands coming up behind but, hey, this was the 1980s, when greed was good.

Op and Hobie still led the American market, but Gotcha and Quiksilver were in hot pursuit, with numerous other Californian start-ups, plus Australia's Rip Curl and Billabong, filling in the factory grid between Huntington Beach and Laguna Beach – a stretch of Orange County fast becoming known as 'Velcro Valley'. Gotcha's edgy blend of surf and rock culture had put it ahead in domestic sales, but Quiksilver's authentic surf roots gave it plenty of long-term market muscle. The major difference between the two brands, however, was that Michael Tomson could take his brand anywhere and do anything he wanted, while at Quiksilver, Bob McKnight felt constrained by directives he received from a licensor far removed from the brand's biggest market.

By 1986, board shorts, Quiksilver's core product, represented only thirty-five per cent of the American business, while T-shirts and walk shorts had reached forty per cent. This represented significant diversification for a brand that still called itself 'the board shorts company'. At the same time, sales distribution had spread from coastal surf shops to a nationwide mix of 1300 surf, specialty and department stores. From a quiet beginning at Liberty House in Hawaii in 1984, department store sales had jumped to nearly twenty per cent of the company's $18.6 million revenue for 1986. Whichever way you looked at it, Quiksilver USA was leading the core surf brand into a brave new world.

Meanwhile, Quiksilver Australia posted just under $5.5 million in sales in 1986, representing less than a quarter of the brand's global sales. With the American market on fire and the European market looking very promising, it was clear that growth in the future was going to be driven from the northern hemisphere, and yet many of the decisions governing those growing markets were being made by a small licensing company in Australia.

Since Jeff Hakman's departure in 1983, Bob McKnight had made every attempt to bond with the three amigos from San Marino who were now his partners. With Charles Crowe, who surfed and was a regular guy, he had no problem. Charles's brother Larry and Randy Hunt were more difficult, but McKnight was trying, and moreover, Larry Crowe was making the company lean and accountable, not that he couldn't break out and have some fun now and then. When the company accountant gave them the good news that they needed to spend some money or give it to the IRS, Larry led the posse to a high-end car dealer in the South Bay, where they paid cash for four gleaming new Porsches.

It was Larry's idea to float the company. With big Randy Hunt in tow, he went to see McKnight, who was initially horrified by the idea. Buying into the Wall Street game by going public would make him answerable to a whole bunch of people who didn't even surf. But then, other issues came into play. He, like the other directors, had cash guarantees over the company's line of credit (nearly $4 million per partner in 1986, and growing fast), and he had a young family. He didn't want to risk their future. And he could be outvoted on the private board of his own company, a situation that grated deeply with him. Taking the company public might, in McKnight's words, 'leverage some independent thinkers into the picture'.

McKnight sought the best advice he could afford, and it was all pretty much the same. Taking the American company public would be a brilliant growth strategy, but only if it had control of its own destiny. So when the Quiksilver USA team flew to Melbourne in September 1986 to seek approval to take the American licensee public, they also had a secondary agenda – to buy the trademarks for the US and Mexico. Cutting the umbilical cord between parent company and biggest licensee was the point at which Quiksilver would really cease to be an Australian brand, despite the marketing hype. McKnight was anticipating a fight with the founder, but instead there was resignation, perhaps tempered by the fact that the deal was going to make Alan Green and John Law considerable wealth.

But there was plenty of lobbying over the terms. Greeny recalls: 'It was only the lawyers that complicated it. Once Lawro and I got Bob into a cab and talked privately, we nailed the whole thing in a few minutes.' McKnight remembers it a little differently: 'Their biggest fear was that the brand would fall into the hands of suits who didn't know and didn't care. They wanted to know if I would still be the guy. I said, "Alan, read my lips. I'm not going anywhere. I will be the guy."'

When the initial public offering was completed on 16 December 1986 and the stock quoted on the NASDAQ exchange, Quiksilver became the first publicly traded surfwear company in the world. The first board of directors of Quiksilver, Inc. consisted of the four working partners – president McKnight, thirty-three; vice-president and chief financial officer Larry Crowe, thirty-four; vice-president Randy Hunt, thirty-five; vice-president Charles Crowe, thirty-one – and two external members, Arthur Crowe, sixty-three, and Robert G Kirby, sixty-one. McKnight and his partners sold half their stocks and made millions, while the Australian shareholders split $3 million and equities.

While Quiksilver was quietly going corporate, Gotcha was going ballistic, riding a wave of neon, surfing's new, vivid look. The look was drawn from California's emerging volleyball culture, with heroes like Karch Kiraly suddenly all over the media, leaping high into the air to smash the ball, clad in fluorescent short shorts and muscle shirts in green, pink and orange, while long-legged Californian beauties completed the look with neon tanks and bikini bottoms. It was sex on the sand, and the look rapidly transcended the beach and hit the malls. Quiksilver's veteran sales manager, Tom Holbrook recalled:

> Echo Beach was bright, fun and core, and it really loosened up the whole marketplace. It captured the mystique of Australia for us, and that was very strong at the time. But then there was the volley, elastic-topped shorts as worn by Karch Kiraly, in those bright colours with a big logo on the butt. They were typically American, and they went right across the country. Retailers love those single items they can lock and load on. The volleys evolved into the whole neon thing, and it went crazy.

Surfing didn't start it, but the astute surfwear brands quickly embraced it. Among the brands to go neon were Jimmy'z, Catchit, Maui & Sons and Billabong, but nobody did it with the punk flair of Gotcha, which hit $75 million in sales in 1987, compared with Quiksilver's comparatively modest $30 million. In fact there was not a lot of difference between Quiksilver and Gotcha's neon product, but Gotcha's bold marketing gave it the edge. Bob McKnight recalled: 'It was the over-the-top, rock star way they did stuff that got everyone's attention. At Surf Expo in Florida, they pulled off this New York–style fashion show, with Michael (Tomson) on the back of a flying saucer with all these chicks. It just blew us all away. We were shocked by their act.'

Michael Tomson:

I created an unbelievable cell of creative people. After a while they were coming to me because I took chances and I created conditions in which they could flourish, and it really paid off. A lot of the big direction ideas were mine, but also we were winning art director's awards through having this fucking great workshop of terrific and talented people.

The primary reason we clicked with the market was that the advertising we were doing was shocking but memorable. And we were doing great airbrush art things. I just figured kids have minds, let's open them up a bit, and they responded. Laguna Beach [where Gotcha was headquartered] became a real hotbed of creativity, the organic centre of the surf industry. The fact that it was a fine arts centre put us in a context, but we were much more street/surf oriented. We'd have fashion shows that were events, man. We'd have naked women, James Brown impersonators, psychedelic stuff … that's how the brand exploded. It became a cult. If you look at the ads and catalogues you can see why the brand succeeded. You could run them today and they'd work. We'd run with a look for no more than six months, then we'd change. We had a computer look, for example, before they were even thought about in a social context.

Gotcha also led the way into the malls of America, selling in quantity to upscale department and specialty stores such as Nordstrom, Robinson's and Bullock's. Quiksilver started appearing in some of the majors too, but Gotcha's 'it' status and urban sensibility took it places competitors couldn't reach.

In summer 1987 Quiksilver, Inc. moved another step closer to the kind of professional management it felt the shareholders required with the recruitment of May's department stores executive John Warner, who started as vice-president of sales but was CEO and chairman of the board by the end of the year, on about double McKnight's salary.

Warner was to be the first of several professional managers brought into the company to help steer it through phases of extraordinary growth, creating a mix of executives that came to be known as 'the salts and the suits'.

John Warner was not the easiest CEO to love and obey. His bluntly authoritarian management style rubbed underlings up the wrong way. He just wasn't cool. Warner put out memos telling people to clean their offices because someone important was coming to visit. In response, McKnight hung a sign on his own office door: 'Director of Groovology'. But if he and John Warner were not exactly on the same page, they were at least reading the same book, and they were reaching the chapter where partner and chief financial officer Larry Crowe had to go.

Crowe, an uneasy presence at Quiksilver for years, had introduced Warner to the company, and at first the two men had shared an alliance, but as Warner's power base grew, he came to see a different side of Crowe. For his part, McKnight had found Larry Crowe increasingly difficult to work with since his vicious handling of Jeff Hakman's sacking. Now that a reborn Hakman was co-founder of the second most successful Quiksilver company in the world, the memory of that spiteful episode rankled even more. Who was this asshole to treat the legendary Hakman like dirt? Moreover, McKnight had begun to question the validity of Crowe's business directives, particularly when it came to margin over quality. (This was to become a familiar refrain, not just in Quiksilver but throughout the industry in the battle of the salts versus suits. And at its core was the question, is it a company like any other company, or is it a surf company?)

Crowe went, but not before it got very ugly. An extraordinary board meeting was called to hear both sides, and the board then hired a law firm to conduct an independent investigation. The investigators found in favour of McKnight and Warner, and Larry Crowe left the company with a fat settlement. His father, Art Crowe, resigned from the board in protest at the treatment of his son but, strangely, brother Charles stayed, and is still there.

While Harry Hodge and his partners at Quiksilver Europe struggled to stay afloat through the late 1980s, a new twist in the market made their long-term future look great, but at the same time put additional pressures on their already inadequate cash flow. Snowboarding had its beginnings in 1965 when an American named Sherman Poppen bolted two skis together and called it a 'Snurfer'. Different forms of mono-ski were subsequently tried through the next two decades, before the modern snowboard evolved in the early 1980s. By 1986, Quiksilver riders Jose Fernandes and Serge Vitelli were pioneering the sport in Europe, and for winter '89, Quiksilver Europe introduced its first ski/snowboard winter range. Surfing sensibilities had come to the mountains.

Alan Green had envisaged a commercial as well as a cultural link between surf and snow when, twenty years earlier, he chose as his logo an image of a mountain and a wave, and now, finally, it was to become the lifeblood of the European surf companies, offering them year-round sales in a cold climate. But Hodge wasn't on the snowfields enjoying the success of his winter range that year. He was hunkered down with his bankers, trying to keep Na Pali SA capitalised. Hoping to sell twenty-five per cent into the venture capital market, Hodge hit the road that summer, meeting with investors in Paris, London and Barcelona. Hodge recalls: 'It started to feel like we were bashing our heads against a wall, because when you analysed it, we weren't particularly attractive to people coming in. The financing package would only be a Band-Aid.' The partners began to look closer to home.

In 1990, while Quiksilver USA continued to ride high on booming sales of surf's 'neon' look, Hodge approached Warner with a proposal that the US company invest in Europe. Neither Warner nor McKnight was interested in a minority position. As negotiations ensued through the summer, it became clear that there was only one positive outcome as far as the Americans were concerned. Hodge recalls: 'It was a difficult decision for all of us at Na Pali, but I guess I was better prepared than my partners because I'd already had to consider the various possible outcomes. But the bottom line was that [selling] was the right thing to do for the growth of the company and for us personally.'

On 3 October 1990, Quiksilver USA announced its purchase of Quiksilver Europe for $10.5 million, plus an injection of $5 million of working capital. The deal was signed in Paris the following February, with the four Na Pali partners agreeing to a two-year earn-out period, during which time Hodge would be the boss and the others would maintain their old roles. So for Quiksilver Europe, there was no immediate or earth-shattering change. For the Quiksilver brand, however, the balance of power had shifted forever.

While the acquisition of Na Pali made Quiksilver USA a licensee again – Green, Law and licensing boss Raymond had no intention of selling the trademarks for Europe – and theoretically should have created stronger ties between the Quiksilvers around the world, the reality was that it began to place strains on the brand's entire licensing strategy. Since the 1986 IPO, Quiksilver USA had been building its business through an aggressive five-year plan that required fundamental shifts in what they made and where they sold it. Board shorts now accounted for less than seven per cent of total sales, while John Warner had opened up new channels of distribution where few surf companies had gone before, and those that dared [with the exception, thus far, of Gotcha] had suffered the consequences in their core markets.

With American sales heading towards the $100 million mark, McKnight, Warner and their board knew that this diversification was essential, but down in Australia, Green and his key executives saw it as a strategy that was increasingly dangerous for the credibility of the brand. The general feeling, too, was that there was a possibility that America would grow away from the core values of Quiksilver. As early as 1988, licensing boss Bruce Raymond had written to Bob McKnight: 'Our strength has always been that we produce products from an attitude, about two or three years ahead of products produced for the purpose of feeding a trend ... If we start taking notice of trend reports and surveys, we will end up producing for the ninety per cent who are not intuitive and generally lack taste … I feel Quiksilver USA has momentarily lost its way.'

Raymond offered to fly to California immediately to sort the problem out, but an angry McKnight responded: 'Quiksilver, Inc. has been incredibly successful in the marketplace, growing and gaining momentum, and yet at the same time retaining our roots … We don't believe a trip from you would be useful right now.'

In November 1989, McKnight flew to Sydney for a celebration of the twentieth anniversary of the Quiksilver brand. Two decades had passed since the yoked shorts with the 'duck' logo had first appeared, and the brand had made all of its top executives rich. The party took place at the Red Onion restaurant and bar in the Rocks tourist strip adjacent to Sydney Harbour. Inspired by the original Red Onion in Newport Beach, California (a notorious Quiksilver hang), it was a venture backed by Green, Law and McKnight – another glowing testament to the fabulously entrepreneurial lifestyle afforded by Greeny's humble board shorts.

More than two hundred of surfing's A-list slogged back the margaritas until the early hours, dancing and laughing like crazy at the 'celebrity roast' conducted by Skyhooks singer 'Shirley' Strachan and the author. The photographers snapped pictures of Green, Law, McKnight, Raymond and Hodge arm-in-arm in lavish displays of bonhomie. The party was a blast, a raucous final fling for the brand's boom decade. But within months, the restaurant had gone, awash in debt, and the Quiksilver founders were at each other's throats.

In 1989 Michael Tomson and Joel Cooper sold forty per cent of Gotcha to investment bank Merrill Lynch, who saw this as a great opportunity to fund the future success of the fastest-growing surf company in the world. But Gotcha's bubble was about to burst, along with the entire Californian surf industry. The neon fad had pushed surfwear sales through the roof over three or four seasons, taking the beach message to places it had never been. But it's the nature of fads that they end, and no one had more exposure than Gotcha when that happened. Sales went south at a frightening rate while the executives cannibalised each other looking for a solution. Similar scenes were being played out in board rooms all over Velcro Valley.

14 THE CHAIRMAN IS AN ASSHOLE

I more or less built this thing up on instinct. I think my instincts and morals are good. I try to run the company fairly and honestly and from the gut. I probably break all the rules about being a good CEO, but I don't really give a shit.
Bob McKnight, *Transworld Surf Business*, 2004

Air France flight AF7638 from Paris's Charles de Gaulle banked in a tight arc over the Bay of Biscay, then straightened for its final approach into Biarritz. Bob McKnight lifted his head from the *International Herald Tribune* and looked out the window at the hundreds of dots beyond the breakers at la Côte des Basques.

As the plane continued its descent, the dots became people, people on surfboards. Big crowd for a weekday, McKnight thought. Good for business. But then it *was* the season. Not 'The Season' as in Parisian couples in matching Lacoste golf shirts with upturned collars dragging their poodles along the crowded and turd-dotted promenades, but the *surf* season. Mid-September, normal people back at work, endless days of sunshine and offshore breezes, with strong ocean swells rolling in from the Irish Sea.

McKnight loved the south-west of France, particularly at this time of year. He closed his eyes and recalled images of sunlit waves peeling across the white Hossegor sands ... Why then, as the plane's landing wheels engaged with a clunk, did he feel such a sense of dread about this visit?

A driver whisked McKnight and his wife, Annette, through the narrow streets of the old resort town to the Hôtel du Palais. Their room looked out over the pool to la Grande Plage, dazzling in the afternoon sun, but after an eighteen-hour journey, all Bob and Annette were interested in was sleep. 'Shit!' The phone's ring was louder and shriller than it had any right to be. McKnight sat up, checked his watch and cursed again. Fifteen minutes of quality power nap. 'Yeah, who is it?'

'Bob, it's Greeny. I'm in the bar. We need to talk.'

McKnight scanned the scene in the hotel bar and made straight for a cloud of blue smoke in a far corner. A tanned and bony hand reached out and gripped his. 'Good to see ya, Buzz. Sit down and I'll get you a drink.'

It was 1992 and Quiksilver was in trouble. The dogs were barking it and the investment analysts were passing on the message. On 9 September, just a few days before McKnight flew to France, the company reported a seventy-four per cent plunge in profits for the third quarter. This was horrible enough, but not exactly a shock. Both sales and profits had been dropping alarmingly for five straight quarters, while thirty per cent of the company's retail account base had just disappeared. America was in the grip of a recession, and at retail counters all over the country, discretionary items like sportswear were languishing. But the economic downturn was only the beginning of the problem for Quiksilver.

While most apparel manufacturers' profits were headed south, the *Investor's Business Daily* reported, 'highflying Quiksilver, Inc.'s earnings headed to Antarctica'. 'I'm still checking for a pulse,' quipped Gary M Jacobson, an analyst for Kidder, Peabody & Co, who just eighteen months earlier had rated the stock a buy with the equally flip endorsement, 'Hey dudes, surf's up – looks radical. (That's good.)' The fashion trade's *Daily News Record* noted, 'Surfwear got really big because of the neon craze, but that was a number of years ago. You can't ride the crest of a wave forever.'

And so the obituaries were stacking up. On top of recession and changing fashions, the past year or so had seen consumer confidence take a major hit from the global tensions surrounding Operation Desert Storm in Iraq, and closer to home the surfwear market had suffered from widespread media reports of syringes on the beach in New Jersey, pollution in California and shark attacks on three coasts. The beach looked bleak, and in a modern world of gas masks, riots and bomb explosions, young consumers had started to make a statement by embracing the street, or hip-hop, culture – the sounds of the ghetto and the look of the op shop.

By 1992 Quiksilver was taking severe blows to most parts of its corporate body. In the toughest decision of his career thus far, McKnight and his CFO, Randy Herrel, had laid off almost fifty people. Domestic sales revenue had dropped from a high of $91 million in 1990 to less than $60 million in 1992, assuming that the fourth quarter went to hell in a handcart like everything else … and it did. Still, if you took fifty American jobs out of the equation, the consequences were not that dire. Sixty million dollars in sales was a workable number. McKnight only had to look back to 1988 to remind himself of that. And then there was Europe, the new star in the Quiksilver constellation. At almost $30 million in sales and growth at an average of thirty-five per cent, the France-based licensee was well positioned to put some serious black ink back on Quiksilver, Inc.'s bottom line.

The real problem that McKnight and his company faced was much more deep-rooted and fundamental than the ebb and flow of money. The glue binding Quiksilver USA and its Australian parent company was called a 'sharing agreement', in which there was meant to be a free flow of ideas, product designs and marketing concepts. But the agreement was totally reliant on the goodwill of a small group of friends who had started out a decade or so before on the basic premise that integrity and authenticity were everything, and that Quiksilver was all about board shorts. But McKnight knew that the wheels of industry would not turn, and the investors would not write their cheques, on the basis of surf trunks alone.

At the height of surf's neon boom in 1988, with beach fashion going ballistic, Quiksilver USA looked either side of the surfers on the waves and saw speedboats racing out beyond them, and volleyball nets on the sand in front of them. It seemed logical to McKnight to embrace both these robust markets, but for Quiksilver's founder and his team in Australia, it amounted to treason. As McKnight would later say: 'To us it was all salt, sea and sand, and the growth was so quick, so seductive, that the sound of a bunch of guys down in Australia saying "board shorts, board shorts, board shorts" was, well, a little annoying.'

Quiksilver USA's acquisition of Quiksilver Europe in 1991 should have brought the Quiksilver family back together, since it made the Americans big licensees again (after the sale of the trademarks, Quiksilver, Inc. had retained licences for only a few small Central American territories), and therefore bound by certain contractual codes of conduct. But instead it fuelled the mounting antagonism between licensee and licensor. In the interests of getting the Europe deal done, the Australians had accepted a lesser royalty than they felt was fair, and months later the smell of the deal lingered on. To Alan Green, John Law and Bruce Raymond, it was further evidence of the unacceptable corporatisation of Quiksilver's American operation.

After overseeing the European acquisition, CEO John Warner left the company, another victim of McKnight's inability to create a balanced boardroom. In an effort to redress the perceived imbalance between the salts and the suits, McKnight then took over as CEO, with a focus on product and marketing, while CFO Randy Herrel ran the backroom business. But as the crisis in domestic sales deepened, he realised that he needed a dynamic merchant on the team, someone who could oversee a rollout of diverse products for a future survival plan in the post-neon world, and he hired Shaheen Sadeghi from Gotcha as company president.

Above: Jeff Hakman on his way to winning Bells in 1976. *Photo: Jeff Divine*

Right: The winner. A whacked Hakman and friends, Bells '76. *Photo: Martin Tullemans*

Lightning Bolt ad, 1976.

McKnight and Hakman (centre) in Bali, 1974. *Photo: Quiksilver Archives*

By the late 1970s, Rabbit Bartholomew had emerged as the outrageous spokesman for his generation. He had the right attitude and look to be Quiksilver's first brand ambassador. *Photo: Quiksilver Archives*

Above: Mark Richards. *Photo: Jeff Divine*

Right: Mark Richards, cover boy for Quik.

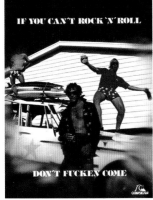

Left: 1980 shock poster.

Design sketches. *Courtesy Simon Buttonshaw*

Pioneer Quiksilver designer Simon Buttonshaw.
Photo: Aitionn

Bob McKnight and author Jarratt celebrate twenty years of Quiksilver, Sydney,
November 1989. *Photo: Author's collection*

Echo Beach US launch, 1980. *Photo: Jack McCoy*

Quiksilver exec Bruce Raymond takes the drop at Sunset. *Photo: Jeff Divine*

Kelly Slater's first press conference, 1990. *Photo: Joli*

Kelly, Pipe Masters '95. *Photo: Sean Davey*

Above: First day on the New York Stock Exchange. *Photo: Quiksilver Archives*

Left: Alan Green and John Law, 1998. *Photo: Rennie Ellis Archive*

Right: Reluctant cover boy, Alan Green, 2002.

Below: Harry Hodge and Bernard Mariette, France, 1999. *Photo: Quiksilver Archive*

The Beach Boys

Greenie and his best mates are unlikely tycoons. They've built two surfing empires and created Australia's strangest company town.

Above and below: Rip Curl in the ascendancy with world champs Mick Fanning and Steph Gilmore, 2007. *Photos: ASP*

Left: A new and salt-free career for Bernard Mariette. *Photo: Coalision*

Hiring Iranian/American Sadeghi seemed a masterstroke. Not only was he an aggressive merchandiser who could be expected to reignite retail, but he was a star player at Gotcha, still leading Quiksilver in sales but experiencing the same difficulties. Quiksilver's gain would be Gotcha's loss. In an interview with the author in 2006, Sadeghi recalled:

> It was a very interesting time in the surf industry because we were discovering that surf wasn't necessarily transferable to the fashion market. All that neon product had started to back out and the companies that were up around the $100 million mark were trying to work out how to deal with it. There was a lot of turbulence around. The greatest effect of me going to Quiksilver was to take out their biggest competitor. Within a year, Gotcha had stumbled and Quiksilver was the leader.

But leader of what? The sales figures of many surf companies were in free-fall. Sadeghi continues: 'A lot of people went out of business at that time. Department stores got out of the surf brands because they didn't understand them. All the big surf retailers were in trouble too. So we had to look at how to grow without simply loading up the surf shops with product. The answer was in diversity. We introduced girls' lines, snow lines, denim, shoes.'

As the industry crisis deepened, the management and sales force of Quiksilver descended on an Orange County hotel in June 1992 for an annual meeting that on this occasion was tantamount to a council of war. At the top of the agenda was the company's bold strategy to rebound through a new program of fiscal restraint and product diversification. McKnight, eager to introduce his key strategist, asked Sadeghi to deliver the keynote address. Sadeghi stood on stage, looking crisp and elegant in his designer threads, beaming at his audience – most of whom had helped propel Quiksilver to the top of the market by selling surf shorts and surf shirts into surf shops along the surfing coasts of the US – and said: 'Ladies and gentlemen, surf is dead!'

In certain parts of the room, Alan Green's anguished groan could be felt, if not heard, from across the Pacific. Sadeghi: 'Is that what they say I said? I don't remember using those exact words, but that was kind of my message in part. I felt the heat immediately. But that was why they hired me, to fix the product because it was no good. That was just classic overreaction and paranoia. Fashion was moving into surf, we all know that now. All I was saying was that we had to integrate these other influences – fashion, music, skate.'

Back at the bar of the Hôtel du Palais in Biarritz, Greeny said: 'You had to get rid of him, Buzz. It was the right thing to do.' He blew a curtain of smoke, and perhaps didn't see the anguish in McKnight's face. Of course Sadeghi had to go. You can't come into an industry for five minutes and then read it the last rites. Greeny had won that battle with Sadeghi's departure in late July, but he was still firing his artillery. McKnight nursed his beer while the founder droned on. It was going to be a long week.

Quiksilver's Global Directions meeting convened at Quiksilver Europe's headquarters on the northern fringe of the resort town of Saint Jean de Luz. All the major players were there, and in conversations over coffee in the corridors, McKnight began to sense a common goal coalescing. 'Globalisation' was a word much used and little understood, but in Saint Jean de Luz it seemed the time had come to pay it more than lip service. As the Quiksilver executives moved into the meeting room, for the first time since leaving California Bob began to feel that some positive outcomes were a possibility.

Alan Green stood in front of the group and scrawled the company's credo on a flip chart:

> To be a worldwide surfing/boardriding label based on authen-
> ticity and reputation of excellence.
> To provide our markets with purity of concept.

To give our customers products they can wear with pride because they represent quality and value from a real foundation.

Authenticity, purity, real foundation … board shorts, board shorts, board shorts, thought McKnight, squirming in his seat and wondering what it was that Alan Green didn't get about supply and demand.

The chairman of the Global Directions meeting scribbled on the flip chart and asked rhetorical questions throughout the morning session and into the afternoon. Everyone at the meeting respected the plain-talking Aussie for building the brand from scratch over twenty long years, fighting fiercely to retain its integrity every step of the way. Quiksilver was Alan Green's creation and always would be, despite the fact that he had moved out of the driver's seat a long time ago. Everyone knew that, and Greeny's advice was to be accepted as one would accept the wisdom of a tribal elder. But this, McKnight thought, was too much. Greeny had arrived in France pissed off, and he wasn't getting any happier as he worked himself into a lather, scribbling and pontificating. During the afternoon coffee break, McKnight, sensing the general disenchantment, quietly slipped back into the meeting room, closed the door behind him, threw back a few sheets on the flip chart and wrote a message in thick, black capital letters.

Chairman Green attacked the final session of the day with new energy, invigorated by his caffeine and nicotine break. Hopefully the bastards are learning something, he thought as he scrawled mission statements on the chart. Twenty minutes on, he flipped back another sheet and turned to write his bullet points. He stopped and drew a long breath. Confronting him on the sheet was the message: 'THE CHAIRMAN IS AN ASSHOLE'.

He spun and faced a giggling audience. 'Right, fuck the lot of you. If you stupid bastards think this is all a fucking joke, you can sit here and giggle by yourselves.' Greeny spoke more in sorrow than in anger, but as he packed his things the fury rose in him. Pens, keys, cigarette packs bounced off walls as he made his way to the door.

McKnight followed him into the corridor and chased him down the stairs. 'Alan, I wrote it. It was a joke, right? I'm really sorry.'

Greeny stopped, turned, and lit a cigarette with one hand while he spoke. 'Of course you wrote it, Buzz, but you're the joke, mate, and I don't want you in my face right now.'

Alan and Barbara Green had organised a getaway dinner for that evening, across town at le Chambre d'Amour, a cluster of cafés on the beachfront at Anglet, not far from the McKnights' hotel. The idea was to relieve their French hosts for one night, while enjoying some family time with their spouses. And, Greeny had thought, such a social occasion away from the rest of the crew might help heal some of the wounds that had surfaced between the Americans and the Australians in recent months. Now, as he sat in his hotel room with a cigarette and a glass of red wine, he reorganised. He phoned John Law, telling him that McKnight had to be 'sorted out', and that it had better be done quickly and quietly. Fearing an ugly scene, Lawro arranged a separate dinner for the spouses.

At the Hôtel du Palais, McKnight was on the verge of tears. Just when it looked as if the meeting might actually achieve something, he had turned it all to shit with the dumbest of dumb classroom stunts. On top of five lousy quarters, every analyst on Wall Street calling for a post mortem, fifty sackings, top to bottom pay cuts and ever-increasing boardroom pressure, this was just too much. Maybe he was the wrong guy in the wrong job.

McKnight and the Australians sat in the back corner of a beachfront café around a small table covered with a salt-grimed plastic tablecloth. Salads, mussels, sardines and shrimp sat untouched. Only the bottles of wine at the centre were being consumed, and even these with less than the usual gusto. A cool breeze had sprung up from the ocean, bringing with it thick, dark clouds. The light was disappearing, the summer was ending. Green and Law were at McKnight's throat. The abuse was deeply, intensely personal.

Bruce Raymond stared at his uneaten food. 'It was brutal to watch,' he recalled years later. 'Not many people in business can treat each other like that. It wasn't about the dumb joke in the meeting, that was just what set it off. It was about Bob stepping up to the plate and taking responsibility. Greeny was just sick to death of this string of people who came into the company and stood between him and Bob. We all were, to some extent.'

As far as McKnight was concerned, the founder of the brand was coming on like a Monday morning quarterback. As much as he loved and respected the guy, Greeny had never run a $100 million company. There were things about this level of business that he simply didn't get. Greeny swigged some wine, then banged his glass on the table to underline his next point about McKnight's failings. Suddenly McKnight could take it no more. He dropped his head to the table, cradled it in his arms and wept.

Green looked at his friend for a moment, then sighed, stood up and touched McKnight lightly on the shoulder as he left the table. 'It's all right, Buzz,' he murmured as he passed. 'It's all right, mate.' They'd hit rock bottom now. The only way to go was up.

While Quiksilver's top brass licked their wounds and considered new strategies, the ground was moving fast beneath them. In 1986, as the company went public, they had almost lost marketing wizard Danny Kwock (regarded by some as Quiksilver's 'rainman' for his intuitive feel for the market), who truly believed that corporatisation would kill the brand. Kwock was turned around, but the sentiment remained alive at Quiksilver's Costa Mesa headquarters as suit after suit came through management's seemingly revolving door. As much as Bob McKnight liked to think of himself as the 'director of groovology', the young punks in marketing often felt otherwise.

The leader of the rebellion was former team rider Richard Woolcott, who finally came to McKnight and Kwock and told them he couldn't stand the direction any longer. Like Kwock a few years earlier, he had decided to start his own brand with Quiksilver colleague Tucker Hall. McKnight was disappointed, but not devastated. He had seen it coming for a while. He liked Woolcott, and even as he wished him well, was thinking he'd take him back after the kid's fingers had been burnt a little.

Woolcott and Hall called their start-up Volcom (for no apparent reason), and financed their initial small range through investment from family and friends. Woolcott's father, Rene, stumped up $5000, while mentor Kwock eventually contributed $15,000, after a couple of investors pulled out. From the very start, the brand's approach was edgy, combining influences from the world of surf, skate, snow and urban music, always with an element of self-deprecatory humour that endeared it to a small but loyal market. Above all else, the brand's positioning statement explained its immediate appeal: 'youth against establishment'. Volcom had outrageous parties, threw money at neighbourhood skate parks and supported young punk rock bands. They went where the big guys had become too frightened to go, and the kids loved them for it.

Essentially, Volcom's anti-establishment catchcry was an echo of Gotcha's, but falling sales and panicked management had diluted that company's once clear message. By 1993 part-owners Merrill Lynch had run out of patience with their zero returns and company revenue down below $50 million, and wanted out. They found a buyer in Marvin Winkler, an entrepreneur who at one stage had been a Body Glove licensee. Winkler was cashed up and had big ideas for Gotcha, but they didn't involve Michael Tomson. Says Tomson:

Marvin was a charismatic guy, but an insatiable deal junkie, always wanting to bring more stuff to the table, no focus on finishing anything. He made me seem like a librarian, but his energy was corporate, not creative. He could really pitch well and he was always coming up with schemes. One day I made a list, and this guy had twelve deals in the air ... licensing deals, mergers, all at the same time and none of them going anywhere. Joel and I needed grounding but Winkler didn't have it, and in fact he destabilised us further. I was the president and Joel was the CEO, but we never defied Winkler's authority, no matter where he seemed to be taking the brand, I suppose because he was just a fabulous salesman. He strung together funding for the Gotcha Glacier theme park, which I thought was impossible and destined to fail. It turned out I was right, but for a while he had all this funding for a $200 million deal, he had the ear of the mayor of Anaheim and we were going to be the new Disneyland. Mad!

As he was selling part of Gotcha to Merrill Lynch, Michael Tomson decided to take out some insurance in the form of a new brand. He created MCD (More Core Division, aka 'Michael's Core Division') as a rootsy sibling that could take over if Gotcha faltered. Now, with Winkler's empire-building becoming more outrageous, Tomson hid under the covers at MCD, having fun again as he built the brand into an $8 million business.

By the early 1990s, Billabong had successfully opened up the American market, while Rip Curl continued to struggle. The most obvious reason for Billabong's success in the world's biggest (and most crowded) surf market was Bob Hurley, a cool, calm and well-connected operator who seemed to make things happen with little apparent effort. Hurley had a good feel for cost-effective marketing, creating a regional profile in his key markets by sponsoring kids on the way up and staging small junior and pro-am events. But he also had one eye on the big picture, working with Gordon Merchant to secure big international stars, like Hawaii's Sunny Garcia, and creating the prestigious Billabong Pro on Oahu's North Shore. Hurley also had the knack of pushing sales through majors like Nordstrum, without offending the brand's core surf retailers.

Billabong had also started to make a breakthrough in the European market, under the direction of a young surfer and former plumber from Victoria, Derek O'Neill, whose first move was to relocate Billabong from frosty Cornwall to Hossegor, France. O'Neill struggled at first, selling small quantities of clothing imported from Australia, but by the nineties he had created a self-sustaining division that was beginning to nip at the heels of Quiksilver.

Another reason for Billabong's continuing hot streak (its global revenues more than doubled between 1988 and 1991) was a small, ponytailed man who sat in a small office at the rear of Billabong's Burleigh Heads headquarters, feverishly working two phones and a pocket calculator. Doug Spong had left Rip Curl in late 1988, having built the garments division into more than half the business. He moved to the Gold Coast with no real plans, other than to surf and play golf, but Gordon Merchant was soon on the phone with an offer. Merchant wanted to create a worldwide accessories division, manufacturing high margin goods such as wallets, hats and backpacks, and he knew that no one in the surf industry knew Asian sourcing better than Spong.

What interested Spong was the fact that Merchant wasn't offering him a job, he was offering to sell him a licence for Billabong accessories, an opportunity to build his own enterprise that had been denied him at Rip Curl. Spong's Thin Air Manufacturing was soon delivering Billabong-branded accessories to all the markets, and within a couple of years he had stretched the licence to cover denim, wetsuits and snow-wear. Says Spong: 'Gordon wanted to attract licensees and I could do that by broadening the line.' Merchant, who hasn't had a lot of praise for Spong in recent years, was gracious in the brand's 2003 history, *Only a Surfer Knows the Feeling*: 'We'd never been a very good accessories company. Doug's strength was always in product. It became a really good partnership, his products and our branding. That was part of a major move forward for us.'

Billabong surged ahead through the nineties on the back of the humble backpack, which helped the company balance its books while it, along with the rest of the surf industry, began to move all production to more cost-effective labour markets. But there were clouds on the horizon. A mum-and-dad operation since the beginning, Billabong's founders were starting to feel the pressures of any married couple running a business. As the company grew bigger, Gordon and Rena grew apart. She moved out of home but not the office as they tried to dissolve one partnership without damaging the other.

15 FILTHY FUCKING RICH

*Rena Merchant, co-founder of the $1.5 billion Billabong surfwear
empire, lives in a large tin shed in Queensland's Sunshine Coast
hinterland … 'I think you would be quite horrified at how I
live,' she says in her ever-so-slight South African accent.*
BRW magazine, 2004

In the summer of 1982 Quiksilver's Danny Kwock and Jeff Hakman
(on one of his last missions before being fired) travelled to Florida
for the Surf Expo trade show, where local surf identity Dick Catri
introduced two of his young protégés. 'Guys, this is Sean Slater,
from Cocoa Beach, one of our hottest young surfers, and this is his
kid brother, Kelly. Kelly's just a dweeb right now, but he's got some
talent too.'

Hakman shook hands with the two little kids and Kwock gave
them each a pair of Echo Beach board shorts. Neither of them thought
too much more about the meeting. They had hot kids thrust at them
at every trade show, every surf meet. But ten-year-old Kelly Slater
thought about it a lot. It was the first time he'd been given stuff. Man,
he was sponsored! Less than a decade later, the 'dweeb' from Cocoa

Beach was signed (by Kwock) to Quiksilver in the first year of his pro career – a career that was to become the greatest in the history of the sport.

In the beginning, to be a 'sponsored' surfer meant very little in cash terms. Through the 1960s and early '70s, most name surfers were more than happy to be flowed surfboards, shorts, T-shirts and most other of their surfing needs. There were exceptions – Nat Young, David Nuuhiwa and Jeff Hakman were all on cash retainers by the end of the sixties – but the concept of the professional surfer remained somewhat vague. As late as 1976, Quiksilver (board shorts), Rip Curl (wetsuits) and Lightning Bolt (surfboards) could rightly claim just about every major surf star for their teams, and virtually none of them received any payment.

In late 1977 Rabbit Bartholomew became Quiksilver's first paid team rider, when Alan Green and John Law offered him $5000 a year, plus a bonus of $3000 if he won the world title. Bartholomew recalls:

> It was all fairly low-key, no lawyers, no real demands placed upon me, other than to wear the product and surf in all the contests. Quiksilver got me around the world in 1978, and I won the title, so I guess it was a sound investment. But there was a whole other side to it, too. Greeny later expected me to go to the board meetings in Torquay whenever the tour allowed, and they turned into real screaming matches. I believed wholeheartedly in the future of pro surfing as the way to build the surf brands, but Greeny was more about soul surfing. For me it was uncharted waters. I never expected to be going into a boardroom and going toe-to-toe with my boss in this huge philosophical debate.

Greeny took his idea to bring a sponsored surfer into internal company politics a step further with his second money signing, Bruce Raymond. In a letter to him in June 1979, Greeny described, for the first time, the mentoring philosophy that would become a Quiksilver trademark: 'I'm convinced that you really do have Quiksilver at heart, and I'm certain we can offer you a lifestyle-compatible future. When that happens, it will mean WORK. Now's the time to play, travel, surf, learn, build your name and your knowledge. When you're ready, we'll involve you more in the business side of things.'

It wasn't just words. Alan Green, and ultimately Quiksilver around the world, nurtured and mentored every surfer who displayed enough company loyalty to become a long-term investment. They weren't alone in this, as all of the major brands realised the importance of star power in their marketing platforms, but Quiksilver certainly led the way, breaking new ground in 1988 with the signing of Tom Carroll to a five-year, million-dollar contract. At the time, this was the biggest money deal a pro surfer had ever done, and much marketing capital was made of that, but it was a historic deal in another way, too, because it demonstrated Quiksilver's commitment to lifestyle rather than contest results.

Ironically, Carroll had been sacked by Quiksilver over attitude issues just prior to his winning consecutive world titles in 1983 and '84. (Michael Tomson was quick to pick up a punk with attitude for Gotcha.) By 1988, in his late twenties, the pocket dynamo from Sydney was an older and wiser surfer, but it still took a considerable leap of faith for Quiksilver to welcome him back with the fattest offer in surfing history. Bruce Raymond negotiated and signed the deal, and for him it was all about vindication of Alan Green's stance on sponsorship. Carroll might never win another world title (he didn't) but he was one of the most respected surfers in the world, and he would go on to become a brand ambassador and surf adventurer well into middle age.

By 1990, Quiksilver had more than two hundred surfers, skaters, skiers and snowboarders on its books, but that summer all attention was focused on one young athlete who was not yet in the company colours. Kelly Slater, now eighteen and just finished his junior year in high school, got a manager and turned pro, just as his contracts with Rip Curl and Op expired. He was the hottest property in surfing, and he was on the market. Danny Kwock began negotiating with agent Bryan Taylor, but it soon became apparent that Op was going to fight for their guy, and that Slater was going to be expensive. Kwock had been given a ceiling price, but as the bidding intensified, he threw caution to the wind. He recalls: 'I was pumped, man. I knew I was going higher than I should, but I knew it was the right thing to do.'

The first contract for the teenage sensation from Florida was $108,000 plus bonuses – about double what Quiksilver was paying volleyball megastar Karch Kiraly at the time, just to put it in perspective – but with the participation of all Quiksilver licensees, this was soon massaged into $320,000 for surfing's first '100 per cent' sponsorship. This meant that Quiksilver owned all branding rights to Slater, with the one caveat, that he could ride boards with the logo of long-time shaper Al Merrick of Channel Island Surfboards. The Kelly Slater sponsorship would soon become the company's underpinning marketing statement, not to mention one of its biggest annual investments in image, and would remain so for the next twenty years. And the concept of 100 per cent sponsorship would soon be adopted by all the major players in the surf industry.

The very next beneficiary of Quiksilver's new '100 per cent' policy would become almost as important as Kelly Slater in the evolution of the company, but the signing came at a fraction of the price, for one simple reason – the signee was a girl. The tear-filled Global Directions meeting in France in 1992 had resulted in Quiksilver's corporate leaders signing off on a manifesto designed to keep the brand closer to its surfing roots, 'avoiding tangents, dilutants and programs devised to support mass'. In simple terms, that meant no straying from the roots boardriding culture, which, a generation after Gidget broke the ice at Malibu, was still very much a boys' club. Despite the fact that Frederick Kohner's 1957 novel about his teenage daughter's surfing and social awakening at Malibu had spawned a girl surf cult through the sixties, and despite the fact that champion surfers like Linda Benson, Joyce Hoffman, Phyllis O'Donnell, Margo Oberg, Pam Burridge, Lynn Boyer and

Frieda Zamba had broken down the competitive barriers, in 1992 Quiksilver's brand gurus were compelled to write: 'Women's ranges are out. We are not sexist, we are a boardriding company and so we make clothes and outfits for boardriders.'

But the women were not that easily pushed back into the kitchen, particularly when the arrival on the scene of petite and pretty Floridian Lisa Andersen fortuitously coincided with the near heretical decision by Bob McKnight and Danny Kwock that it was time for Quiksilver USA to launch a girls' swimwear line. Kwock chose the name Roxy, after his favorite LA club, and a small line shipped in 1991. But before Roxy had time to settle in, all brand extensions were scuttled by the growing recession, never to be seen again according to the authors of the Global Directions paper.

In the meantime, Quiksilver International's Bruce Raymond signed Lisa Andersen, 'the foxy chick who surfs like a guy', according to the surf mags, for $6000 in 1992. Ironically, Raymond's hand can be seen all over the manifesto that banned girls, but he was also an astute judge of surfing talent, and she simply couldn't be denied. Ultimately, Kwock and McKnight couldn't be denied either, and Roxy relaunched in 1993. As Lisa Andersen emerged as a multiple world champion – forming a dream team with Slater in the mid-nineties – so Roxy emerged as the benchmark of women's surf apparel, with every major brand soon following in its wake. But in the initial stages, Roxy, like many young girls (and boys), struggled to find its identity. Bob McKnight claims the 'lightbulb moment' came in 1994, as he and a Roxy designer watched the finals of the Pipeline Masters in Hawaii: 'The sun was shining, the surf was going mental, and suddenly this gorgeous little Eurasian babe walks by, and she's wearing a pair of men's board shorts, rolled down over her hips to show the thong of her bikini. We watched her walk by and we went, "Aha!"'

Girls' board shorts became the engine of Roxy, now cleverly branded with back-to-back Quiksilver logos forming a heart. But the genius of the Roxy assault on the marketplace (it soon became thirty per cent of Quiksilver apparel and accessories) was not so much in finally recognising the existence of women in the surfing landscape, but in aligning the brand with an exotic South Sea Islands imagery that spoke of romance as well as of a healthy outdoor lifestyle, and spoke it to romance-seekers way beyond the normal parameters of the surf culture. Roxy chicks weren't po-faced models sulking on catwalks. They were out there doin' it in the sun, just like Lisa, free as birds and twice as pretty. Middle America lapped it up and the rest of the world followed.

Since Quiksilver, Inc.'s acquisition of its European licensee, Quiksilver Europe, in 1991, the Quiksilver board had become increasingly disenchanted with that company's co-founder and CEO, Australian Harry Hodge. A former journalist and one-time film-maker, Hodge was a gifted leader and a courageous deal-maker, and there was no question that his flair had been largely responsible for establishing the brand in Europe. But he was a big-picture guy who had little time for the mechanics or fine print of business, and the French CFO he hired for those purposes became equally unpopular with the California-centric board. The bottom line was that, despite quarter after winning quarter as the business grew at an astounding rate, the Americans didn't feel comfortable about the Aussie and his French buddies running the business alone. What they needed was, well, their own Frenchman. At the conclusion of the two-year executive earn-out (when the balance of the purchase price was paid, plus performance bonuses) they started to look around.

In early 1994, Hodge wrote to his mentor, Quiksilver founder Alan Green: 'I have trouble with the board. Not me. Them. This I am sure of. I sat there late last year and copped a fucking hiding. Hakman said afterwards he thought I'd gone mute and was paralysed because I didn't tell them to stick it and deck someone. Thankfully those days are behind me ... I believe as soon as [Quiksilver Europe's] figures don't measure up (for whatever reason) I'll be replaced.'

In the late northern spring of 1994, an executive of global corporate headhunting firm Korn Ferry phoned a young manager at Timberland France, based in Nice, and asked if he would be interested in interviewing for a position at Quiksilver Europe. Bernard Mariette, about to turn thirty-two, with two MBAs to his credit and a fast-tracked career path certain at the fast-growing outdoors lifestyle brand, was not remotely interested. In fact he had never heard of Quiksilver. But he was already an accomplished operator, and he knew enough not to diss a headhunter who might one day have an offer too good to refuse. He agreed to a meeting.

Born in Valence, in south-east France, in 1962, Mariette was the oldest child of a former air force pilot whose failing eyesight had cut short his career. Mariette *père* ended up flying a desk and Bernard and his two siblings grew up in a middle-class home near their father's base. But Bernard's early life was saved from provincial ordinariness by virtue of the fact that his paternal grandfather had married an Indian woman and lived a regal existence in Pondicherry, where Bernard would repair for his summer vacation. One-eighth Indian by birthright, and blessed with the swarthy good looks of the subcontinent, Mariette grew up with a broader cultural sensibility than many of his French peers, and with a certainty of social position born of his Indian summers rather than his French realities.

The young Mariette wanted to fly the hours denied his father, so he studied for a mathematics degree in Paris as the first step to becoming a fighter pilot. But his eyesight, like his father's, soon began to deteriorate. He wasn't going to fly a desk, so he quit and enrolled instead at a business college in Montpelier. He fell in love with the adventure of business, telling the author in 2005: 'This was where I caught the virus of business. The professors were not just my teachers, they were my friends, and I worked with them on consulting projects. I felt I was a businessman before I even graduated.'

Mariette went on to win a second MBA at Bradford, England, before joining cosmetics giant L'Oréal as a London-based financial controller. Here he met a rough-and-tumble manager named Peter

Bloxham, who was in the process of rebuilding the company's ailing hair care division, Garnier. To save the division, many heads had to roll, and the two men found a shared passion in administering the guillotine, and laughing about it in the pub later. As a boss, Bloxham was a gnarly piece of work, but he was an effective operator, and he soon became a mentor to the young Frenchman, who had only recently learned English but had quickly perfected the delivery of 'You're fired'.

Mariette managed to combine ruthlessness with great charm and a quirky sense of fun, and those who worked for him soon learned that to question was to risk exclusion from the fun team – possibly forever. No one wanted that. Bernard was a rising star with runs on the board at L'Oréal, and was soon headhunted to Timberland at double salary, where he again built a protective core of committed lieutenants around him. So why the hell did he find himself flying down to sleepy Biarritz to interview for a job he didn't want? Because Bernard Mariette was nothing if not a risk-taker, and if there was some action going on in this surfing scene, he wanted to sniff it out.

In a scenario that was to become symptomatic of Quiksilver management style at the turn of the century, Mariette arrived at Quiksilver Europe headquarters to find himself being interviewed by two people, at least one of whom he thought he would be replacing. CFO Daniel Marthan kept his distance, but typically, Hodge embraced the guy. He might have seen the writing on the wall about his own position but, hey, even if Mariette didn't know surfing from Scrabble, he loved a beer, a laugh, a good red, skiing and Formula One ... what was to dislike about him? And Hodge was also canny enough to know the wisdom of accepting what you can't change, and the preferability of piss being aimed outside the tent rather than in.

Mariette, for his part, wasn't convinced that Quiksilver would be a good career move. Bob McKnight flew him to California to convince him, having heard, from no less a judge than Harry Hodge, that Bernard wasn't your average Frenchman. That much became clear halfway through dinner at quirky Five Feet in Laguna Beach. The

Quiksilver wives loved his nose for a red and his cute accent, the guys loved his cut-to-the-chase assessment of a market he knew nothing about and his ability to feign interest in a Lakers game. As McKnight told the author: 'He was smart, he was funny, he was respectful ... man, he was the guy.'

So 'the guy' arrived in Saint Jean de Luz in September 1994 to take up the position of director general, which he found was already filled by Daniel Marthan. This oversight was soon remedied by creating two DG positions, with Mariette responsible for all the money stuff, even though Marthan was the accountant. It didn't matter because everyone knew, except Daniel, that Daniel would soon be gone. And anyway, there was a more pressing issue. Mariette might have been the guy, but as far as the European executive was concerned, he was the new guy, and they didn't want him.

In view of all of this, it is legitimate to ask why Mariette took on the job, having had initial misgivings, and Mariette's shorthand answer to this has always been that he fell in love with Bob, with Harry, with the brand. A more plausible reason was suggested to the author by a former colleague of Bernard's at Timberland: 'He was a mid-range executive at Timberland who was believed to have a solid future, but he was also a loose cannon who had made enemies, some in high places. Perhaps this was a factor.'

The culture that Harry Hodge had built at Quiksilver Europe over a decade, despite the great success of the company, in some respects mirrored a locker room. It operated on the time-honoured principle of 'work hard, play hard', and the playing involved not just surfing and snowboarding, but also long drinking sessions with the boss at watering holes such as the Carlos Bar and the Bodega Beau Rivage. Hodge went out of his way to include the new man in his after-hours fraternity of expatriate surfers and rugby players, but no matter how silly with drink Mariette got, he could not shed his image as a 'suit' charged with replacing bonhomie with boring management systems. As time would reveal, nothing could have been further from the truth, since Mariette's management style was neither systematic nor boring.

Much of the initial problem for Bernard Mariette lay in the indisputable fact of Hodge's success. His methods may have been unorthodox, but they had delivered twenty per cent growth in Europe in the face of recession. Now Mariette had orders to fix the system, and that meant the joyful sliding song of the guillotine. Says Hodge: 'The first thing he had to do was to tear our business ethic and our systems to shreds. He started to make profound and necessary changes, and he didn't have time to mount a charm offensive, so he ruffled a few feathers.'

Contrary to the expectations of the American board, Mariette and Hodge began to forge a working alliance that Hodge would later refer to as 'the dynamic duo'. Certainly, it was against all odds and the normal laws of the corporate jungle, but Mariette played second fiddle to the ebullient Aussie, got the company straightened out, and kept booking twenty per cent plus growth, no matter how hard those numbers had to be bent. And slowly, the Quiksilver Europe executive came around to Mariette's waggish humour and undeniable charm. When France was to play out the 1998 World Cup final against Brazil in the Stade du France in Paris, before flying to the game as a guest of player Bixente Lizarazu (a god in the Basque country), Mariette confided in the author: 'I have done something absolutely crazy, and I don't care if Harry sacks me, because I do it for France.' A couple of hours later, the entire executive of the company gathered on the corporate deck for a champagne toast. As trucks passing on the Route Nationale began honking their horns madly, Mariette led everyone to the edge of the building to see a huge *tricoleur* French flag being lowered to cover four storeys. Alongside it were the words, 'Allez Lizarazu!'

Bernie's big flag had stuffed the schedules of the samples sewers and caused all sorts of minor production problems, but it was hardly an indictable offence, and in the light of the excesses he would be guilty of in the future, would be relegated to nothing more than an expression of understandable excitement of the moment. But the gesture endeared him to the French executive, and never again would Bernard Mariette be in fear of Harry Hodge showing him the door.

By 1998, Billabong had begun its advance on Quiksilver's market dominance, leaving Rip Curl in its wake as it ramped up marketing efforts and product offerings around the world. But internally the company faced major problems. The first of these was a long-simmering boil-over between brand founder Gordon Merchant and former board shaper Bob Hurley, who had built the brand from nothing to sales of $60 million in the US. Although they had both graduated from 'mowing foam', the two men shared none of the shaping bay bonhomie typical of that hard game. They pretended to be friends, then they just tolerated each other, and then it really wasn't working anymore.

Hurley had an astute business mind and would not be pushed into places his market wouldn't go. Merchant had a simplistic founder's view, common in the surf industry, that he alone knew best. Conflict was inevitable, and yet Billabong head office was completely blind-sided when in 1998 Hurley simply relinquished his Billabong licence and took most of the Billabong USA staff with him to establish Hurley International. The *Los Angeles Times* called this 'the biggest surf industry news in two decades', quoting Quiksilver's Bob McKnight as saying, 'It's shocking to everyone.' McKnight would have been more delighted than shocked, seeing a rising competitor split asunder, but Billabong had been wounded somewhat less than mortally, and no one knew that better than Gordon Merchant, who set up camp in Velcro Valley and started the rebuilding process immediately.

The second problem facing Billabong was even more wide-reaching and more insidious. Something big was going on and only Gordon Merchant seemed to know what it was. Hurley had already felt it when he declined the licence for Billabong Girls and Merchant set up his own operation in San Francisco. The wagons seemed to be circling even more when Doug Spong was granted the girls' licence for Canada, but Spong, like most of the other Australia-based executives, wasn't sure what was going on either. The mystery deepened when

Billabong's management team gathered at the Huntington Hilton in California for their annual global meeting. Billabong had become a big company, but not so big that the top brass didn't know each other. So who were these two tall guys lurking in the shadows and looking uncomfortable in Billabong beachwear right out of the box?

As it turned out, they were the Perrin brothers, Matthew and Scott, Gold Coast property developers, lawyers and racetrack touts who had been brought into the Billabong inner sanctum by Colette Paull, the long-time personal assistant to both Rena and Gordon Merchant. Paull approached the Perrins initially because Billabong had run out of warehouse space, and they patched together an $11 million real estate package at Burleigh Heads. But the Perrins, who were known as aggressive young deal-makers, had their eyes on a bigger prize.

It had been widely known for several years that Rena Merchant wanted to get out. Long after the Merchant marriage ended, Rena felt uncomfortable in the business relationship. According to one insider, she would sometimes surround herself with crystals at board meetings to protect her from 'Gordon's bad vibes'. After helping arrange finance in the US for Gordon Merchant's rebirth of the Billabong operation as a wholly owned division, the Perrins turned their attention to Rena's forty-nine per cent stakeholding in the fastest-growing surf company in the world.

In a rare interview with *BRW* magazine in 2004, Rena Merchant denied she was stalked by the Perrins, or that there was any pressure on her to sell. 'Billabong had become a numbers game and I didn't want any part of it,' she said. A consortium led by the Perrin brothers and including former Qantas chairman Gary Pemberton bought Rena's shareholding in late 1998 for $26.4 million, a figure Rena has steadfastly refused to confirm. After twenty-five years of hard work, she walked away to build a sustainable golf course near Noosa, giving a one per cent holding to Colette Paull to prevent the Perrin bloc from gaining majority control. Billabong general manager Greg Woods, who was squeezed out soon after, told *BRW*: 'Rena was stitched up.'

Another Billabong heavy feeling the pinch was Doug Spong, whose licensed accessories division was a huge money-spinner for the brand. Spong suddenly felt himself an outsider. At a company meeting at the Sheraton hotel in Noosa, Spong was completely ignored by both the Perrins and Pemberton. Outside the meeting, Scott Perrin came up to him in the car park and said, 'We'll get around to dealing with you in a couple of months. Until then, carry on as normal.'

Spong soon realised what was afoot. No one would admit it, but Billabong was centralising ownership in preparation for floating the company on the stock market. It was the end of the nineties, greed was still good, the dotcom bubble hadn't burst yet, IPOs were making new millionaires every other week, and if the Y2K bug didn't kill everyone, the future was rosy. The family, the surfing cowboys, the trusted retainers, the old salts ... they all had to go to make way for the masters of the universe. And when Billabong's ducks were all in a row, the public would be invited to play and the A-team would make a shitload. Doug Spong eventually sold Thin Air, the accessories licensee, for $28 million, most of it in company shares at $2.30, which made him a very rich man after the successful float. But not in comparison to the Perrins, who would become the most successful corporate raiders in the history of the surf industry.

Gary Pemberton used his considerable boardroom muscle to put together a formidable board of directors that included Qantas chair Margaret Jackson and the then-head of Foster's, Ted Kunkel, and in 2000 Billabong announced a $295 million float, debuting on the Sydney Stock Exchange later that year with spectacular results, soon achieving $500 million market capitalisation and sending Gordon Merchant's personal wealth into the stratosphere. Soon after the float, it was valued at $255 million; by 2004, *BRW* estimated it at $491 million.

Billabong's rags to riches fairytale dominated the financial news in Australia for months, and the combination of good public relations, a platinum-ranked board, and the fact that its retail sales in Australia had just pipped Quiksilver's created a public perception (fuelled by lazy finance writers and never denied by the brand itself) that Billabong was the biggest surf brand in the world. It wasn't, by a long shot. In 2000, Quiksilver's global sales were almost double Billabong's. After moving to the New York Stock Exchange (from NASDAQ) in 1998, Quiksilver fast became the darling of Wall Street, and with good reason. The Roxy women's wear brand had taken off around the world, opening doors to department stores that the men's brand could not enter. Meanwhile, the rollout of retail concept stores, known as Quiksilver Boardriders Clubs, continued apace with high-profile openings in New York, London, Paris, Sydney and Los Angeles. And all the while, the European division kept delivering phenomenal growth. Over the five years between Mariette's arrival and the turn of the century, Europe averaged thirty-two per cent growth per year. The man perceived as its architect, Bernard Mariette, could do no wrong.

Harry Hodge exited France for Australia as his sons reached high-school age, and Mariette took over as president director general of Quiksilver Europe. The following year he was invited to join the board of Quiksilver, Inc., and immediately became its most valuable market analyst and strategist.

Meanwhile, just as Billabong had consolidated its ownership prior to going public, Quiksilver, Inc. moved to buy back the farm, even if the farm was still owned by the founders. By early 2000, Alan Green and John Law saw that global consolidation was inevitable, and sold Quiksilver International, the licensing company, for $70 million. Realising that if you were going to sell the farm there was not much point in keeping the land the farm had been built on, in 2002 they sold Ug Manufacturing, which included Quiksilver's Australian and Japanese operations, for $166 million. The deal made Green and Law Quiksilver, Inc.'s biggest individual shareholders.

As the new century got under way, it seemed that everyone in surfing was stinking rich. Doug Spong summed it up best in a conversation with the author: 'Can you believe it? I'm fifty-something, I'm fat and I'm filthy fucking rich!'

16 THE BLOWTORCH BROTHERS

Careering in 45 minutes late for our interview, no excuse forthcoming, flanked by three PR flunkies ... [Quiksilver president Bernard Mariette] lets rip. No subject is left unturned: losing money, making money ... how much he loves his colleagues, his ignorance of the Brazilian economy ... surfing, cars ... His language can get confused amid the general excitement ... He speaks impeccable English, but the odd lapse of concentration leads to gems such as 'piggy-pig', as opposed to the more generally favoured piggyback.
Independent on Sunday, London, 2004

By the turn of the century, surfing had become immensely popular around the globe, and its attendant fashions and cultural leanings were adopted as cool by millions of young people who had never ridden a wave, and perhaps had never even seen one. They all seemed to think they could buy into the dream by wearing the T-shirt or the trunks, but within the core culture, the dream had begun to mean many different things to different people.

Rising on $4 billion in global sales, the surf industrial complex had long since moved from a manufacturing to a marketing base.

While the government-controlled sweatshops of the Third World and China and India mass-produced the same beachwear with hundred of different logos, the surf companies ploughed as much as twenty per cent of their revenues into their dream factories, using branded surfers (and skaters and snowboarders), events and films to prove their brand was cooler than their competitors', even if their product was identical.

Surfers, however, were not identical, and while the big brands had spent fortunes creating a world professional 'dream tour' to help showcase their stars – like Quiksilver's Slater and Andersen, Billabong's Irons and Occhilupo, and Rip Curl's Mick Fanning – they also invested heavily in the projection of their commitment to free surfing, beyond the restrictions of a points system. This resulted in some bizarre and brilliant marketing schemes, such as Rip Curl's global hunt for the perfect wave, The Search, Quiksilver's twist on the same theme, The Quiksilver Crossing, and Billabong's Odyssey. These multi-million dollar campaigns became ongoing location shoots (The Crossing lasting seven years) and the resulting flood of videos and later DVDs, given away through their concept stores or sold at below cost, effectively killed the independent film-makers. The smartest of them, like veterans Jack McCoy and Albe Falzon, stood up and caressed the enemy rather than being raped and pillaged, and some of these dance-with-the-devil collaborations were actually very good. So it wasn't necessarily what the big surf brands were doing that pissed a lot of people off, it was the fact that they had such muscle in the market that they could dominate virtually everything they touched, and homogenise it. An increasing number of surfers didn't want to be homogenised. It wasn't in their genes.

For a dozen years after Australian surfer/shaper Simon Anderson had introduced the tri-fin 'Thruster', virtually no serious surfer rode anything else. On every beach with waves around the world, the boards looked the same and the surfing was defined by the stock manoeuvres of the top pros – the leg-pump and the gouge. But then something happened. Demographers may have seen it coming, but they didn't tell the surf industry. The baby boomers started to get old and fat, but unlike their parents' generation, they didn't want to stop having fun. The longboard came back, reviving the careers of ageing gurus like Bob McTavish, Robert August and Donald Takayama.

Longboarding extended the involvement of many surfers into and past middle age, but it also introduced to the sport hundreds of thousands of wannabes who would never have persevered with the much more difficult shortboard. So the big brands soon took the side of the young and the cool, leaving the old fat dudes, the late adopters and the mature women to the supermarket surf brands or, in many cases, to the old cottage-industry companies that could once again eke a living out of something they loved. But just when the market was neatly segmented, the Gen-X surfers started to get middle-aged spread. Never having ridden longboards as kids, they turned instead to fattened-up retro models of twin fins and fish, or the sleeker lines of pre-Thruster single fins.

The retro movement touched a nerve with seriously cool surfer/ musicians like Donovan Frankenreiter and Dave Rastovich, leaving the big brands totally rattled. And while the punk nabobs in the marketing departments were attempting to deal with that one, the pop-out surfboard re-emerged, bigger and better than ever, with a financial imperative of turning every human in the world with a grand of disposable income into a surfer.

The mass-produced pop-out surfboard had made many forays into the market since the 1950s, and some had actually found price-point niches for a time, but the majority had been rejected for very good reasons. Their manufacturing was invariably inferior and their design nonexistent. In the 1980s, however, Santa Barbara shaper John Bradbury made a styrofoam/epoxy resin lightweight board for pro champion Martin Potter, putting the spotlight back on the possibilities of mass-producing performance surfboards. In the early 1990s, Santa Cruz designer Randy French, who had worked with moulded sailboards for a decade, transferred the technology to surfboards and created a company called Surftech. Signing up some of the biggest name shapers in the industry, he took his templates to Thailand and formed an alliance with the Cobra manufacturing company, thus creating a new benchmark for mass-produced surfboards. Initially ridiculed, Surftech was doing huge business by the turn of the century and had spawned a raft of competitors in moulded boards.

Into this increasingly confused youth culture came the dotcoms, leapfrogging over the extant surf media to promise all things to all people, through a process known as 'convergence'. No one actually knew what that meant, but the digital entrepreneurs just kept spruiking it as they hit the beach car parks in the summer of 1999. In those naive, not so distant days, websites seemed to be the answer to everything, and the surf culture's dream factory was an easy target. Cashed up with other people's money, the dotcoms raided the surf companies and surf media for talent. By 2000, there was no one who didn't have some kind of gig on a dotcom! Hardcloud, Bluetorch, Surfline, Swell.com, they were all going to change the way we thought about surfing … or something.

Gotcha's new sugar daddy, Marvin Winkler, fresh from failing to set the world alight with his plans for the Gotcha Glacier theme park in Anaheim, was the brain behind Bluetorch, which was funded by Orange County chip manufacturer Broadcom Corp. Bluetorch CEO Matt Jacobson, a fringe player in sports television, talked up the new media the loudest: 'Our goal is to reach our target audience of young male surfers across multiple media platforms, combining traditional and next generation interactive media.' But no one really believed him.

And then somebody burst the balloon. It turned out that a slick name and a bunch of psychobabble was not enough. We weren't about to forsake all other media, we liked what we had, and the only surf websites that would survive the inevitable withdrawal of funding were those that offered a genuine service, like wave cams and swell prediction. Dotcom mania came and went fairly quickly, but what remained was the fact that the world of communications was rapidly changing and fragmenting, and while this lot of cowboys had ridden off into the sunset, more and bigger posses were on the way. An already fragmented industry would have to learn how to impart its message through newly fragmented media channels, and it wouldn't be easy.

The challenges of the 2000s were not lost on Rip Curl, which had remained truer to its roots than most other surf brands, even as founders Doug Warbrick and Brian Singer stepped back from the reins. Rip Curl's penetration of the US market had always lagged behind Quiksilver and Billabong, and at times it had appeared nonexistent in Europe. But at $300 million sales and with one of the most respected brands in surfing, it was still a force to be reckoned with.

While speculation mounted that Rip Curl would soon go public, as Warbrick and Singer moved toward retirement, the company announced the appointment of James Strong as chairman of the board. The dapper, bow-tie loving former Qantas CEO was one of Australia's most dynamic and interesting businessmen. A cultured man, chairman of the Australian Opera ... what the fuck was he doing slumming it at the Curl?!

The answer was that Strong was having a ball. A long-time friend of Singer's (they had been in the Young Presidents Association together), Strong was an adventurer and a mountain climber, both passions of Brian Singer. While sharing an igloo at the South Pole, Sing Ding had invited the opera buff to join the board, and Strong had accepted. In his first public appearance as the Rip Curl chair, at a winter trade show at Grenoble in the French Alps, Strong told the author: 'I love these guys and I love the way they've built their company. I believe that at this stage of Rip Curl's development I can contribute meaningfully.' (Almost a decade later, Strong again combined his passions for the outdoor world and clever business by leading the late 2009 float of Kathmandu on the Australian Stock Exchange.)

On the morning of 11 September 2001, surfing conditions were near perfect on both coasts of the US. By nine a light offshore wind was caressing the beaches of the Jersey Shore, while across the continent dawn was revealing classic late summer lines at First Point,

Malibu. Optimism was in the air, and then two planes rammed the Twin Towers in Manhattan and the whole world changed.

With three thousand people dead, it seemed crass to ruminate on what effect this might have on the surf industry, but the fact was that aftershocks ripped through American consumerism over the next year, with a major dip in retail spending. Americans were hunkered down at home, worried about the future of their families, and no surf company seemed to take this on at corporate level more than Quiksilver. Perhaps it was the fact that the industry leader had a president and a board right out of the heart of Californian conservatism, and that this assault on American values was harder to take than it was, say, for Volcom (youth against establishment). Perhaps 9/11 had just hammered home the staleness of its management team, or perhaps it was the fact that the company had serious inventory issues that no one seemed able to address. For whatever reason, the Quiksilver board considered that the company was in crisis, and urged Bob McKnight to make an appointment, from within or without, to fix the inventory and address the ongoing morale of the executive. McKnight decided to bring in Bernard Mariette.

According to an insider, the American management group was stunned by the revelation that an untried Frenchman was coming in above them, but the inertia that had become their modus operandi kicked in again, and after some minor bleats, they just got ready to meet and greet the French guy who was now 'the global guy'.

Mariette's new brief was to be global president of Quiksilver, Inc., while retaining his position as president of Quiksilver Europe. He would move his family to California, but commute between Saint Jean de Luz and Huntington Beach on a week-to-week basis. This was a recipe for disaster for any high-powered executive, putting undue stress on family relationships and creating a scattergun management. In Mariette's case, it compounded the propensity he had already shown for the grand gesture over the fine detail. In practical terms, the Quiksilver management found, when you needed a decision out of Bernard, he was never there to give it.

None of this is to diminish Mariette's capabilities as a corporate strategist. Scattered, prone to flights of fantasy, overly excitable, manipulative and ruthless, you could argue persuasively that he was not a great leader of men, but he had brought to Quiksilver a keen sense of its defining opportunity, and while he never understood the brand ethos, he saw its potential. 'He's our mad Mozart,' a board member confided in the author soon after Mariette's global appointment. And the board loved it. They loved the black ink on the quarterly reports and they loved the urbane Frenchmen he kept stacking onto the board, such as Danone's Franck Ribout.

Bernard Mariette was a serious businessman – a suit in salt's clothing – but he was also a serious bon vivant, and by 2002 he had begun to take Quiksilver's global management way beyond its standard level of naughtiness. Mariette had learned his pit skills with some of the finest winers and diners in the business, and as his influence at Quiksilver grew, he brought more of their ideas (and often the people themselves) into the corporate culture.

In the late 1990s, Quiksilver, by now with a billion in sales in its sights, started to emulate larger corporate cultures. The Quiksilver HQ, once known as 'the factory', became known as 'the campus', just like at Nike. The core management group, in both Europe and America, became known, more generically if more grandly, as 'the office of the president'. In Europe, where titles mean everything, membership of the OTP became a platinum pass into the WOB (World of Bernard), and Mariette's old mentor from L'Oréal, Peter Bloxham, now general manager, became the gatekeeper.

While, in the US, the office of the president remained an occasional forum for the exchange of views on issues of corporate policy, in Europe (where it was also known as the management committee) it quickly became a boys' club in which the exchanges of views were always robust, and frequently complemented by exchanges of blood, skin and even bodily fluids. Bloxham, a corporate bareknuckle boxer from Birmingham who loved a good stoush, chaired the group and convened its monthly meetings around a network of the fun cities of

Europe. With Quiksilver's growth rate, there was always a shop opening or a marketing exercise to justify a junket to Barcelona or London or Paris or even Marrakech.

Some serious business was achieved at these affairs, but not much in comparison with the mind play behind the scenes. Since their sacking of the staff of Garnier, Mariette and Bloxham had perfected the 'blowtorch' negotiation, and frequently brought this into play at management committee soirees. Either man was capable, after a generous dinner, of applying the blowtorch to the belly of a corporate victim. When both men were involved, the results could be life-changing, if not psychologically damaging. A double blowtorch was simply devastating for an executive who thought he was doing his best for the company. It might begin with a sneering, 'Why are you smiling? Your figures are shit.' And it might finish as a sinister fireside chat, away from the comfort of friends, when the offender is told over and over again, with increasing venom: 'You are fucking our company, you are a piece of shit and you will walk away with nothing if you don't deliver the numbers next quarter.'

For the members of the European management committee, the most wonderful moment in any junket, and this was not uncommon, was when the blowtorch bro's got so drunk they turned the torch on themselves instead of on their team. On these occasions, drinks were hurled, tables were upturned and punches were thrown, and in the morning nothing was remembered. Such was the character of Quiksilver's European management committee. Everyone at the top was a rock star, and behaved as such.

The 'money doesn't matter' approach hit new levels in the summer of 2002 when Bernard Mariette convened a 'directions' conference over three days at the historic Marmounia Hotel in Marrakech, Morocco. As one eyewitness reported:

> After a travel day and a drunken poolside binge that lasted long into the night, the conference convened in the usual manner, with a hungover president barely able to set a real working

agenda. Invariably these things revolved around Bernard scribbling some unrealistic numbers on a whiteboard, then demanding that the various sales managers agree to meet them. There were some quite personal attacks, but the real 'blowtorch to the belly' was reserved for the drinking sessions later ...

The Marrakech party hit its low point the following night, when the Quiksilver group descended on a luxurious estate in the Palmerie district on the fringe of the desert, at the invitation of the Moroccan architect who had designed it. Our group arrived for the aperitif an hour or so late with several senior people already drunk. We were to spend an hour over drinks, then all leave for dinner at one of Marrakech's finest restaurants, but at the appointed time for our departure, Bernard was loudly making champagne toasts and showed no inclination to move on. 'No,' he told his assistant, 'tell them we will eat here. They have staff.' In fact the house kitchen staff had prepared the aperitif and gone home, but now the gracious host ran around and tried to put together a dinner for thirty people at no notice. By night's end, the president of Quiksilver was stretched out on the grass beyond the pool, champagne glass still in hand, tearfully muttering to himself. It was a revealing glimpse into his personal style, but it was also a little bit sad. Sometimes the bravado was covering up the enormous pressure he was under.

In April 2003, Quiksilver's leading executives converged on the ultra-chic Delano Hotel in South Beach, Miami for a conference that would cost the corporation an estimated US$300,000 and had just one stated purpose – to unveil a strategy to quadruple, over five years, the corporation's then revenues of $1 billion plus. There was, of course, another agenda, this one set by Bernard Mariette. It was, quite simply, to announce a changing of the guard. Mariette was now the man, and Mariette did things his way.

Over-the-top, enormously expensive corporate talkfests like this occur as regularly as bowel movements, and with much the same results. This one was a tad different. Traditionally, Quiksilver conferences had been held adjacent to a world class surf break, like Cloudbreak in Fiji or G-Land, Java, but the corporate landscape had been changing rather rapidly since the elevation of Bernard Mariette to the office of president of Quiksilver, Inc. The Delano was a mock art deco pile on the most un-surf beach in Florida, packed with pimps, Cuban hoods and New Yorkers with too much money.

The European contingent, of which the author was a member, arrived in Miami via an overnight stay in Paris for a Quiksilver shop opening party, recovering from hangovers in the first class cabin of a British Airways 747. The light- to welter-weight execs in the group were fairly impressed by all this, but as it turned out, they were slumming it. Their American counterparts flew in from California on a fleet of executive NetJets. When executives checked into plush poolside cabanas, they found welcome packs that included a Mont Blanc pen and notepad set with a message on a Quiksilver calling card: *Hello all. Thank you for a fantastic first semester. Let's make sure that the second six months are just as good! I'm looking forward to spending more time with each of you. – Bernard.* Underneath the calling card was a cheque for US$5000. Welcome to the new Quiksilver!

After a champagne-fuelled night, the president arrived at the conference centre sweaty of lip and shaky of hand to deliver the keynote address. Barely able to speak, he threw instead to an audiovisual presentation of Quiksilver's planned leap from the $10 billion 'universe' of *glisse*, or sliding sports, to the blue skies of 'outdoors', which also encompassed golf, cycling and hiking. Hungover as he was, Bernard Mariette watched and noted the reaction of every executive in the room to this bizarre plan to rip the guts out of surfing's iconic brand, for in Bernard's world, you were with him all the way, or you were out the door.

If Bernard Mariette's extravagant behaviour seemed to exemplify how surfing had strayed from its roots, then the Perrin brothers in Australia represented an even more blatant victory of the suits over the salts, and these suits were shiny and worn with pork pie hats and racing binoculars! After the successful float of Billabong, the Perrins had become seriously rich, entering *BRW* magazine's 'Rich 200 List', alongside Gordon Merchant (the richest man in surfing), Quiksilver's Green and Law, Rip Curl's Warbrick and Singer and Globe's Hill brothers, who were suddenly making a mint on surf and skate. The *BRW* 200 was an elite club, and some of the members were destined to be temporary, but for Matthew and Scott Perrin to be so rich so soon, on the back of Billabong, did not sit well with many people who had devoted their working lives to the industry.

'I picked them for raiders the first fucking day,' said Doug Spong. He was right. For two years, Matthew Perrin, aged just twenty-eight at the float, guided Billabong into better corporate governance, better financial reporting and better all-round performance. Despite the fact that he knew nothing about surfing, like Quiksilver's Mariette, he was potentially a great corporate leader for the brand. But Matt Perrin and his brother Scott liked fast cars, fast horses and fast money. From the day they came in, they were on their way out. In fact Scott Perrin took his profit and left before the float.

In January 2003, without consulting his board, Billabong CEO Matthew Perrin dumped eight million of his company's shares, realising more than $66 million in cash, causing the stock price to drop more than two dollars and prompting an Australian Stock Exchange investigation. While Billabong was still in recovery mode, with Perrin long departed, he sold his final five million stock, at a somewhat reduced price, but adding considerably to his wealth. Board chairman Gary Pemberton reportedly cashed up during this period too, but managed to avoid the headlines.

In the context of the plundering of Wall Street that was going on in the first few years of the new century, it hardly even rated, but the surf world was rocked, and rightly. The Perrins had been on a mission – to infiltrate surf, pick its bones dry and get the hell out of Dodge. And surf had welcomed their money and their ideas, and let the raiders have their way. When the Perrins left the field of play, some who stayed were much richer and the Billabong brand remained basically untarnished, but there was a loss of innocence that was felt way beyond the brand's headquarters in Burleigh Heads, Hossegor and Irvine. It seemed the surf industry had finally come of age, in the most unpleasant manner.

As the major surf brands became better known in the mainstream business community, many corporations sought a genuine surf company for their brand stables, resulting in a mid-decade industry phenomenon known as 'consolidation'. But for others, the solution was simply to invent a surf company. The most blatant – and most successful – of these was American retail giant Abercrombie & Fitch's invention of Hollister Co in 2000. A&F chief executive Michael Jeffries saw that the push into the retail sector by genuine surf brands like Quiksilver, Billabong and O'Neill was beginning to pose a threat to his dominance of the teenage market, particularly with the spectacular rise of Roxy and Billabong girls' wear on the back of the media blitz surrounding the movie *Blue Crush* and the MTV show *Surf Girls*. So he created a surf brand of his own, giving it a fictitious history that closely paralleled the real history of a brand like O'Neill. In Jeffries's Hollister history, a man called JM Hollister, a 'Pacific merchant', had founded the company in California in 1922, 'inspired by the sun-drenched spirit of California'. Jack O'Neill, probably the real inspiration, founded his company in 1952, so Jeffries had stolen an entire generation of authenticity on him. The name itself came from Hollister Ranch, a private coastal estate north of Santa Barbara long known for its excellent surf.

The Hollister mythology didn't stop there. They decorated their shop walls and catalogues with old photos of surf contests and Hawaiian beach boys – ending up in court when the Makaha surfers challenged their right to associate them with the brand – and while real surf companies spent millions sponsoring real surfing events around the world, Hollister made millions selling T-shirts that celebrated nonexistent events like 'San Onofre Hollister Surf Pro'.

Surf company CEOs who'd been in the business five minutes and had never felt sand between their toes started banging on about 'stolen heritage' and 'ruthless exploitation', but many secretly admired the audacity of the Hollister concept. And the worst aspect of it for the surf industry was that not only had Hollister stolen their image, but they were better at projecting it. Across the malls of America, the cashed-up teenagers who entered the cavernous Hollister 'experiential concept stores' felt that this was a totally authentic surf brand, and they voted with their wallets. By 2007, Hollister had 450 stores across America and $1.6 billion in sales, and they still hadn't put a cent into surfing.

The first of the genuine surf brands to become part of the consolidation process was Hurley International. When Bob Hurley walked away from his US Billabong licence in 1998, he simply took down the sign and put up a new one and pushed out the new season's range under his own name, retaining Billabong designer Lian Murray and most of the sales team. It was a $30 million start-up, just like that. But Hurley was an astute businessman and realised that he would have to do more than just produce Billabong garments with a new logo. He developed new technical products, like stretch board shorts, broadened the brand image through sponsorship of punk musicians and soul surfers like Rob Machado, and created a market niche for himself. Then, just four years after hanging up his shingle, he sold to Nike for an estimated $120 million. Hurley had become a respected brand in no time at all, largely due to the fact that Bob Hurley himself was one of the most respected figures in the American surf industry.

Other major corporations wanting to buy into surf had to dig deeper into history. Ocean Pacific, founded by Jim Jenks in 1972, had all but disappeared by the 1990s, but it was revived at the turn of the century by an astute, California-born entrepreneur named Dick Baker. Baker, who had come from high-powered positions at Esprit and Tommy Hilfiger, picked up the moribund Op brand for a song on behalf of a San Francisco investment fund, and proceeded to revive it to its glory days. He hired Hawaiian beachwear pioneer Nat Norfleet to carefully blend Op's design heritage with modern sensibilities, and rebuilt Op's industry cred by sponsoring key surfers like Joel Tudor, and bringing back the Op Pro. Op didn't infiltrate the core surf market the way it once had, but its broad distribution quickly made it a serious player again.

Naturally, the offers started coming. Baker sold Op to the Warnaco Corporation (makers of Speedo, among many sportswear brands) in 2004 for $40 million, staying on as a consultant. Two years later he helped Warnaco flip the brand to the Iconix Group for $54 million. It wasn't the surf industry as we knew it, but Baker, who passed away in 2009, spent his time away from the negotiating table mentoring new young surf brands, through his role as president of the Surf Industry Manufacturers Association.

The San Diego–based Reef, which began as a sandals company in 1984 and ultimately made a fortune for Argentinian brothers Fernando and Santiago Aguerre, was purchased by VF Corporation in 2005, to complement its 2004 purchase of skate shoe brand Vans, and further strengthen the corporation's Outdoor Coalition. Later in the same year, Gotcha, Michael Tomson's innovative industry leader of the 1980s, was snapped up by fashion group Perry Ellis, after years of slumming it in the supermarkets. 'My baby's turned into a whore,' moaned Tomson.

17 ALL FALL DOWN

When Bernard first came to the States to become president of the company, there were doubters. How is this French guy going to pull this off? How? By asserting his leadership through his intelligence and charisma. Alternatively challenging and charming, Bernard is a confident natural leader.

Quiksilver counsel and board member Charlie Exon,
The Mountain & The Wave, 2006

It wasn't just the big mainstream companies that got the consolidation bug. Within surfing the major brands were looking to grow laterally as their market penetration maxed out in the mature markets, like Australia and California. Billabong ensured its ongoing cool factor by acquiring Element Skateboards and Von Zipper Sunglasses in 2001, then added Kustom Shoes and the twenty-two store Hawaiian retail chain Honolua Surf Co in 2004. None of these acquisitions fundamentally changed the direction of the company. Rather, they strengthened it around the edges, and created new platforms for growth. Billabong turned Honolua into a wholesale garment brand, successfully targeting an older demographic, while Element branched into skater clothes and Kustom, an Australian brand, tackled the US market.

These were all challenges for Billabong, but they were manageable and, in the main, they were successful. If Matthew Perrin brought anything tangible to Billabong, it was that this growth strategy began on his watch, and it continued under his successor, Australian Derek O'Neill, the former plumber from Victoria who tapped away at the pipes in the European office for a decade until his brand held respectable market share, then showed remarkable poise in taking the global reins in the midst of the Perrin sell-off. With former South African pro surfer Paul Naude running a tight ship in North America, Billabong emerged from the Perrin raid a disciplined and focused company.

Quiksilver, on the other hand, was used to leading from the front, with flamboyance. When Quiksilver made an acquisition, the earth had to move, as it did in 2004 when the company purchased DC Shoes for slightly more than $100 million. DC, founded by skate/snow bums Damon Way and Ken Block, and fast-tracked to profit through the success of Damon's kid brother, skate star Danny Way, was the coolest shoe brand in the boardriding sector, and Quiksilver had proven over many years that it did not do good shoes. So the acquisition made sense, particularly in light of the fact that Quiksilver had just joined the billion dollar club, with revenues rising from the previous year's $975 million to $1.3 billion in 2004. The conventional wisdom was that, over a billion, you grow as fast as funding will allow, or you die.

But $100 million was a lot of money, and while the significant issues of a cultural and operational merger with DC were addressed, one might have expected the industry leader to kick back a little. But one would not have understood Bernard Mariette's motivation. By 2004, Mariette was at the height of his powers, strutting the world stage with a curious mix of breathtaking pomposity and audacious corporate positioning. Virtually everything he did in the name of Quiksilver courted serious risk, and yet he seemed above question, beyond the normal checks and balances.

The rollout of Quiksilver concept stores throughout Europe, for example, continued at warp speed even as the Euro economy showed signs of a wobble and Britain went into a retail decline. Shop leases on high streets and malls were signed even though the fit-out construction crew had no chance of scheduling them for months, and the once-immaculate look of a Quiksilver Boardriders Club became shabby and makeshift as a result of the unholy rush to complete and move on to the next.

At a time when pay TV networks in Europe were struggling for market share and advertising revenue in an increasingly crowded marketplace (and advertising rates were consequently more affordable than they'd been in years), Mariette announced a joint venture with Rip Curl to create their own boardriding channel, and put a stop to networks like Eurosport and Fox showing Quiksilver's growing library of branded footage. The joint venture never materialised, but relations with the pay sports networks suffered hugely.

Mariette worked feverishly in Europe to build his profile, but most news organisations were not that interested in a surf boss without a surfboard. When he did score a big interview, he invariably blew it with braggadocio. London's *Independent on Sunday* caught him after a big lunch with his pal Peter Bloxham, and made mild fun of the situation, painting him as a slightly mixed-up rev-head in a surf hat in an article titled 'He'll have fun, fun, fun – except for "stupid questions from analysts"'. Bernard was predictably furious.

Mariette's behaviour was more circumspect in the American market, where he felt the board was still judging him, despite the fact that he well and truly had the numbers. In Europe he could do whatever he liked, because he felt he owned it. And, in a sense, he did. Old ally Bloxham was the hands-on boss of the territory, while the heir apparent, Pierre Agnes, was still being groomed for the job. Oddly enough Agnes, a former top French surfer who got his business start managing Quiksilver's first retail store in Europe, had been one of the leading critics of Mariette's original appointment, believing that suits like him had no place in a surf company. Mariette's charm offensive got him in the end, and the first thing the global president of Quiksilver did on each return to France was to drag 'Blox' and Pierre, and others of the inner sanctum, off to former rugby player Christian Laroque's Ferme Ostalapia, a charming Basque restaurant not five minutes away from the Quiksilver campus. These lunches usually segued into dinner, and then some, with everything going on the company account. And even when there seemed no purpose in staying, the night staff closing down all around him, Bernard would be steadfast in the bar, refusing to allow his drinking companions to leave. To some habitués of Ostalapia, he was known as 'Cape Horn', because you couldn't get around him.

As power flowed to him, Mariette became more and more of a corporate bully who ruled by fear. Conversely, he was also tremendously loyal to those who showed appropriate subservience, and to the few within the company whose skills and style he genuinely respected. Despite their ugly drunken brawls, he and Bloxham were joined at the hip. As time went on, Bernard's relationship with Pierre Agnes also blossomed. For one thing, they shared a love of fast cars, but more importantly, Agnes had something Mariette wanted but would never have – respect as a boardrider. It seems a silly thing, but it defined the relationship, and Bernard never stopped trying to compensate for the fact that there was no salt in his veins.

By 2003, with the assistance of vast and expensive teams of public relations hacks, strategists, fortune tellers and mind readers, Bernard Mariette had convinced everyone that mattered that his particular vision for Quiksilver's future was the only logical way forward. The vision was bound up in a theory known as 'The Five Universes of Outdoors', an impressive body of work compiled by market researchers in support of a position that Mariette had long since reached – that Quiksilver was growing too big for the surf market.

The Five Universes paper, first presented to Quiksilver's global management at an extravagant conference at Miami's Delano Hotel in April 2003, examined the $42 billion (projected for 2004) outdoors market, which represented approximately one-third of the

$120 billion sports goods market. Its five universes were defined as country ($15 billion), snow ($10 billion), mountain ($7 billion), water ($6 billion) and street ($4 billion). Quiksilver was represented in three of the five universes, but while its market share in surf was approaching forty per cent, and in all board sports (surf, snow, skate) was a healthy sixteen per cent, across the five universes of the outdoors market it had only three per cent market share. A lot of blue sky there, and, moreover, the report noted, many areas of outdoors were not being serviced well by the existing brands.

Within its five universes, outdoors encompassed everything from golf to mountain biking to scuba diving to in-line skating. Quiksilver had already flirted with golf, through an apparel line called Fidra, and gone nowhere. The rest of the turf was anathema to a surf company, apart from the places where they had already planted a flag – snow, skate and surf. Nevertheless, the Five Universes paper was an interesting road map of the market, and might have been used effectively to position Quiksilver, Roxy and their new stablemate, DC Shoes. But Bernard Mariette's big idea was much more grandiose than that, and it centred on a chance meeting he had had with Laurent Boix-Vives, the septuagenarian chairman of the century-old French ski company, Rossignol, in the French Alps in the winter of 2001.

Boix-Vives, seventy-eight years old when first approached about selling to Quiksilver, had bought out the founding Rossignol family back in 1956, and had presided over a successful family of brands for almost forty years. But in the last decade the company had struggled to retain a thirty per cent market share while its profits had declined dangerously.

The story of the Boix-Vives connection was an interesting one that varied with each telling, dependent upon geographic location and tactical advantage. When a merger of Quiksilver and Rossignol was first mooted, it was said that the Mariette and Boix-Vives families went back decades, and that Bernard had learned to ski at the side of the chairman. When the minority shareholders of Rossignol protested that a sweetheart deal seemed to be cooking and that the arrangement between friends might sell them short, it was said that Mariette and Boix-Vives barely knew each other, and that the relationship was recent and built on commercial opportunity. This latter version was actually the truth, but when the acquisition possibility hit the US radar, the old family friends scenario seemed to work better again.

Rossignol was indeed still a great name in snow sports, but it was a French hard goods manufacturing company that had not moved with the times, and had been haemorrhaging money for years. Despite the potency of its brand, and its ski offshoots Dynastar, Lange and Look, it had no apparel product to speak of. The group's golf brand, Cleveland, was in better shape, but not by much. The company's biggest issue was margin, for which the solution was relocation of manufacture, but this was a French iconic brand, and moving offshore was unthinkable.

Exactly how closely the Quiksilver board looked at these issues has never been revealed, but the entire Quiksilver executive seemed to be in the thrall of the charismatic Frenchman, who kept repeating his mantra, in forum after forum, from analyst conference calls to late-night boozy tete-a-tetes, that Quiksilver had no option but to march forward into the outdoors market. The spin was that Quiksilver with Rossignol would rocket from one billion to three billion overnight, and become the biggest player in a huge and growing market. You knew it was working when even Bob McKnight started talking about the five universes. It was only a matter of time. If anyone in Quiksilver thought the emperor had no clothes, he was too frightened to say it. Mad Mozart was unstoppable.

Over the Christmas/New Year break in December 2004, Bernard Mariette met with Laurent Boix-Vives at Rossignol headquarters in Voiron, and again over several days at Meribel in the Alps, and reportedly made an offer to acquire the Boix-Vives shareholding of forty-five per cent, which carried with it sixty-three per cent of voting rights. Quiksilver would then offer to acquire all remaining shares from private shareholders. Boix-Vives, who had been concerned about succession issues for some time, with neither of his daughters in the running to take over, is said to have agreed in principle, but asked for time to think. He didn't get it.

As soon as Europe went back to work on 3 January, Mariette revealed to the French newspaper *Les Echos* that Rossignol was Quiksilver's leading target for acquisition. Rossignol's chief operating officer, Yves Barnoud, was forced into a face-saving admission that yes, there had been talks, but the family had made no decisions. As far as Mariette was concerned, it was a done deal, and by March it actually was. The purchase price of US$550 million (A$700 million) made it by far the biggest acquisition in the history of the surf industry, and ironically, it was designed to take Quiksilver beyond the industry it had for so long dominated. The private shareholders had been mollified and their shares acquired by July, giving Quiksilver 100 per cent ownership of the ski company and a substantial shareholding in the US golf subsidiary, Roger Cleveland Co. Laurent Boix-Vives took up a position on the board of the company that was now to be known as Quiksilver-Rossignol.

The acquisition took Quiksilver's revenues from $1.3 billion in 2004 to $1.8 billion in 2005, and throughout that year Mariette out-lined to investment managers and analysts his plan to reach $3 billion through leveraging the Rossignol brand in apparel. But the acquisition had blown out Quiksilver's level of debt from under $200 million to almost a billion, and worse, while Rossignol's $600 million in sales certainly added to the revenue line, it detracted from the company's overall profitability. While the Mariette posse was toasting its own cleverness all around the world, the 2005 annual report (the first to carry a tiny 'Quiksilver-Rossignol' name on the spine) contained a significant warning light for shareholders on page 82:

> Our acquisition of Rossignol is expected to have a significant impact on our financial results. Our revenues and expenses are expected to increase substantially. However, our overall profit margins are expected to be negatively impacted because Rossignol has historically generated lower profit margins than

we have, and this trend is expected to continue in the foreseeable future … Further … we will be substantially more leveraged as a result of debt incurred in connection with the acquisition, and we will have an increased amount of capital committed to manufacturing functions.

So what was the good news? According to the majority of analysts, there wasn't any. The day the Rossignol deal was confirmed, its stock rose twelve per cent while Quiksilver's fell almost twenty per cent, and the negative market perception grew almost as fast as Quiksilver's ballooning debt, as it spent more and more to try to turn Rossignol around, including massive investment in employee relocation and the construction of a huge winter sports headquarters in Park City, Utah. Within Quiksilver, the standard line, from chairman down, was that the analysts simply 'didn't get it', and that the sophisticated five universe plan would soon be on track to deliver major profit.

Bob McKnight joined Mariette on corporate roadshows to shore up weakening shareholder confidence, but the stock price kept slipping, and often there seemed to be an air of desperation creeping into the explanations of what the world's greatest surf company was doing. In a 2006 conference call with analysts, Mariette patiently explained:

By the end of the nineties, we could see that surf and even snow would slow down, and to protect ourselves we needed to go to the outdoor world. So we started looking for an acquisition. In outdoors there are five categories and we are in four of them now, with big potential growth in all. With Rossignol, from a financial point of view … it's number one in brand awareness in snow, number five in golf. Our priorities were one, to reorganise the group from its 1980s set-up; two, to make it an outdoors icon, not just a winter sports icon; and three, to reinvent our snowboard division by going to Park City.

It sounded confused and not very convincing, and came at a time when a warm European winter had further decreased Rossignol hardware sales, and golf had hit a flat spot. The external pressures also seemed to be having an effect on senior management. While McKnight and Mariette operated from offices only a few metres apart, the chairman and CEO became increasingly unaware of where his second in command was or what he was doing. The easygoing McKnight seldom got visibly angry, but he did when he discovered that the governor of Utah was in the next office, discussing state tax breaks for the Park City operation. 'A fucking governor is here and nobody told me!' he bellowed to an associate.

While the cracks may have been starting to emerge, for most in the Quiksilver management and beyond, Mariette was still a conquering hero, the architect of the most audacious expansion plan anyone had ever imagined. And it was working, or so Bernard said. Although he had been distanced from the running of the company for years now, as the biggest individual shareholder, Alan Green carried tremendous influence, and occasionally used it when he felt the brand was losing its way. Given how far the Rossignol deal was taking Quiksilver from its roots, it would have been reasonable to expect him to fire a few rounds over the bows of what was increasingly looking like a sinking ship. But Green had become an unabashed Mariette fan, regarding him as 'a bloke with balls surrounded by fucking weaklings'.

In February 2007, Quiksilver executives and leading sponsored athletes from around the world were invited to Paris, ostensibly to celebrate the launch of the French edition of *The Mountain & The Wave*, a major book on the company's history (a book that Mariette had sent back to its author for a rewrite because, he maintained, it devoted too much space to events prior to his joining Quiksilver in 1994). As the guests arrived they discovered that, coincidentally, Bernard was to receive a *legion d'affaires* medallion from the French government at the treasury offices that very evening. This honour, bestowed twice-yearly on a significant number of French businessmen, was described in Quiksilver circles as 'a French knighthood'. And so it appeared at a celebratory dinner later, when 'Sir' Bernard was lauded in toast after toast. Perhaps the most bizarre of these, and one that flabbergasted the French speakers in the room, was from salt-encrusted surfer Pierre Agnes, who sounded like a Mafia made man when he professed 'love for life' to his boss and mentor.

But within weeks the jig was up. With the stock price still labouring, something had to give, and golf was the sacrificial lamb. But there was a catch. In order to sell Cleveland, Quiksilver had to acquire it 100 per cent. This it did in September, preparatory to selling the company to Japanese SRI Sports Limited for $132.5 million in October. Bernard Mariette commented: 'We believe this transaction is a key strategic action for our company that will drive immediate value and enable us to reduce both our exposure to the hardgoods space and our degree of leverage.' Both of which had been caused by Bernard's acquisition of Rossignol. Debt remained at $1.1 billion and growing.

The board was running out of patience with Mariette, who rapidly became the scapegoat for everything that was wrong with Quiksilver. It was easy to blame him because he was undeniably culpable, but of what? Well, he had managed to convince the all-powerful, all-knowing board of good ole boys from old money San Remo that the five universe plan would make them all wealthy beyond belief. And while the conduct of the board may have stopped short of negligence and neglect of due diligence, it raised serious questions about the ability of the Quiksilver board to direct the future of a company now with sales of $2.4 billion.

For Bob McKnight, one of the most respected figures in the surf industry for thirty years and someone whose genuine love of the Quiksilver brand and all that it stood for was unquestioned, the demonising of Bernard Mariette didn't alter one salient fact: it had all happened on his watch.

How quickly we go from hero to zero. In another conference call to analysts in late 2007, Mariette said: 'We continue to believe that the Rossignol business will improve over the course of the next two seasons.' Mariette went on to outline the possibility of offloading the hardware part of the business while retaining the apparel, but he was dreaming, and at Quiksilver, the believers had long since left the building. Not only had Rossignol continued to drag the company's numbers down and trash its stock price over more than two years, now there was a new threat looming just as Quiksilver reached the most vulnerable point in its history. The ongoing sub-prime mortgage crisis was beginning to threaten the stability of the banks, and the US economy was teetering on the brink of a major crisis. At the time of its greatest need, Quiksilver had nothing in the war chest and nothing in the think tank.

'We have seen and overcome difficult market conditions at a variety of points in our history and have always emerged a stronger company,' Bob McKnight breezily told the recipients of a conference call, then went straight into a huddle with his lawyers to discuss the most pressing mission facing the company – to get rid of the architect of the five universes plan. On 12 February 2008, he emailed a letter to Quiksilver's key employees, some three thousand of them:

> It's clear that the Rossignol transaction has hurt the company. We continue to believe in the power and potential of the Rossignol brand, and we think we have positioned the company for long-term success. Nevertheless, we recognize that the seasonality and the general nature of the hard goods business is not manageable ... Therefore, we have decided to sell it. It's also clear that, even in our core business, consumers are being cautious with their spending, and there are concerns about recession, or at least economic contraction, both in the US and abroad ... What we will control is our commitment to reduce the losses from our hard goods business and increase the operating profitability of our core apparel and footwear brands. In this context, you've no doubt seen our announcement today concerning Bernard's departure ... Bernard Mariette has been, for the past fifteen years, one of this company's leaders and

innovators. There is perhaps no one here at Quiksilver with a greater passion for the company and our brands … His passion and dedication are the two things that make it so hard for me to tell you today that Bernard and Quiksilver are parting ways.

Bernard Mariette may have brought a great company to its knees with his tunnel vision, but the light at the end of that tunnel was tinged with a golden glow. He 'resigned to pursue other interests' (including, apparently, a plan to purchase Rossignol) with a termination package of $3.9 million. Quiksilver's stock immediately rose six per cent. 'This is great news for Quiksilver,' surf industry commentator Bob Mignogna told the *Los Angeles Times*. The analysts agreed, sending notes to their clients that McKnight would now restore focus on the company's core brands. Nobody said the analysts didn't 'get it' anymore, least of all McKnight. But getting rid of the instigator of the Rossignol mess didn't solve the situation. The corpse of the venerable French ski company was still in the room, and it was starting to stink.

On 27 August 2008, Bob McKnight once again wrote to his staff: 'Great news. We've found the best buyer for Rossignol, and we expect to close the sale in the next couple of months.' If McKnight really believed this was great news, it was an indication of how far Quiksilver's expectations had fallen. After chasing down any number of false starts, Quiksilver's David Morgan, appointed Rossignol boss on Mariette's departure (with a brief to hold it together while he found a buyer, any buyer), came up with a European consortium led by a former Rossignol CEO and fully funded by Australia's Macquarie Group. The company, Chartreuse & Mont Blanc, signed a heads of agreement to buy Rossignol for a cash component of $70 million, but before the deal could be concluded, the global financial crisis began to peak, sending Macquarie, along with other major firms around the world, into a tailspin of overcommitment. But Quiksilver was desperate to offload, and eventually accepted $37 million cash.

In just three years, Rossignol had cost Quiksilver more than half a billion dollars, and all but destroyed the surf industry leader, built from nothing over almost forty years. It was time to retreat, regroup and try to summon the energy required for the greatest fight in the company's history – the fight for survival.

18 SURVIVAL STANCE

Whether you got Cult or you didn't, hats off to Spong ... He put his money where his mouth was and gave it a good crack, truly living up to his statement to Times Online back in 2006: 'Who wants to be the richest guy in the graveyard? You can't have fun when you're dead.'
Caz Ridings, *Australian Surf Business* magazine, 2009

The impact of the economic meltdown wasn't just the biggest surf industry story of 2008: it was the *only* story. Of course, this was not the first time that economic events beyond their direct control had adversely affected the big surfwear brands and their retailers – in recent history think 9/11, the diabolical rockabilly summer of '91 (when no-brand white tees ruled and pollution closed beaches) and the Wall Street crash of '87. And when the big guys sneeze, the entire industry catches cold. But, even when the equities markets staged a comeback in late 2007 and it seemed for a hopeful minute that the sub-prime crisis was just a storm in a teacup, there were significant differences between this calamity and those that had preceded it.

For one thing, previous crises were like child's play compared with the shit-storm the surf industry was now suffering as a result of a generation of corporate greed. For another thing, the industry could no longer throw its hands up and say, hey, we're just surf dudes so let's just surf until the storm blows through and the market glasses off. The surf sector might still have been but a blip on the radar of big business, but the big brands were as culpable as the next multinational corporate sausage machine, paying the honchos and buddies too much and investing in the future too little. And while America's two biggest surf retailers, Pacific Sunwear and Zumiez, took a lot of heat for their seriously diminishing returns in 2008, the biggest hurt was reserved for surf's biggest manufacturer.

In a thoughtful article on Swellnet's 'Surfpolitik' page, posted on 20 November 2008, commentator Stuart Nettle noted that 'the ripples from the Wall Street crash have finally reached the coast … One could say that there is never a good time for an economic crash, though in Quiksilver's case, the timing was particularly bad.'

Credit raters Moody's gave Quiksilver a junk bond rating as its shares slid below a dollar (from more than $15 a year earlier) and short-term debt became due for refinancing. The unthinkable had happened. Bulletproof Quiksilver was on its knees, and if it could happen at the top, it could happen anywhere. That was the salutary lesson of 2008. And why had it happened? The deepening of the global financial crisis and the credit squeeze of the second half of 2008 were certainly major factors, but the life-threatening malaise was the giant leap from boardriding into the unknown universe of outdoors. Despite the company's claims that it had saturated existing markets so much that it had no choice, the fact was that Quiksilver had not conquered the snow market and only the 2004 acquisition of DC Shoes had given it real cred in skate. Quiksilver had other growth options, but it chose to take the scary leap and suffered the consequences.

Conversely, the big corporations who bought into surf, notably Nike and VF Corporation, fared relatively well in the crisis. Nike's lead surf brand, Hurley, acquired in 2004, recorded its best ever results in the first quarter of 2008, with revenues increasing thirty-three per cent, according to its parent company. This seemed like a lot in a tough economy, but in fact even the strugglers (like Quiksilver) were helped enormously by the dive in the US dollar increasing the value of their export sales in Europe and Asia. VF Corporation, the thriving brand stable that is home to Reef and Vans, keeps its internal sales numbers cleverly disguised, but the company overall defied the downturn and posted excellent numbers in its surf and skate division.

Of the other major brands, Billabong probably hurt the least, due to its sound management strategies of vertical growth through the acquisition of manageable and culturally fitting companies to fill in gaps in their product offering or increase their retail reach – accessories company Da Kine in August 2008 was the fifth acquisition in twelve months – but they did take a few hits, like everyone else. In the US they backed out of opening a high cost retail store in Chicago, and in Australia went to court to try to recover $600,000 from failed retailer Brothers Neilsen. Still, there were plenty of surf companies that would have been quite happy to have problems of that ilk. The brand reported a 5.5 per cent lift in full year net profit to 30 June 2008, off revenue of A$1.3 billion. Said CEO Derek O'Neill: 'It is a pleasing result, but [with eighty per cent of revenue offshore] we would have liked to have a lower Australian dollar.' O'Neill got his wish. The Aussie had dropped thirty per cent against the greenback by December, although it rebounded in mid-2009.

Rip Curl, meanwhile, continued in its quiet way to add value for its private shareholders, issuing a special dividend of A$34 million. A prominent member of the brand's business-savvy board, National Australia Bank CEO Ahmed Fahour, increased his investment in the company by A$1.8 million. At the shopfront, the Curl kept up its solid and respected product offering, while marketing received a huge boost from having dual Aussie world champions Mick Fanning and Steph Gilmore as a double act. (Gilmore backed up for a second title the following year, and in 2009 both Fanning and Gilmore were the champions again.)

In the US, Volcom had its first really tough year, with a flagging share price and internal problems most out of character for the happy, hippie troupe that Richard Woolcott had led for years, with 'Wooly' vacating the president's chair in July 2008. The brand also had serious inventory problems by year's end, with retail business on both US coasts and in Europe decidedly down. And while US retailer Pacific Sunwear had its own share of problems, it also seemed to be the answer to Volcom's, with sales to PacSun increasing by an enormous eighty per cent.

In Australia, leading retail chain Brothers Neilsen, held together by a rescue mission eighteen months earlier, finally collapsed after more than thirty-five years of trading. Devastated founder Paul Neilsen toughed it out as he had always done as a pro surfing champion in the 1970s, blaming no one but himself. Nevertheless, the shockwaves and fallout filled the blogs for months, with the Australian surfing public divided as to whether the creditors – in large part, the 'big three' of Quiksilver, Billabong and Rip Curl – should be hostile or sympathetic. In Billabong's case, as noted above, it was the former.

Meanwhile, struggling footwear brand Globe pulled out of its world tour event in Fiji – perhaps not the last $2 million event to fade away from the Association of Surfing Professionals' Dream Tour – while Globe stocks languished at twenty cents and angry shareholders began to ask questions about the management style of the founding Hill brothers.

Also on the ropes, with its advertising and real estate disappearing in tandem, was Cult Industries, the brainchild of former Billabong heavy Doug Spong. Cult headquarters in Burleigh Heads, a cathedral-like edifice designed to dwarf its neighbours, Billabong and Rip Curl, was the first to be put on the market. Cult's high profile Main Street, Huntington Beach retail store soon followed. After months of speculation, Cult Industries was placed in voluntary liquidation in April 2009, with debts of more than $15.4 million.

Despite, or perhaps because of, the prevailing doom and gloom, new and young brands continued to surface, and yesterday's new brands, like RVCA, continued to thrive. Insight, an Aussie-based board brand reinvented as edgy apparel in the US by former surf journalist Jesse

Faen, won best advertising campaign and breakthrough brand at the SIMA Summit in 2008, but the brand's strengths went beyond smoke and mirrors. Faen and his team managed to create a new and exciting twist on the art/music/surf axis, much as Volcom had done a decade earlier, and Gotcha had done a decade before that, and to back it with quality product. While Insight continued to fight for shelf space in an ever-introspective market, their support base grew stronger where it counted.

Australia's recent start-up Rhythm could have chosen a better time for its run on the American market, but it still managed to make some inroads on the trade show circuit and achieve placement with core retailers. Still the 'it' brand in Australia, Rhythm was looking to achieve similar status in global markets through its fun approach to the surf lifestyle, when it seemed to hit a wall in 2009. Insiders blamed management conflict, while other observers noted that the strain of trying to crack new markets in the midst of a recession had simply taken its toll.

By the middle of 2009, there was cautious optimism in Australia and less panic in the US. The economy seemed to have bottomed, and most of the major surf brands were still on the field of play, if limping and somewhat bloodied.

Following a January Wall Street tip that Quiksilver was about to be taken over by Nike (the stock price jumped forty-six per cent on the back of it) the company secured a refinancing package with private equity firm Rhone that enabled it to stay in business while it restructured, but at a massive interest cost that itself threatened the future of the brands. Quiksilver's interest costs in 2009 were more than $100 million. Meanwhile, global CFO Joe Scirocco presided over more than 500 sackings (saving more than $60 million a year), pay cuts of up to fifteen per cent for top executives (himself and Bob McKnight included) and a major culling of Quiksilver's vast retail network, which had peaked in 2006 at more than 500 stores, half of them company-owned. Thirty non-performing stores were closed immediately. Quiksilver also pulled out of the January Action Sports

Retailer trade fair in San Diego – traditionally a pissing contest between major brands to show who has the most marketing muscle – and flagged a reduced presence at the summer show. By September, the draconian cost-cutting measures had been favourably noted by Wall Street, but the huge interest payments had kicked in.

It was definitely one day at a time for Quiksilver, but the comforting news was that the vast majority of consumers remained oblivious to the fact that the company behind the Quiksilver, Roxy and DC Shoes brands was struggling to survive. Retail sales were flat in all markets, with the Surf Industry Manufacturers Association reporting a 3.4 per cent decline in US receipts with sales down from $7.48 billion in 2007 to $7.22 billion in 2008, but industry research by companies like California's Board-Trac and Leisure Trends showed that consumer sentiment was still very much with Quiksilver's brands. In a show of faith to its core market, Quik reconfirmed its commitment to sponsorship of ASP pro tour events, and re-signed nine-time world champion Kelly Slater to a five-year contract that would see the iconic star into his forties. The message from McKnight and his team was loud and clear: we're down but we're not out.

Meanwhile, at Billabong, CEO Derek O'Neill had also assumed the survival stance, legs bent to withstand the impact of the long-term effects of recession. Billabong slashed executive pay, with O'Neill himself dropping a million dollars to $1.7 million in 2008, while the company issued an entitlement offer to help reduce its debt. The share price suffered from the capital raising, and dipped again when Billabong announced a thirteen per cent drop in profit in the 2008–09 year. But Billabong seemed to be better positioned than most surf companies to ride out the storm.

Around the world in 2009, the little people in the surf industry were still copping set after set of financial turbulence on the head. Ma and Pa surf shops were barely in business: some just shut their doors and walked away after years of work. The mass production of surfboards in China and South East Asia had turned many custom surfboard operations into non-profits, while even the best shapers found that getting into bed with the enemy was the only sure way to survive. And, generally speaking, the mass production distributors like Surftech, Global and Bic were generous in their success. It was a two-way street, of course. They needed the credibility of shapers like August, McTavish, Webber and Walden, as much as the shapers needed the extra income.

But there were some rays of hope. The growing popularity of the stand-up paddle board was keeping many businesses viable, even if the number of SUP riders in the break was sending surfers around the twist. Surfers were still buying boards and wax and leg ropes and rashies and boardies and tees and thongs and shoes. Non-surfers were still buying all of the above plus anything else they could find to help them live the dream without getting wet. The surf media (real and cyber) were surviving despite dire predictions, and sales of surf-themed DVDs were actually on the upswing. Surf was going to survive.

Interviewed for the *New York Times*, surf industry veteran Randy Rarick commented: 'I have a little saying. When the stock market is down, the surf is up. No matter what, you don't have a pay cheque coming in, you're not doing anything, you can still go out and catch a wave.' And, as if to prove his point, Rarick stood on stage at the Blaisdell Centre in Honolulu in July 2009 while more than US$800,000 of surfboards and surf memorabilia went under the hammer at his Hawaiian Islands Vintage Surf Auction. Many of the surfing world's leading personalities and some of the industry's leading lights engaged in fierce bidding wars that saw records for top prices crash all night.

When the hammer went down at US$40,000 for a half-century old Bob Simmons 'foam sandwich' board, the highest price ever paid for a surfboard, a well-known collector leaned over and whispered to the author: 'Looks like the recession is over.'

WHERE ARE THEY NOW?

Hobie Alter

Industry pioneer, surfboard and surf shop pioneer and creator of the Hobie Cat, Hobie divides his time between Palm Desert, California and Orcas Island in Washington state, where he still sails the picturesque waterways with wife Susan.

Duke Boyd

The surf industry's first marketing man and co-creator of the Hang Ten and Golden Breed brands lives in Honolulu, Hawaii, where he still enjoys attending surfing events, like the Quiksilver in Memory of Eddie Aikau opening ceremony at Waimea Bay. He is still coming up with ideas for surf brands.

Dick Graham

Duke Boyd's partner in crime and surf marketing guru in his own right, Dick lives in Laguna Beach, California, where he dabbles in real estate.

Alan Green

The Quiksilver founder is another inveterate traveller who spends as much time as possible surfing remote Indonesian reefs from the comfort of a boat, or heli-skiing the world's finest powder. He also loves golf, the races and the footy.

Jeff Hakman

Quiksilver USA and Europe co-founder, Jeff still lives and works in France, where he plays a vital role in Quiksilver's European marketing. Loves to get away and surf exotic breaks in Morocco, Indonesia and Mexico.

Harry Hodge

Quiksilver Europe co-founder, Harry lives in Sydney where he oversees his many business interests, including an interest in fashion brand ksubi, and can help coach his three sons, rising stars of surf and snow.

Walter and Flippy Hoffman

Still both active in Hoffman California Fabrics, the mentors of the surfwear industry live in Southern California and surf 'where the water is warm', disappearing to secret spots around Los Cabos every month or so.

John Law

Alan Green's long-time business partner drifts between homes in Torquay, Noosa and Bali, playing golf and loving life with his extended family.

Gerry Lopez

The Lightning Bolt icon and co-founder divides his time between homes on Maui and in Bend, Oregon. Still surfs and snowboards with great style, and has added stand-up paddle to the repertoire. Writes books in his spare time.

Bob McKnight

Quiksilver, Inc. guru for more than twenty years, Bob is firmly in the driver's seat again at Quiksilver, as chairman of the board, president and CEO. Not quite where he imagined he'd be at this stage of his life, but he won't be moving until Quiksilver is back on track. Still finds time to surf and snowboard all over the world, and has homes in California and on Kauai.

Bernard Mariette
Fifteen months after his departure from Quiksilver, the former president of the brand accepted the role of chief executive of Montreal-based snow-wear group Coalision and moved with his family to Canada.

Bill and Bob Meistrell
Wetsuit pioneers and founders of the Body Glove brand, the Meistrell twins shared active lives built around the ocean until Bill's passing in 2006. Bob celebrated his eightieth birthday by going on a scuba dive, wearing a Body Glove wetsuit, of course.

Gordon Merchant
The Billabong co-founder still plays an active role in guiding his brand, when not surfing at one of his many bases around the world. Still the wealthiest man in surfing, he has homes on Queensland's Gold Coast, at Angourie, on the North Shore of Oahu and at Jeffrey's Bay, South Africa.

Jack O'Neill
The founder of the O'Neill brand and wetsuit pioneer still lives on the beach in Santa Cruz.

Matthew Perrin
The former Billabong CEO and company raider sold his stock for around $100 million in 2002 and 2003, was said to be worth $150 million in 2008, and was declared bankrupt, owing $28 million, in March 2009. Gambling debts were said to be part of the problem.

Bruce Raymond
Quiksilver's long-time licensing boss now lives in semi-retirement on Sydney's northern beaches. A dedicated all-round waterman, the

former pro surfer spends a part of each day surfing, paddling and doing yoga.

Jack Shipley
The Lightning Bolt co-founder is still a Honolulu businessman, still involved in running Hawaiian amateur and junior surfing events, and can still climb up the tower to judge a heat, despite an artificial leg.

Brian Singer
Rip Curl co-founder, with Doug Warbrick, and the two still guide their brand, while no longer active on a day-to-day basis. 'Sing Ding' enjoys a relatively laidback lifestyle, split between homes in the snowfields and at Bells Beach. He skis, surfs and travels to feed both habits.

Doug Spong
The surf industry veteran's Cult Industries went into voluntary liquidation in 2009, nominating Doug as one of its significant creditors. 'Spongy' took it on the chin.

Dale Velzy
The legendary shaper, surf shop proprietor, surf stylist and rough-riding cowboy was celebrated by the industry until his death at seventy-seven in 2005. Thousands crowded into Doheny Park to farewell him, many shedding a tear when his cousin, Righteous Brother Bill Medley, sang Dale's favorite song, 'Desperado'.

Doug Warbrick
Rip Curl co-founder. 'Claw' Warbrick divides his time between several waterfront homes, surfs every day there are waves and is one of Australia's fiercest senior longboard competitors.

ACKNOWLEDGEMENTS & THANKS

This book has been growing inside me for a long, long time, and has sat to one side of the brain while other projects took precedence. But it was always there, and because I have stored away information gleaned over half a lifetime of commenting on the surf industry and culture, many people who are quoted herein did not talk to me specifically for this book. Wherever the circumstances dictate, I have made mention of the context in which the quotation was derived.

The idea to write an insider's account of the history of the surf industry came from a degree of frustration I felt at having parts of this great story vetoed by the brand that was paying the bill for its publication at the time. When I mentioned this frustration to many friends in the industry, I was urged to publish my account independently, and for the opportunity to do this I wish to thank my publishers, Hardie Grant.

In its depiction of recent tumultuous events in the surf industry, this book pulls no punches, but nor does it point the finger at anyone in particular, and it is my sincere hope that all those who have helped me in ways great and small to gather the information presented here will see this as a true and fair account of the fascinating growth of an industry, particularly over the last dramatic twenty years.

For insightful on-the-record interviews over many years, and for background information gleaned over the dinner table, in the surf, and on trains, planes, boats and automobiles, I wish to thank the following:

Bob McKnight, Alan Green, Bruce Raymond, Harry Hodge, Jeff Hakman, Doug Warbrick, Brian Singer, Doug Spong, Paul Neilsen, Rod Brooks, Duke Boyd, Dick Graham, Michael Tomson, Shaun Tomson, Martin Potter, Peter Townend, Rabbit Bartholomew, Greg Noll, Randy Rarick, Jack Shipley, Kelly Slater, Paul Holmes, Jeff Bradburn, Norm Innis, Stephen Bell, Michael Owen and Tim Baker.

No book, article, movie, TV documentary or website has ever covered the surf industry in the depth that it receives here, but my task in presenting this information would have been that much harder – and in some areas, impossible – without reference to the following secondary sources:

Tom Blake, *Hawaiian Surfboard*, (reprint Mountain & Sea Publishing, 1983), 1935

Joe Brennan, *Duke of Hawaii*, Ballantine Books, 1968

Mike Doyle, *Morning Glass*, Doyle, 1993

Midget Farrelly and Craig McGregor, *This Surfing Life*, Rigby, 1964

Finney and Houston, *Surfing: A History of the Ancient Hawaiian Sport*, Rutland, 1966

Alain Gardinier, *Les Tontons Surfeurs*, Atlantica, 2004

Paul Holmes, *Velzy Is Hawk*, Croul Family Foundation, 2006

Rod Holmes and Doug Wilson, *You Should Have Been Here Yesterday: The Roots of British Surfing*, Seas Edge, 1994

King David Kalakaua, *The Legends and Myths of Hawaii*, Webster & Co, New York,1888

Jack London, *Cruise of the Snark*, MacMillan, 1911

Carey McWilliams, *The California Revolution*, Grossman, 1968

C Bede Maxwell, *Surf*, Angus & Robertson, 1949

Greg Noll and Andrea Gabbard, *Da Bull: Life over the Edge*, North Atlantic Books, 1989

Derek Rielly (ed.), *Only a Surfer Knows the Feeling*, Rolling Youth Press, 2003

John Severson, *Modern Surfing*, Doubleday, 1964

Albie Thoms, *Surfmovies*, Shore Thing, 2000

Murray Walding, *Blue Heaven*, Hardie Grant, 2003

Matt Warshaw, *The Encyclopedia of Surfing*, Random House, 2003

Nat Young, *The Complete History of Surfing*, Palm Beach Press, 1983

I have also quoted from my own works, including *The Wave Game* (Tracks Publishing, 1977); *Mr Sunset* (General Publishing Group, 1997); *The Mountain & The Wave* (Quiksilver Inc, 2006) and *Kelly Slater: For the Love* (Chronicle Books, 2008).

In addition to the above, I have been fortunate to have had at my disposal a vast library of surf magazines, including, but not limited to: *Surfing World*, *Surfer*, *Surfing*, *Tracks*, *Surf International*, *The Surfer's Journal*, *The Surfer's Path*, *Australian Surf Business*, *Transworld Surf Business*, *Nalu*, *Longboard (RIP)*, *Pacific Longboarder*, *Wavelength* and *Surf Europe*. My thanks to all those journalists and editors who contributed to the industry information vault over many years, but most particularly, for their sharp insights, to John Witzig, Drew Kampion, Steve Pezman, Paul Holmes, Kirk Willcox, Nick Carroll, Jimmy O'Keefe, John Brasen, Jamie Brisick and, in more recent times, to the midnight mailer Ben Marcus, whose capacity for the sharing of information knows no bounds. I have also ventured into the blogosphere, and mainly found it wanting, but to whoever is responsible for Randominium, keep it up, you crazy bastards!

My thanks, as always, to my wife Jackie and my wonderful daughters and their extended families, particularly to my three gorgeous grandsons, who *will* surf, and who will no doubt one day come a-knocking on your door, dude, looking for that great job at Quik, or Bong, or Curl. Please don't hold me against them!

Finally, I want to dedicate this book to the greatest non-suits I know in surfing, even though one of them wears one every Saturday, and the other used to prowl the Beverly Hills party circuit in one on a regular basis. I refer to Bob McTavish and the late Miki Dora, neither of whom ever made a serious buck out of the industry, and yet helped sustain it over the last half-century, Bob through his fearless history of surfboard innovation and spirit of adventure, Miki through his absolute dedication to the philosophy that a day worked was a day wasted, and that there had never been a problem conceived that a good surf couldn't wash away. Amen to that.

GLOSSARY

While the author has tried to avoid surfing terminology, in a few instances the following definitions may be helpful.

backside	riding the wave with your back to it
booster	PR man or promoter
dweeb	nerd, annoying small person
femlin	sixties term for girl surfers
flow	to gift board shorts or surfboards for promotional purposes
frontside	riding the wave while facing it
goofy-foot	right foot forward stance on surfboard
gouge	savage cutback, leaving deep fin trail on wave
gremmie, grom	semi-derogatory term for young surfers or beginners
hotdogging	trick riding as opposed to functional
leg-pump	pump action designed to increase speed along the wave
natural-foot	left foot forward stance on board
pig	popular, broad-backed surfboard shape of the 1950s
pop-out	derogatory term for mass-produced boards
semi-gun	big-wave surfboard
stoke, the	elation caused by the surfing experience

talk story   Hawaiian pidgin for storytelling

tube-riding   riding inside the spilling wave, the ultimate thrill

A note on measures: Imperial measures have been retained as for most of the period covered they are part of the lingua franca of the surfing culture and industry. For those whose minds are metric:

1 inch = 2.54 centimetres
1 foot = 0.305 metres
1 yard = 0.92 metres
1 acre = 0.405 hectares

INDEX

Van Straalen 138
Vans 223, 239
Velcro Valley 173, 181–2, 206
Velzy, Dale 42–3, 45, 84, 247
Velzy Jacobs 44–5
Velzy-Jacobs 'pig' board 54, 56, 71
VF corporation 9, 223, 238, 239
Victory Wetsuits 157
Viertel, Peter 71
Vitelli, Serge 179
Volcom 1, 5, 6, 192, 215, 239–40, 241

Waianae Lions Club 46
Waikiki 15, 17–18, 20, 40, 46
'Waikiki' sportswear 39
Waikiki Surf Club (France) 71
walk shorts 97, 103, 118, 173
Wallace, Bill 56, 61, 71, 82–3, 88, 93
Wall, Terry 93
Warbrick, Arch 94–5
Warbrick, Doug 9, 89, 92–3, 94–6,
    103–4, 106, 108, 109, 110, 121, 122,
    125, 161, 162, 214, 220, 247
Warnaco Group 9, 223
Warner, John 177–8, 179, 180, 186
Warren, Mark 130, 139
Warshaw, Matt 75–6, 128
Water-Logged 81
Way, Damon 225
Way, Danny 225
Weber, Dewey 73, 84, 92, 243
Weeks, Bob 69

West, Claude 32–3, 55
West, TJ 28–9
wetsuits 44, 45, 62, 65–6, 96, 100, 106,
    108, 109, 110, 122, 123, 126, 161
Wetteland, Max 80
White Stag Wetsuits 96, 106
Whyte, Louis 33
Wickham, Alick 26, 29
Wiles, Ken 61–2, 98
Williams, Frank 158
Williams, Freddie 26, 27–8
Wilson, Brian 67
Wilson, Peter 2, 149
Windansea 41, 90
Winkler, Marvin 192–3, 213
Winship, John 169
Winton, Glen 171
Witzig, John 79, 84, 88, 89
Witzig, Paul 57, 80, 81, 84, 89, 113
Woods, Gordon 54, 56, 62, 71, 82–3,
    88, 138
Woods, Greg 207
Woolcott, Richard 5, 6, 191–2, 240

Young, Nat 79, 81, 83, 85–6, 89, 90, 91,
    92, 96, 97, 112–13, 120, 123, 140, 197
Young, Ray 36, 79

Zahn, Tommy 53, 55, 57
Zamba, Frieda 199–200
Zanuck, Richard 71
Zumiez 238